Analyzing Children

Dear Barbara,
Hope you enjoy
the book!
Warmest regards,
Chister

The Vulnerable Child Book Series

Series Editors:

M. Hossein Etezady and Mary Davis

The Vulnerable Child series is based on work that comes out of an ongoing Vulnerable Child Study Group, founded by Theodore Cohen, MD, in 1969. It is sponsored by the American Psychoanalytic Association (Committee on Social Issues), and in the past was co-sponsored by the Association for Child Psychoanalysis. For many years the group has met regularly to discuss what life events render children more vulnerable to developmental and emotional disturbances, and what interventions help to reduce that vulnerability. The study group presents a workshop looking at various aspects of these issues at the meetings of the American Psychoanalytic Association. Co-chairs of the study group are M. Hossein Etezady, MD, and Mary Davis, MD; Until his death, Dr. Cohen remained involved as Chair Emeritus. The Vulnerable Child series publishes volumes which arise from the work of the Study Group, and looks toward expanding offerings to other publications that address the issues which make children more vulnerable to mental health problems, as well as interventions that help to ameliorate that vulnerability.

Titles in the Series

Vulnerable Child Volume 1, edited by Bernard Pacella, Theodore B. Cohen, and M. Hossein Etezady

Vulnerable Child Volume 2, edited by Bernard Pacella, Theodore B. Cohen, and M. Hossein Etezady

Vulnerable Child Volume 3, edited by Bernard Pacella, Theodore B. Cohen, and M. Hossein Etezady

Clinical Perspectives on Reflective Parenting: Keeping the Child's Mind in Mind, edited by M. Hossein Etezady and Mary Davis

Mothering without a Home: Attachment Representations and Behaviors of Homeless Mothers and Children, by Ann Smolen with Alexandra Harrison

On Thought Disorder: Organizational Mastery and Regulating Unprocessed Affect from a Psychoanalytic Perspective, by Theodore Fallon with Susan P. Sherkow

Analyzing Children: Psychological Structure, Trauma, Development, and Therapeutic Action, by Edward I. Kohn, Christie Huddleston, and Adele Kaufman

Analyzing Children

Psychological Structure, Trauma, Development, and Therapeutic Action

Edward I. Kohn, Christie Huddleston, and Adele Kaufman

ROWMAN & LITTLEFIELD
Lanham • Boulder • New York • London

Published by Rowman & Littlefield
An imprint of The Rowman & Littlefield Publishing Group, Inc.
4501 Forbes Boulevard, Suite 200, Lanham, Maryland 20706
www.rowman.com

6 Tinworth Street, London SE11 5AL

British Library Cataloguing in Publication Information Available

Library of Congress Cataloging-in-Publication Data

Names: Kohn, Edward I., 1949– author. | Huddleston, Christie, 1952– author. | Kaufman, Adele, 1940– author.
Title: Analyzing children : psychological structure, trauma, development, and therapeutic action / Edward I. Kohn, Christie Huddleston, Adele Kaufman.
Description: Lanham, MD : Rowman & Littlefield, [2019] | Series: The vulnerable child book series ; No. 7 | Includes bibliographical references and index.
Identifiers: LCCN 2018058342 (print) | LCCN 2019013545 (ebook) | ISBN 9781538121047 (Electronic) | ISBN 9781538121023 (cloth : alk. paper) | ISBN 9781538121030 (pbk. : alk. paper)
Subjects: LCSH: Child psychology.
Classification: LCC BF721 (ebook) | LCC BF721 .K635 2019 (print) | DDC 155.4--dc23
LC record available at https://lccn.loc.gov/2018058342

♾ ™ The paper used in this publication meets the minimum requirements of American National Standard for Information Sciences Permanence of Paper for Printed Library Materials, ANSI/NISO Z39.48-1992.

Printed in the United States of America

Contents

Preface

Edward I. Kohn

In recent years I have had the opportunity to discuss child analytic cases that have been presented at national meetings. Mrs. Adele Kaufman presented the analysis of Ella at the annual meeting of the Association for Child Psychoanalysis that focused on contemporary technique in child analysis, and Dr. Christie Huddleston presented the analysis of Isabel at the Discussion Group of the Vulnerable Child Study Group during the annual meeting of the American Psychoanalytic Association.

Though there was much in common with these two girls' difficulties, their parents' concerns, and their initial presentations in the analysts' offices, their analyses suggested to me that their minds were working in significantly different ways. Both girls were action oriented, and managing their behavior was often a challenge. Yet, especially early on, there was something different about the qualities of their actions and the impact of their behavior on their analysts. Mrs. Kaufman found that her usual interventions and interpretations did not work with Ella, so she found different, more effective interventions. While Isabel was a handful and Dr. Huddleston was often off balance, Dr. Huddleston did not feel a need to vary her analytic technique. When considering both analyses, there is an obvious question: What was going on in each girl's mind that led her to respond to her analyst in the way she did? The answer to that question, unsurprisingly, is not easily put into words.

In my mind, the internal worlds of these two girls were different in two significant ways. For one, their minds were structured differently. Ella's outbursts were the result of fragmentation. The structure of her mind was such that she could not sufficiently tolerate certain stresses or circumstances. Some of her extreme and uncontrolled behavior was a manifestation of disintegration of the self or the collapse of ego structures. Other behaviors, like her need to control Mrs. Kaufman's actions, were caused by a desperate effort to fend off this psychic collapse. In my discussion of Ella's analysis, understanding the structure of her mind was essential to understanding the treatment process and its therapeutic elements.

Isabel, however, had reached the stage of development where her mind had achieved substantial structure, the oedipal phase, but she had endured certain traumatic events earlier in her life that made entry into the oedipal phase an overstimulating and incendiary experience. This, of course, influenced the kind of material that emerged in her analysis, but I was impressed by the differences between a child who had a more intact psychic structure—a cohesive self—and a child who did not have a cohesive self.

Initially, each case and discussion stood alone. When Drs. Mary Davis and M. Hossein Etezady, the chairpersons of the Vulnerable Child Discussion Group, suggested that Dr. Huddleston and I expand our presentation into a book, my first response was "A what?!" Then, I began to think about the intriguing differences between Isabel and Mrs. Kaufman's analytic patient, Ella. Dr. Huddleston, Mrs. Kaufman, and I began to discuss the prospect of comparing these two analyses. The task seemed to grow rapidly, which was both daunting and exciting. It would not be sufficient to reproduce the original case reports and discussions. I recognized that the concepts that informed my understanding of these children and their analyses were very useful to me in my own mind, but in order to make a convincing case to a reader and to satisfactorily lay out the similarities and differences in the girls' inner worlds, these ideas had to be more fully explained and explored. It began to appear that a book was at hand.

What does it mean to have a cohesive self? What is different between a child's mind or self that is cohesive and one that is not? What does it feel like to be that child? What is his or her world like? Many important contributors to the fields of psychoanalysis and child psychoanalysis have studied the way the child's mind changes in the first years of life. While these psychoanalysts' languages, terms, and concepts are generally different, they all come to grips with a fundamental change in the working of the child's mind. S. Freud's (1923/1953–1974d) oedipal phase, with its new structure, the superego, is one example of the monumental transition in the functioning of the mind. Bion (1963) refers to alpha elements and beta elements, and Melanie Klein (1975) lays out the paranoid/schizoid position vs. the depressive position. Mayes and Cohen (1996) describe an important transition in the function of the mind when they discuss development of a theory of mind, while Fonagy and Target (1996, 1998; Target & Fonagy, 1996) discuss the capacity for representational thinking and mentalization. Margaret Mahler, Fred Pine, and Anni Bergman (1975) studied the process of separation-individuation, referring to the achievement of object constancy. Kohut describes the establishment of a cohesive self, addressing the same transition, except that he emphasizes the fate of the self, while object relations scholars emphasize the fate of the object.

The second major difference between Ella and Isabel, particularly early in their analyses, is that they were dealing with different developmental issues. Ella was dealing with separation-individuation and fears of abandonment. The developmental accomplishments of these preoedipal years include laying down psychic structure. Interferences in this process leave a child with a fragile self, vulnerable to fragmentation. The child and parent must deal with the little girl's growing independence and autonomy and development of her own unique self. Important functions, like the capacity to calm herself, have not yet been internalized, and the child relies on her parents to serve this function.

While Isabel had achieved the oedipal phase of development, she was not managing it very well. Her life was significantly hampered by anxiety and inhibitions, and the intensity of her emotions created strong winds. Isabel had a cohesive self, but the traumas of her earlier years were reignited by the fantasies and preoccupations of the oedipal phase. I realized that I had to delve more explicitly into the similarities and differences between trauma and fragmentation. In order to understand the profoundly important differences between Ella and Isabel, I looked to find a way to imagine myself into their minds in order to apprehend their different psyches and experiences.

Chapters 1 and 3 immerse the reader in Isabel's and Ella's analyses, respectively. These case reports by Dr. Huddleston and Mrs. Kaufman draw the reader into the room, bring the experience of child and analyst to life, and demonstrate the analyst's approach to interventions, while leaving room for the reader to look around the room and develop his or her own understanding of each case. Chapter 2 is my original discussion with Dr. Huddleston of the analysis of Isabel, and chapter 4 is my original discussion with Mrs. Kaufman of the analysis of Ella.

In chapter 5, I discuss psychological structure. I draw on different authors to present various models of the mind and ideas about the way the mind is structured. This includes ideas about how that structure develops and the functions it serves. Understanding the development of psychic structure is also relevant for understanding the collapse or disintegration of psychic structure.

Sandler and Rosenblatt's (1962) paper "The Concept of the Representational World" provides a useful metaphor for the structure of the mind: They compare the representational world to a stage on which the internal performances of self and object representations occur; the theater is analogous to the ego, whose apparatuses support the stage and the performances. There are a significant number of authors who address psychological structure, and they provide different models or visual representations of the structure of the mind. Kohut (1977) posits that the self is the supraordinate structure of the mind. Bromberg (1996) focuses on dissociation and explains that the self is an illusion created by the increasing integration of dissociated states of self. Fonagy, Moran, Edgecume, Kennedy, and Target (1993) provide two models for the development of psychic structure: the mental representation model and the mental process model. Chapter 5 also includes the work of A. Freud (1965) and Rapaport (1960).

Wilson and Weinstein (1996) discuss the zone of proximal development (ZPD), and they look at the interchange of words between analyst and analysand to explain the minute additions to psychic structure. Tolpin (1971) draws on Kohut's concept of transmuting internalization in order to demonstrate how a child internalizes parental functions and psychic structure is created. Like Tolpin, I repeatedly look at the capacity to soothe oneself to represent a function that reflects internalization of psychic structure.

In chapter 6, I examine the concept of trauma and compare it to the concept of fragmentation. I begin with Freud's (1920/1953–1974a) model of the mind as an apparatus whose purpose is to manage stimuli. Freud's view of trauma as a consequence of flooding the mental apparatus or overwhelming the ego has influenced the subsequent study of trauma. Krystal (1978) wrote extensively about trauma, including the process of being overwhelmed: "In the catatonoid state, we are dealing with the very moment of the self being overwhelmed with a phylogenetically determined surrender pattern" (93). Anna Freud (1964/1967) made many contributions to our understanding of trauma in children. Among them is her observation that the word *trauma* is often loosely applied. She provided criteria to help us understand what we mean when we talk about trauma.

Grotstein (1990a) compares the traumatic state to a black hole. In his vivid descriptions, the depths of a traumatic experience and fragmentation are not necessarily distinguishable. Boulanger (2002) and Bromberg (1993) discuss trauma with dissociation in mind. Boulanger explains that, for a traumatized child, the integration of the bits and pieces that normally form memories is interfered with, and memories are stored in dissociated states. For Bromberg, dissociation is an effort to contend with an overwhelming input. Both authors stress that these dissociated states interfere with the capacity to symbolize, leading to concreteness of subjective experience (Bromberg) and indelible memories (Boulanger).

I look at fragmentation from a developmental perspective. During toddlerhood, prior to the oedipal phase, psychological structure is created. Mahler, Pine, and Bergman (1975); Kohut (1971); Fonagy and Target (1996); Bion (1963); and Klein (1975) all describe a transition in the mind that is associated with a strikingly new kind of functioning. I examine the clinical material in Isabel's and Ella's analyses in conjunction with these concepts in order to understand the workings of their minds and clarify the concepts with examples from their analyses. While the girls' surface behavior often seems similar, I point out the significant difference between the moments when Ella's self is fragmenting and those when Isabel is overstimulated or overcome by anxiety.

In order to understand how psychic structure is laid down, one needs to understand the magical quality of the parent–child relationship. I discuss this in chapter 7. Dahl (1996) explains that the developmental needs of the child and the ways in which the child–analyst relationship facilitates developmental growth are more evident and available than in adult analysis. Edgcumbe (1995) paraphrases Anna Freud and explains that the child's needs shape the analysis; he takes from the analysis, one way or another, what he needs. Child analysts refer to the developmental object (Hurry, 1998; Miller, 2013), but other writers address these phenomena with their own terminology.

Spitz (1956), Khan (1963), and Gitelson (1962), among others, use the concepts of the auxiliary ego and stimulus barrier. Spitz and Gitelson also refer to the diatrophic function of the mother. Winnicott (1965) talks about the holding environment, Bion (1965/1977b) refers to the container, Kohut (1968) talks about the selfobject, Baker (1993) and others describe the new object, and Bollas (1979) writes about the transformational object.

Winnicott (1960) explains that the infant sees herself in her mother's face, and this process gives the child back to herself. Bion (1965/1977b) and Brown (2011) describe how the child or analysand finds her own mind in the mind of the other. Lyons-Ruth (1999) emphasizes the importance of being open to the child's state of mind, while Fonagy and Target (1998) write that the child sees her intentions, desires, and beliefs in the mind of her parent. Mayes and Cohen (1993b) describe this process with the parents' response to the child's aggression, and Kohut (1959, 1968) emphasizes empathy.

Additionally, in chapter 7, I examine vignettes in which the interactions and processes I have just described occur with Isabel and Ella. I pay particular attention to the girls' capacity to modulate affect as evidence of the development of psychological structure (Tolpin, 1971). I also point out how their play activity, fantasies, and dreams reveal that new psychological structure has been created during their analyses.

In chapters 5 through 7, I establish the importance of the phase transition in the developing mind when a new cohesive structure has been achieved. In chapter 8, with this understanding in mind, including metaphors that enable us to picture the structure of the mind, I go inside the experience of a fragmenting self or a severely traumatized individual so that we can conceptualize the process and the experience. Then I turn to Ella's analysis in order to demonstrate how her work with Mrs. Kaufman created psychic structure, leading to a cohesive self.

Considering my view that Ella and Isabel have minds that are structured differently, we would expect differences in how their minds function, the kinds of dysfunction that occurs, and the ways in which psychoanalysis facilitates change in the functioning of their minds. In chapter 9, I begin the task of discussing the therapeutic action of psychoanalysis and apply the concepts presented to the changes within each of the girls.

I start with a discussion of the role of insight and S. Freud's (1895/ 1953–1974n, 1915/1953–1974o, 1923/1953–1974d, 1933/1953–1974k) changing models of the mind and theories of cure. Much of Freud's thinking remains and becomes a starting point for subsequent theorists. Freud, for example, talks about the transformation from id to ego, while Fonagy et al. (1993) created the mental representation model in an effort to explain how ego structure develops. Sugarman (2006) focuses on the process of gaining insightfulness rather than limiting himself to insight as an awareness of mental contents. He sees this perspective as a way to do away with the dichotomy between relationship and interpretation. Wilson and Weinstein (1996) emphasize the verbal interplay within the ZPD. It is not the specific word that is learned that is most important but the stimulation of budding processes when the pair (mother and child or analyst and analysand) are within the ZPD.

Bollas (1993) believes that it is the moments when analyst and analysand miss each other that provide the greatest opportunities for growth as the pair playfully and creatively try to refind each other. Opening creative capacity—fantasy, myth making, free-associating, and dreaming—is therapeutic. Baranger, Baranger, and Mom (1998) explain that trauma leads to closed systems, and Mitchell (1996) explains that transference can collapse the myth-making potential. Analysis has the potential to facilitate a new opening of the system. The role of the analyst as developmental object, the enduring potential within the psyche to move forward developmentally, and various ways to think about optimal frustration are other important ideas in this concept-laden chapter.

It is obvious that the young child engages with her analyst in a way that is very different from the adult. Lack of understanding, limited self-control, and propensity to action all complicate the analyst's task. In chapter 10, I discuss the rich and complex world of analytically informed play with a child. Play is natural for a child, and she may not even recognize that something therapeutic is going on. The child's natural immersion in imagination and fantasy, play's closer access to the unconscious, and its freedom from the constraints of reality all help to provide remarkable access to her inner world. In this chapter I discuss the child analyst's ways of understanding play activity, techniques of intervention, and the process by which play leads to intrapsychic change.

In chapter 11, I delve into the ways in which the relationship, the varieties of interplay between analyst and child, and the things they talk about come together and facilitate the unfolding and transformation of the child's mind. I begin with a line of development described by Ekstein and Friedman (1957) in their paper "The Function of Acting Out, Play Action, and Play Acting in the Psychotherapeutic Process." I devise my own version of this continuum: action, play action, play-acting, play in the microcosm, symbols, and words. I also examine play interruptions and action that is associated with words. The latter refers to situations where the child is taking action while the analytic pair are also engaged in verbal exchange. Play interruptions and action that is associated with words give us an opportunity to see the relationship among action, relationship, and words at any point along the continuum.

In chapter 12, I discuss the oedipal material in both analyses. Isabel's analysis was organized around oedipal themes pretty much throughout the work, while Ella moved from a central focus on separation-individuation and abandonment to more consistent oedipal themes. This enables us to view the transformation of Ella's world as she moved forward developmentally and to see ways that preoedipal separation-individuation concerns remained imbedded within and added shape to her oedipal experience. By the ends of their analyses, the structure and functioning of Isabel's and Ella's minds had much more in common than they had early in their analyses. When I consider the progression of Isabel's theories of conception, we get to observe the receding of earlier oral and anal preoccupations.

I discuss termination in chapter 13 and observe how both girls remember and reminisce about their analyses. At times, the girls have these conversations consciously and directly and, at other times, unconsciously or metaphorically. We see Ella's poignant review of her analysis when she talks about the rug in the office. Isabel plays with disappearing ink. For both girls, the termination process is an opportunity to rework resolution of internal conflicts and consolidate developmental gains. The grieving process and the significance of object constancy is highlighted when each girl, in her own way, wants to remember and be remembered.

Acknowledgments

EDWARD I. KOHN

I would like to express my appreciation for a number of psychoanalytic institutions that foster a deep immersion in psychoanalysis and welcome the relatively small number of us child analysts into that immersion. I wish to thank the Cincinnati Psychoanalytic Institute, where I trained in adult analysis and where I teach and supervise, thereby learning more and more. I did my child-analytic training at the New Orleans Psychoanalytic Institute (now the New Orleans–Birmingham Psychoanalytic Institute), and these two institutes have joined together to form the Southeast Consortium for Child Psychoanalysis. The dedicated, innovative, and intelligent members of the consortium (faculty and candidates) have fostered an atmosphere for teaching and learning that is rich and rewarding and would not have been available without their willingness to collaborate and come together.

The Association for Child Psychoanalysis (ACP) provides an opportunity for child analysts from around the country and the world to delve deeply into clinical child analysis. One advantage of the relatively small numbers in the child analytic community is that people get to know one another more easily and creative thinking emerges in a relatively informal environment. It was at an ACP workshop on the technique of child analysis that I had the good fortune to discuss Mrs. Adele Kaufman's presentation of her analysis of Ella. The Vulnerable Child Study Group has been exploring the minds of children for decades, and it was at the group's discussion during the annual meeting of the American Psychoanalytic Association (APSaA) that I had the opportunity to discuss Dr. Huddleston's treatment of a traumatized girl, Isabel.

I wish to thank Mary Davis, MD, and M. Hossein Etezady, MD, who lead the Vulnerable Child Study Group and are the editors of the group's book series. It was Dr. Davis and Dr. Etezady who first suggested that we embark on this book project. While there were times along the way that I had second thoughts about this advice, I am pleased and proud that our book is now included in the series. Dr. Davis provided much appreciated encouragement and suggestions, as well as editing, during the writing process.

Sydney Anderson, PhD; Lee Ascherman, MD; and Brett Clarke, MSW, served as indispensable resources as I began putting my ideas onto paper. They spent a great deal of time with me, helping me untangle a morass of ideas, each of which seemed precious and elucidating to me at the time. They helped me to organize my thinking, understand the reader's perspective, and forge a more coherent narrative.

Thank you, as well, to Mark Kerr, Kathleen O'Brien, Courtney Packard, and Andrew Yoder from Rowman & Littlefield, who helped us through the publishing side of things, something of which I had little understanding.

Finally, I wish to underscore my gratitude to my wife, Sandy, whose support, encouragement, and belief in me (even if she is biased) sustained me throughout the project. If you, the reader, return to this acknowledgments page after reading the book, I hope you will be further convinced of the wonderful and magical quality of our developmental objects, selfobjects, or transformational objects throughout our lives.

CHRISTIE HUDDLESTON

I am deeply grateful for those who helped me understand Isabel and guide me in my work with her, most especially Charley Parks, PhD, who, in his thoughtful manner, walked the analytic path with Isabel and me. Hossein Etezady, MD, and Mary Davis, MD, co-chairs of the Vulnerable Child Study Group of APSaA, permitted me the honor of presenting my ideas in their forum and the opportunity to receive valuable feedback on my work. Many others have helped me mature in my analytic work with children, especially the distinguished faculty at the Psychoanalytic Center of Philadelphia and the Southeastern Consortium, including but not limited to DeWitt Montgomery, MD; Ruth Fischer, MD; Lee Ascherman, MD; Sam Rubin, MD; Fred Fisher, MD; June Greenspan, MD; Harold Kolansky, MD; and Wendy Olesker, PhD (geographic supervisor). I have been blessed with analytic colleagues who have challenged and nurtured me in my work. Among these colleagues are Bob Kravis, PhD; Ruth Garfield, MD; Ira Brenner, MD; Ann Smolen, PhD; and Jodi Brown, MD. Finally and equally important are those who helped me on my own analytic journey: Homer Curtis, MD, and Jack Solomon, MD.

ADELE KAUFMAN

My thanks to Dr. Edward Kohn for his vision in conceptualizing this volume. His dedication, enthusiasm, thoughtfulness and collaborative spirit made the vision become a reality. With grateful appreciation to Dr. Barbara Rocah, Dr. Mary Davis, and Edward Kaufman for their careful reading and thoughtful comments on this manuscript. I also wish to thank the Association for Child Psychoanalysis, the Chicago Psychoanalytic Institute, and the Committee on Child Psychoanalysis of the American Psychoanalytic Association, among others, for many rewarding opportunities to present my ideas in clinical papers on teaching, learning, and doing child psychoanalysis. These groups provided opportunities for me to learn from generous and stimulating collegial discussions, a continuation of the lifelong educational journey that is a vital part of being a psychoanalyst.

Chapter One

Isabel

Christie Huddleston

Child analysts are uniquely positioned to gain understanding of the interactions between life experience, intrapsychic pressures, and the push of development. Although all children are vulnerable in ways that adults are not, this is especially true of young children who are under the sway of naïve cognitive abilities and limited mentalization. The relative weights of conflict, trauma, and developmental pressure vary for each child and that child's innate strengths. The child analyst may be able to track the emergence of symptoms and link them to a particular trauma or conflict due to the closeness of the events or symptomatology or both. However, in other instances the picture is murkier, leaving one to speculate about the meaning and origin of dramatic symptoms. It is through steady, close attention to the child's communications that the link between these factors is clarified and understood. This latter position was the one I found myself in as I began to work with Isabel.

DEVELOPMENTAL HISTORY

Isabel's mother had called to set up an appointment because she felt her daughter was anxious. Much to my surprise, during the first meeting, her mother reported that Isabel, age 6½, had stopped speaking 2 years earlier, except at times to whisper in her mother's ear. Her mother attributed this behavior to shyness. She described her daughter as intellectually precocious but inhibited when playing with children. Isabel would stand rigidly next to the school aide during recess and refused to play in their cul-de-sac with neighborhood children. Recently, she had refused to try new activities, would not go to the park with the family, and had stopped riding her bicycle. Her mother emphasized that her daughter had friends but was sensitive to rejection and easily hurt. Two weeks prior, Isabel had told her mother that she did not know if she "could go on in life." Her mother also expressed concern that Isabel refused "to ask" her teacher to use the bathroom and consequently suffered frequent constipation and abdominal pain. Upon questioning, her mother said that Isabel required her to be in the bathroom when using it at home. However, she was proud that Isabel, who was in first grade, was performing well despite being essentially mute.

At home, the mother reported that Isabel was an affectionate child, but her displays of affection were sometimes quite rough, especially with her younger sister. In a much later meeting, she revealed that Isabel's roughness took the form of hitting her and her younger daughter in the belly and breasts. She felt the roughness increased when Isabel was anxious. Another manifestation of Isabel's anxiety was a stubborn and demanding manner during daily routines, which required her mother to constantly accommodate her. For example, Isabel had trouble leaving the house in the morning, so her mother would take her younger daughter to school and then return to take Isabel, who was now late, to the same school. She described Isabel as the more reserved of her two children. Her younger daughter, Eva, she described as friendly and adventuresome. Not infrequently, the mother discovered Eva comforting Isabel at night when Isabel was crying.

In subsequent meetings with both parents, I learned about Isabel's early life. Her parents told me that they had met in college and married shortly thereafter but had decided to wait for children until they were better established financially. Six years into their marriage, Isabel's mother was surprised to find out that she was pregnant. Despite her lack of emotional preparedness, the pregnancy and delivery went well. Six months after the birth, Isabel's mother returned to work part time. She breastfed Isabel until she was a year old, and they had a "family bed" for several years. According to her mother, Isabel walked and talked at under a year of age. Her mother was proud of Isabel's early verbal skills, reporting that she used complete sentences almost from the beginning. Until the age of 3 years, Isabel was in day care for a few hours daily.

Isabel's parents reported a notable series of crucial events during the mother's second pregnancy, when Isabel was between 2 and 3 years old. Soon after her second birthday, Isabel broke her collarbone falling out of the car and then a few months later was viciously attacked by the family dog after admonishing him not to eat her feces in the potty seat. The injuries to her arm required medical treatment, and her mother said she thought their dog would have killed Isabel if she hadn't been there.

Isabel was 2½ years old when her sister was born in an unplanned home delivery. Isabel's father said he had quickly set up a video for Isabel to watch but that he was panic-stricken when he realized that he was going to have to deliver the baby himself. He contacted emergency services, but when he heard his wife screaming in the bathroom, he rushed in to see their baby's head crowning. He had difficulty getting his wife from the toilet to the floor to deliver the baby. Blood was everywhere, and although he tried to close the door, in their small house, it was next to impossible. Within minutes of the birth, their neighborhood was inundated with sirens of the emergency services. Both parents were, of course, preoccupied, so Isabel was taken to a neighbor's home to be cared for until her mother and new sister were released from the hospital. Her parents noticed no significant reaction from Isabel to these events at the time. When Isabel was 3 years old, her father's company moved their business overseas, and the family decided to move in with Isabel's maternal grandparents until they could get back on their feet.

INITIAL PHASE: TROUBLESOME BABY, BIRTHS, AND THE DANGERS IN BEING A WOMAN

At our first meeting, Isabel seemed anxious but came into the office with me. She was a pretty, dark-haired girl, modestly dressed in what she had worn to school. As she settled into the office, she stood looking carefully at the play area. When I noted her curiosity, she began to pull the stuffed animals out of the cabinet in order to feed them. At first, she did this in a controlled manner, but quickly the animals were eating voraciously. I noted aloud how hungry they seemed. In her first words to me, she remarked on the lion's bushy mane and the squirrel's bushy tail. She inspected the doll family and remarked that grandfather also had bushy hair. She became fascinated with "Troublesome Baby," who, she noted, had no hair and was dressed in red. "Troublesome Baby" crawled aggressively into the mouth, nose, and ear of the horse puppet and then into the hind end of a dog that she called "Doggie with No Tail." She said "he" (referring to "Troublesome Baby") went into the tummy of the horse to eat something. In subsequent sessions she eagerly brought me into her world as she elaborated these themes. She made "Troublesome Baby" push a baby bottle roughly into the bottom of "Squirrel." I asked her if she thought that hurt, and she concurred. As she expressed sadism, she wanted me to understand that "Troublesome Baby" was a bad baby and encouraged the animals to be bad.

In our first few months, Isabel would alternate between sessions in which she was quite constricted and performed as a dutiful student might, doing homework and producing drawings, and sessions in which she was excited, intrusive, and physical. Although I thought she was trying to express important feelings that she had previously contained through inhibition, the undifferentiated expression of her feelings created technical difficulties, both in terms of physical safety and emotional or sexual overstimulation. In these sessions Isabel started by jumping from chair to chair frenetically. I believed her compulsive action functioned as a partial discharge of feelings and as a defense against an awareness of it. I felt she did not have the words to tell me about her worries and experiences, and I didn't yet know enough about them to help her more specifically, so I worked to establish a safe environment. She seemed appreciative of my emphasis on safety and at the same time frustrated and defiant at what she felt were my attempts to restrict her. Even trickier were those moments when Isabel jumped into my arms, trying to rub her body against mine, asking for "uppies." I did not want to convey disapproval but felt it was not helpful for her, and I struggled with my discomfort at those aspects that seemed erotic. I positioned myself so her ability to engage in this behavior was curtailed while I continued to work to understand the meaning of it. It seemed as though there was an eroticization of closeness, even as she pushed me for protection from danger.

Six weeks into the analysis, Isabel's father suddenly passed out at work. He was hospitalized for evaluation of syncope, and Isabel's parents did not talk with her about the frightening events. In the office, intermingled with a flurry of action, Isabel recounted her father's sudden collapse and her visits to him in the hospital. I spoke of how disturbing this must have been for her. In this context she reported for the first time that she had had a dream—a "weird" dream—but she was not going to tell it to me. I tried to explore why, and in response she revealed to me that she had seen a movie about Tinkerbell and had dreamed about fairies and monsters. I intervened, "Maybe a part of you is curious and wants to know more, and a part of you says, 'No way.'" She responded that all parts say "No way!" She was elucidating a pattern of silence she used to protect herself from being overwhelmed and a mode of communication that would at times act as a resistance in the analysis. I wondered if she were trying to titrate what she revealed in order not to be overwhelmed and retraumatized.

As if trying another tack, Isabel began to explore a book on my shelf about Greek myths. She read the titles of the chapters to me and was particularly interested in the chapters "The Birth of Athena," "The Birth of Aphrodite," and "The Birth of Zeus." She sat beside me wanting me to read the stories to her. As we read together, I noted that in the past people had used stories to talk about things they were struggling with, and these stories seemed to have themes of births and fights. As this intervention engaged her intellectual curiosity, Isabel's associations moved in a more emotionally laden and overwhelming direction. She spent a subsequent session jumping unrelentingly on my sofa while she told me the story of Purim. She said the king's wife refused to display her body for him, so he wanted a new wife. He chose Esther, a beautiful woman who, unbeknownst to him, was Jewish. Isabel said everyone thought Esther was brave, but she didn't agree. It was Mordechai, a father figure to Esther, who discovered the plot to kill the Jews; he was the brave one! After telling the story, Isabel was spent. She confessed she should have gone to the bathroom and acknowledged she had wet her pants. The next session, again jumping on the sofa, she returned to the story of Purim. She said she now realized Esther had been brave because she used her power as queen to profess her Judaism and protect her people. Esther had risked being killed. Isabel then unconsciously referred to me as Mordechai. It seemed that she was introducing a conflict she had about revealing herself and the dangers inherent in that, as well as her difficulty in becoming over-whelmed by her thoughts and feelings. The early transference was as if I were a trusted father figure.

There followed a series of sessions of intense action in the office and toward me. When I felt I had enough data, I interpreted that I thought her actions were a way of not feeling afraid. She stopped jumping frenetically and, with a sudden ability to contain herself, asked why she would be afraid? I indicated that in recent sessions she had been talking about scary stories, dreams, births, and a woman who risked her life. She smiled thoughtfully, saying, "Oh, yeah!" Through parental sessions I knew that, despite physical-ity with me, Isabel had stopped hitting her mother and her sister and was now talking at school, although with a soft voice.

OEDIPAL WISHES AND FEARS IN PLAY AND ENACTMENT

Aided by having a part of her experience put into words, Isabel felt less at the mercy of being overwhelmed and more able to think about what was on her mind. She was an avid reader and brought in a book, a sequel to *The Wizard of Oz*, which she read silently in my presence for some sessions. When I asked about the book, she told me that it was about Dorothy's adventures after the wicked witch was dead. Obliquely she seemed to be broaching oedipal themes: a yearning for love, the idealization of the wizard, and liber-ation from the wicked witch. I thought Isabel was revealing to me her own strengths and desires, which she was proud of, and beginning to reveal as-pects of the maternal transference. In her silence she had conveyed to me her emotional containment and her separateness but also warmth and connection. In these moments, did the use of silence as a mode of communication reveal her feelings toward me as the loving mother in the positive maternal transfer-ence? In a step toward verbalizing her concerns, she sang to me "If I Only Had a Heart" and "If I Only Had a Brain" as she introduced a theme of wanting to be made whole. She poignantly sang "Somewhere over the Rain-bow," expressing her wishes for a happier family and life.

Gradually, expressions of physicality toward me reemerged as Isabel took up sexual themes. Now she began her sessions routinely by kicking her shoes off and aiming them for my breasts—or "throwing them at your heart," as she described it. At the same time, a transference was developing, involving who controlled whom, who broke whose heart, who was or wasn't in the know. For months she compulsively demanded that I stay between the double doors of my office while she attempted to squash my body with the inner door. Later she would insist that I try to hold my body behind an artificial line drawn while I was between the double doors, which meant that my breasts and belly would be cut off. I made this connection to her and wondered aloud if she didn't have some concern about my having a woman's body and what could happen to a woman's body. Without a direct response, she insisted that I not peek when behind the doors. At another level, was I the sexually immature little girl who was not supposed to look? And what were the consequences if I did? I tried to elucidate the feelings of the little girl and talked about feeling alone and confused. Isabel would further elaborate the play by erecting barricades with me behind the doors. Then suddenly she would feel the need to defecate urgently, and we would rush to the bathroom. The link between this play and her ability to allow herself to defecate was repeated compulsively. As I felt imprisoned, I spoke with her about feeling punished for talking about feelings. She agreed. I wondered why, but she would not elaborate. I thought this play symbolized multiple aspects of Isabel's internal experience. At different levels, I thought, I represented the mature woman whose capacity for sexuality and pregnancy were terrifying to her; I was the baby in the womb who could be horribly destructive, and I was her as a frightened little girl trying to handle the excitement and shock at witnessing the birth of her sister after disobeying the edict not to look. The door seemed to represent a way to contain and neutralize the sexually mature woman, to link her symptom of holding in her stool and her fears related to body integrity and pregnancy, and to remind her of the inhibitions with which she had imprisoned herself physically and psychologically. I also wondered about the anality in her defense of withholding her feelings in silence, and a connection with her symptom of retention of her stool.

One day, while exploring the toy cabinet, Isabel picked up the boy baby doll, pulled down his pants, and exclaimed that he had a penis! Immediately she checked the girl baby. When she found "two mounds and a hole" she tossed the girl aside with disdain. She then wanted to play a game in which each player hit the other with a pillow, trying to "cut off their limbs." The last person standing won. Isabel cheated, and I commented on how important it was for her to win. I did not interpret her feelings about the differences between the sexes, her concerns of body integrity, and a link to her need to win, as it seemed too far from her conscious awareness. During this play she openly acknowledged her struggle to permit herself to defecate. Although I thought this symptom was multiply determined, I spoke to her about a conflict between her desire for order and control and her need to express messy, excited, or angry feelings. After this work her mother reported that Isabel had been able to use the bathroom at school.

As the transference evolved, Isabel was the sadistic teacher, and I, the demeaned student. I was ordered to list 10 observations about the baby boy's penis. She seemed to want to make me feel like she felt when she contemplated the differences between her body and a boy's body. I wanted to engage Isabel about the teacher's harsh treatment while I, staying in the play, complied with the task, but she refused to permit me to speak explicitly about it. When I wasn't fast enough or observant enough, I was punished by having to stand in a corner and not participate in the "fun" other children were having. It felt like I was being forced to take in a confusing and disturbing experience without help, much as she felt she had been, and I voiced these feelings aloud to her. Was she identifying with those aspects of her mother, who could be a taskmaster, as well as explicating a fantasy of her mother's disdain for not knowing or for feeling helpless? Was this identification or fantasy at the root of her harsh superego and her disavowal of vulnerable feelings?

EXHIBITIONISM, SADISM, AND HARSH SUPEREGO MANIFESTATIONS

In the play Isabel would wag her butt and moon me. I protested her freedom in contrast to how controlled I was required to be. She laughed in recognition of the unfairness of my position. In elaboration, moving from the anal to the genital, she would straddle my desk and chair, blatantly exhibiting her underpants as if to reveal her genitalia. I noted that she seemed to want to show me her bottom. She corrected me, indicating that her bottom was her rectum and her "seat" was her genitalia, confirming that she was more informed than I. She then sang "The Itsy Bitsy Teenie Weenie Yellow Polka Dot Bikini," seemingly unaware of its theme of a girl who wanted to reveal her body and her sexuality but was afraid to. She pretended to break an egg over my head, poke me with "needles," and plunge a "knife" into my back, causing "blood to drip down," as she returned to the themes of sexuality, body integrity, and births. She seemed anxious and stimulated by this behavior and wondered if I would tell her mother about the "bad things" she did. I told her that, even though she thought of it as bad, she was trying to show us what she was struggling to understand. A few sessions later, she told me she had dreamed of five chocolate turtles. She had eaten one of them. Thinking of the dream, she thought one of the turtles had been her sister. She wished she hadn't told me. When I tried to explore why, she refused to say. Again, I wondered about the transference: Was I the punitive mother who would punish her for revealing her sadism, and was her withholding from me an expression of her sadism toward me?

I also speculated about links to seeing her mother's bloody and messy genitals at the time of her sister's birth, consequently coloring her understanding of the differences between the sexes, sexuality, and feminine identifications with a heightened anxiety and sadism. What fantasies did she have about the experience? Did she feel that her mother's body in those moments confirmed a belief that the girl or woman had been wounded genitally or castrated? Had her sister wounded her mother, or was her sister wounded in the birth process? What did it mean to Isabel to have been a baby or, in the future, to be a woman capable of giving birth? Was she exposing her genitals to me in a counterphobic manner to express and deny worry about her genitalia? In the transference, was she also trying to shock me the way she had felt shocked? Gradually her exhibitionism diminished, as in her play she was able to sublimate more of her experience.

October ushered in preparations for Halloween. Isabel made costumes for all the stuffed animals. She made a ghost costume for "Horsey" and decided his costume needed to cover his bottom (like a diaper). During this time she made frequent demands of me. I responded that demands might contain feelings that she wanted satisfied but that she was uncomfortable expressing in words, and she stuck her tongue out in response. She made a flower of Kleenex and a pencil that resembled female and male genitalia, and she watered the flower for weeks. Was this need to have both male and female aspects an attempt to defend against a fantasy of the woman as wounded and devalued? Later, Isabel's mother reported that one of Isabel's older friends had gotten her period while Isabel was with her, and subsequently she had trouble sleeping. I wondered if the "diaper" for "Horsey" expressed a fear about the meaning of menstruation. During this time Isabel picked a scab on her leg. When it bled, she became panic-stricken but tried to defend against these feelings through self-sufficient bandaging of the wound. It seemed that picking until she bled was an attempt to turn her passive experiences of menstruation and earlier exposure to genital blood into an experience controlled by her.

VOLDEMORT, MOANING MYRTLE, TOILETS, AND BASILISKS: THE MATERNAL TRANSFERENCE

A year into our work, Isabel began reading the Harry Potter series. She was enthralled! She introduced me to Sirius Black, a scary wizard whom everyone believed was trying to harm Harry Potter. After she left the office, I noticed a length of tape she had left on my desk blotter on which she had written *Voldemort* (the evil wizard whose name must not be spoken). We began months of discussions about Harry and his friends, his scary world, the problems he faced, the traumas he endured, and the manner in which he handled them.

Abruptly, Isabel's mother called to cancel a session because her father had had another syncopal episode and was hospitalized. The following session, Isabel threw candy wrappers on the floor. I observed how upset and angry she must have been feeling. She ignored me so she could obey her mother's instructions to prepare to visit her father by wrapping a gift and making a card for him. I asked how he was, and she said she didn't know. I spoke about how difficult it must be when adults don't explain what is happening. Turning the tables and moving away from her distress, Isabel began excitedly peppering me with questions about the Harry Potter books. Who opened the Chamber of Secrets? Who is Moaning Myrtle? She was disdainful and gleeful when I didn't know all the answers.

Isabel revealed two dreams. In the first dream, she and a friend Mark were living together with their families. She and Mark had mailed away for cricket eggs, and Mark cracked one of the eggs over her head. In the second dream, she and her sister had gone into a shark cage at the aquarium. Her sister saw a sign that said "Eat" and told Isabel, who in the dream could not read, that the shark would eat her, so they ran. Privately, I thought the dreams might involve a fear of being ripped apart as the consequence for sexual feelings and wishes to have a husband and family. In the second dream, she turned to her younger sister for protection, as she had done in life, but also perhaps the dream disguised her own vengeful feelings toward her sister. After revealing the dreams, her associations through play were to understand the life cycle of a caterpillar. She encouraged me to participate in constructing a poster exhibiting models of the life cycle from egg to caterpillar to cocoon to beautiful butterfly. She wanted to know if I knew what came from a cocoon. She seemed to want to reassure herself that, despite life events and her oedipal strivings, there would be a hopeful ending. In working with her dreams, I worked within the play and spoke of her curiosity about maturing. This seemed to give permission to her healthy competitive feelings. After running circles around me to and from the bathroom, she asked me if I knew that the basilisk, a monstrous snake, had killed Moaning Myrtle in the bathroom. Did I know what was in the Chamber of Secrets? She associated secrets adults have and then told me that babies come out of their mothers' bottoms.

In a later session, Isabel constructed a toilet. She wanted me to guess what it was and then what was to be inside of it. Using her earlier associations, I guessed a basilisk. Initially, she was excited by my answer but then stopped herself and said, "No! It was Moaning Myrtle." I chose to explore why poor Myrtle was moaning, and Isabel replied disdainfully that it was because she was a crybaby. I wondered aloud why people thought Myrtle was a crybaby if terrible things had happened to her that might upset anyone. Again dismissively, Isabel retorted that it had happened 50 years ago! I wondered aloud why people looked down on Myrtle for being upset and added that it can take a long time to get past upsetting feelings. This working through in displacement seemed to soften the harsh superego that had constrained Isabel. There was a lessening of her need to disavow vulnerable feelings and to be critical of herself, and she was able to exhibit less irritation with her mother and me.

NEW EGO CAPACITIES AND POSITIVE FEMININE IDENTIFICATION

Over time, Isabel demonstrated enhanced ego capacity. In one of the now-infrequent sessions when she excitedly jumped from chair to chair, she stopped and said, "Let's see, why am I so excited? My best friend is coming. And I have no school!" Isabel was using her ability for introspection to modulate her action orientation. Another time, she reminisced about the owl puppet and asked me if I remembered "Troublesome Baby" crawling in the nose and the belly of owl? She explained to me that owls are born from eggs in their mothers' bellies and they "ploop" them. Suddenly she regressed to her own "troublesome" feelings by lying on the floor, kicking, and crying. The next moment she stopped herself, saying without disdain that she was acting just like a baby. She returned to her difficulty "going to the bathroom," saying bathrooms were creepy, and associated to kangaroos, whose babies crawl into the mother's pouch from the opening in their mother's body where they were born. She seemed to be working on her understanding of the birth process and its impact on the mother, as well as working through an anally tinged unconscious fantasy of birth that underlay her symptom of withholding her stool and avoiding bathrooms.

Abruptly, Isabel's manner became hostile, destructive, and shut down in her sessions. A week and a half later, Isabel's mother told me that she had informed Isabel that she would be changing her sitter and schools in the fall. With Isabel, I linked her shutting down to guilt over feeling enraged and wondered if she wasn't feeling sad over the impending losses. She concurred and laughed bitterly. She drew a picture of Voldemort and wrote "I'm back!" I interpreted to her that, in her hurt, she seemed to feel she had been treated in a callous manner and felt vengeful. With a growing sense of her feelings and how they were linked to her behavior, she felt freed up. As Isabel continued to play, she introduced me to "Shiskapoo," a tiny doll she had constructed. She talked to him in a reassuring tone, as if to a small child. In silence she made him a house and furnished it, making sure that he had a place to sleep, a kitchen, and so on. In the last moments of the session, she told me in a whisper that a friend of hers had gotten her period that day. Isabel said it was a secret and then ran out. The next day I focused on helping her put into words how it felt to have so much thrown at her before she felt ready. In her play she provided "Shiskapoo" with grooming items. She seemed to feel more tolerant of maternal identifications, including nurturing a small messy child (or perhaps a young girl learning to handle periods).

As our August break approached, Isabel began to read throughout sessions. There was closeness, but it seemed as if she were distancing herself. After one of these sessions, I sat in the chair she had been in and noticed potato chips. The next day she threw candy wrappers on the floor. I noted to her that she really liked to make a mess as if leaving behind something of herself for me to remember her. When she became interested and asked how, I told her about finding the potato chips, and she laughed gleefully. She made two moustaches—one for each of us—and we danced "Ring around the Moustache," cavorting as if we were two guys having a good time. The next day she told me of comments she had received from her father and grandfather while wearing the moustache, which thrilled her. It seemed that Isabel was elucidating the paternal transference in which her femininity was confirmed but she was also permitted masculine identification. Was she also protecting herself from the painful feelings of separation through the camaraderie of the paternal transference? Upon return Isabel seemed relaxed and happy. She had seen the movie *Grease* and sang "Summer Nights," with its tale of summer love and sexuality. Isabel loved the refrain, "Tell me more. Tell me more." At first she wouldn't say what the song was about, but later she revealed it to be a story about a girl who falls in love with a boy and their romance. In this context she recalled the birth of her sister, saying that it was exciting. When I asked her if it had not also been scary, she asked me why, and I said that a woman's body can change in exciting but scary ways. She was silent initially but through play associated to my comments. Halloween was approaching, and she pondered what costume to wear. Her mother suggested she could be Medusa and wear a swim cap with plastic snakes attached, but Isabel wanted to be Athena. She proceeded to work on costumes for the stuffed animals. She wondered what their choices would be. Finally, she decided she would insist on being Athena. It seemed she was working through her anxiety about becoming a desirable young woman and the risks that it entailed, including making a choice different from the one she felt her mother might want her to make.

TRAGEDY AND TRAUMA

For a third time, Isabel's mother called to cancel her daughter's session because her husband had fallen from the roof while cleaning gutters and was badly injured. Isabel brought a toy soldier to our next session. Silently, she cut off the base so that the toy soldier could no longer stand. She cut off the soldier's gun, saying that now he looks like a woman. She tossed the toy aside and shifted to pretending to be a mean teacher demanding that I perform. I acknowledged to Isabel that her mother had called about the accident. Her response was detached but angry: "My real mom or my pretend mom?" I was taken aback and felt Isabel was struggling with a sense of shock. I said that it must be hard to put things together, and she accepted my words quietly. Over days she built geometric molds, collected pencil shavings, and layered them in the molds with glue. She wondered if the shavings would hold without the molds. She checked the glued forms for a week and was relieved when she could hold and look at the intact structures. Still, during the next few weeks, her play had a compulsive, restricted quality. It seemed that her father's accident had made her sadistic fantasies feel real; that is, there really was violent retribution for her wish to have her father's exclusive love. Her desire to cheat me during our play expressed her murderous feelings and wish to triumph illegitimately, which she needed to counteract with an oppressive, restrictive moral authority. In displacement Isabel attempted to come to terms with the extent of her father's injuries and psychic impact of the fault line in her idealization of him, while Isabel's homelife settled into a routine without her father, except for weekly visits to the hospital and later the rehabilitation facility in which he was recuperating.

Isabel gradually seemed to find her footing after the shock and upset of her father's accident. As she did so, she elaborated play involving Alvin and the Chipmunks. Alvin, the Chipmunks, and their girlfriends became students in school with me. The boys and the girls went together into the bathroom. As teacher, Isabel went in to monitor their behavior and was surprised by what they were "doing" in the bathroom. She took them to a "private area" to talk to them, and I was not to be privy to their discussions. The harsh, punitive teacher was absent in this play, replaced by a thoughtful one who maintained the appropriate limits for the children. In contrast, Isabel later returned to play in which she gave me a "chill" and then requested I give her a chill. Before I could speak, she pretended to slap my face, saying that an "old lady told a young lady not to do that!" Was she referring to a prohibition on masturbation? Toward the end of the next session, Isabel silently drew a picture of a disembodied arm that was bleeding and insisted on showing it to her mother. Subsequently, her mother told me that Isabel questioned her about being attacked by the family dog. I wondered if Isabel thought she was responsible for the attack when she tried to chastise her dog; I saw a parallel when she admonished me about the chill, testing whether I would viciously attack her.

Isabel crafted a game in which she was a shopkeeper and I was to buy a special fan from her. It was expensive, and I had to go to the bank to get money to buy it, but I was not to be told how much I needed. After several trips to the bank, withdrawing ever larger sums of cash, she finally accepted my payment and gave me the fan. Laughing, she revealed that the fan was a fake and so I was a fool! I reflected that I had been feeling excited and proud of the special fan she had given me, and now I felt humiliated. Isabel was reminded of the time she had demanded I write about the baby boy's penis. She felt that that had been "weird." Isabel was continuing to integrate her early traumatic experience and its impact on her oedipal desires and fantasies. In the transference she seemed to be uncovering a feeling of being cheated by her mother in terms of her body and genitals and a feeling of revenge. Her play also seemed to illustrate Isabel's wish to be cherished by me and her fear that I would humiliate her.

HERMIONE: MATURING SUPEREGO FUNCTION

In play Isabel pretended I was a Muggle (someone without magic) and she was Hermione Granger (a good witch), who was pretending to be a Muggle so as not to be discovered. She surreptitiously made calls to Dumbledore (a kind, fatherly wizard), pleading with him to rescue her from Muggle life. Isabel wanted the magical power of the good witch and wanted to be saved by an older, more powerful, good wizard who would take her away from her boring, difficult reality. She picked up the phone and exclaimed, "There are robbers in my toilet! They are going to steal poop!" Abruptly, she turned and asked if I knew who Professor Moody was. I indicated that I did. She responded, "So you believe in wizards, too." As Hermione, she whispered, "More Muggles are finding out!" She asked me if I knew Professor Umbridge (an evil, cruel witch allied with Voldemort). I said that she was a witch but quite different from Hermione, and she agreed. She felt that Professor Umbridge should be punished. Isabel seemed to be comparing and contrasting her internal representations of the harsh superego of early childhood (Professor Umbridge) and of her current, more mature, modulated superego (Hermione). She wanted to inflict punishment on Professor Umbridge in angry protest of her own self-punitive impulses, which mirrored the partially resolved conflict within herself. In the same context but at a freer intrapsychic level, Isabel made two books. One was *The Tushie Book: Ideas for My Doctor*, with the following chapters: (1) "Everyone Poops"; (2) "The Book of Spooky Secrets"; (3) "How to Go to the Bathroom"; (4) "The Pee-Pee Book"; and (5) "Even My Doctor Pees, Poops, Burps, and Farts." The other book was a diary, with a note on the back: "Secret, Private, Keep Out, Girls Only!"

The next few weeks marked a time of a distinct upsurge in Isabel's aggression in the office. I spoke about her angry, dismissive tone toward me, and she went to the toy shelf and knocked the toys off, confirming her anger. She made a drawing called "Angry Ants," showing a large queen ant lounging and drinking from a glass with an umbrella surrounded by other, smaller ants dancing and fighting in an unruly fashion. She made another drawing called "Annoying Apes," showing four female apes with prominent breasts and bellies swinging on a vine in provocative defiance. While drawing she would alternately call me over to look and push me away, hitting me in the breast. I commented how confusing this was: She seemed to want me to come close and then was irritated by it. Later, I became aware that her father had had a major setback in his recovery and wondered if this was a partial explanation of her hostility.

ENDINGS: GRIEF, ANGER, AND WORKING THROUGH

At the end of Isabel's second year of analysis, after the summer break, her mother and father announced that they would be getting a divorce. They acknowledged that they had been talking about it over the last two years and recently decided that their marital differences were irreconcilable. This information and announcement caught me off balance, as they had not spoken to me about this level of discord. They had not told their daughters yet and did not plan to for a while. When next I saw Isabel, she seemed irritable. Uncharacteristically, she was ambivalent about coming to the session. She showed me her leg, on which she wore a boot from a fracture, and told me how she had an accident at camp. She continued reconnecting with me and recalled a dream in which there was a party with Professor McGonagall, Professor Umbridge, and Peeves. Dumbledore had died, and Professor Umbridge was ordering Peeves to unscrew the light bulb. I wondered privately if there was a connection between her fracture; the death of Dumbledore; and an unspoken knowledge of the tensions between her parents, including a feeling her father was being killed off. Her associations led to the alliance between Peeves and Professor Umbridge, both of whom exhibited behavior that hinted at the return of Voldemort, symbolizing the upsurge of her angry, destructive feelings.

Maintaining her forward movement, Isabel referred back to a game map she had constructed with me that illustrated Harry Potter's world. She wanted to change it and make the paths more flexible. I noted that the map seemed like a work in progress and that she saw ways to improve it. She associated to having met her teacher and being excited to start her new school. The next day I met again with her parents, who informed me that, because Isabel was adjusting well to her new school, they had decided to stop treatment. They noted that, unbeknownst to me, Isabel had been protesting coming to appointments, even before the summer break. Her mother thought Isabel did not want to come and didn't think she should force her. I felt that Isabel's protests had more complex meanings than her parents were aware of and that her mother was in conflict over the decision. I hoped that our bond was strong enough for me to push for time to understand what Isabel's protests were about. Her mother relented and said she would give it a month, but if Isabel's protests continued, the treatment would end. As I considered the state of the transference, I again wondered if Isabel wasn't disappointed in me for not preventing the unfolding of life events: her father's accident and the divorce. During the following month, I wondered how much Isabel had overheard or sensed about her parent's decisions. Was the protest over sessions an attack on her mother and an attack on me in disillusionment? Was she killing me off? Was she behaving as "Troublesome Baby"? From her earlier dream, did she feel she was behaving as Peeves and following the destructive lead of Professor Umbridge in identification of a sadistic part of her mother's personality?

I tried to talk with Isabel directly about her protests, but she refused. In sessions she reviewed our work together and acknowledged the work might be ending. As she pulled out the productions that represented her intra-psychic work and the journey we had traveled together, she seemed thoughtful. She spoke about *Parental Guidance*, a movie she had seen in which parents leave their children in the care of irresponsible grandparents. The children are gleeful about the unruliness but also wish for appropriate guidance. I thought Isabel was thinking about her desires to be rebellious and expressing a concern that her parents were not helping her with these feelings. I spoke with her about the conflicting feelings the children in the movie seemed to have.

In another association to endings, Isabel came in with materials to make friendship bracelets. She was making one for a new friend in her class who was leaving soon. Because her friend had given her a gift, she wanted to make a gift in return. I felt she was also thinking of our relationship. Speaking to an aspect of the transference, she expressed a concern about one of my plants: Was I waiting too long to water it and making it suffer? She continued wondering aloud, "What if Harry Potter had had no tragedy, no deaths, no horcruxes, no hallows, no chambers?" "What if he had won the tournament but his competitor was still alive?" "What if Voldemort didn't return and Dumbledore didn't die?" And, "What if there were no Death-Eaters?" Insightfully, she guessed then that the stories would be boring. I thought her questions were a poignant acceptance that life held deep sadness as well as joy; they expressed a wish that feelings were less difficult and dangerous for her. I acknowledged that it would be understandable if a person were to wish that terrible things didn't happen.

FEARING A TSUNAMI, WISHING FOR A SOFT LANDING

I met with Isabel's mother. She acknowledged that Isabel no longer protested coming to appointments but had preemptively spoken with Isabel about continuing once a week, and she reported that Isabel had agreed. I felt in a bind, that to protest the further reduction in sessions would have risked a complete rupture. I thought it would impact our work together, but I also thought that it was important to let Isabel end in a constructive manner and not one dictated by her rage at her parents or me. Later that day, when Isabel and I met, she pretended to come at me with a tack and threw paper at me. I asked her if she was angry with me. She said, "No, why?" I said she seemed to be showing anger. She moved away from a verbal response and began to make a parachute, adjusting it because she wanted it to have a soft landing. She ordered me to make one and then asked me if I knew what a tsunami was. She informed me that a tsunami was a wall of water from the ocean that smashes onto land. I elaborated her metaphor by saying that it usually came from an earthquake in the ocean that unsettled it and powerful forces mounted until the water crashed into the land. A tsunami could be powerful and frightening. She picked up "Horsey" and rushed me with him. I said I thought there was a tsunami, and she made a face. Isabel seemed to be showing how painful it was to acknowledge her feelings. In a follow-up session with her mother, I uncharacteristically spoke of the play in which Isabel had expressed a wish for a soft landing and fearing a tsunami. For the first time, I thought her mother appreciated her daughter's perspective about premature ending. Her mother reiterated the need to meet once per week but said she would allow the treatment to be open-ended; the decision to end would be mutual.

For the next months, Isabel and I returned to the classroom setting. She was a kindly kindergarten teacher, and I was one of her young students. I was brand new to school, and she helped me adjust. She developed a schedule, listing my classes and activities for each day of the week, and we went through the schedule. It seemed as if she were counting down our time together. She taught me how to find my bus and emphasized that she would show me and then I would know what to do on my own. In English class she taught me to read using Lemony Snicket's A Series of Unfortunate Events series, about lost parents and orphans. In math class I learned that, if I had two puppies and took away one, there would be only one left. In science class she proposed an experiment in which she put ink from a marker into a bowl of water and we watched it disappear. She said the question was "Is the ink there or not?" I compared changes inside herself, her feelings, and relationships to the ink and said that, even though we couldn't see them, they were there. She concurred. I also used her play to elaborate feelings I thought she was struggling with. I complained that the week was going so fast, and I didn't feel ready. She responded by saying I would get through it. I said I wasn't sure. I thought I might miss school. She responded that sometimes we have to do what we don't want to do. Again, she said I would be alright. She noted it was time to end the session and told me to clean up. She seemed to want to be the one to detach and to leave, but she could allow the expression of sadness and a sense that our work together was meaningful. In another time I pretended to have a question and said, "My parents say I have to change schools, and I don't want to change schools. I like it here." She responded that, again, sometimes we have to do what we don't want to do.

Several months later Isabel's mother told me she had initiated the divorce papers and they would be finalized in a few months. With greater ego capacity and a fundamental change in her use of silence as a defense, Isabel had expressed to her mother that she was upset by all the changes and didn't want more. Her mother was able to hear her sadness and respond to it. In one session Isabel read me the epilogue to one of the Series of Unfortunate Events books, which is dedicated to Beatrice, someone the author had loved and whom he missed after she died. She went through her drawer to find the Harry Potter map and made final changes. She began putting in streets that were not on the map and noted that they were from the dark side. I commented that the map she had originally constructed had all the places where Harry Potter spent happy times, and she agreed but was clear that it was no longer sufficient that way.

Her dad's moving-out day was fast approaching. In session, as the teacher, she did roll call, and I commented that some important people were absent. She said she knew what I was trying to talk about but we should just continue our project. She directed me toward building a house for her pretend rat. I replied that she would rather do that than talk about what is happening at home. She met my comments with silence as she continued to work. In the first session after her father moved out, she again reviewed our work. She pulled out items from when she had cheated me and laughed. She reviewed test papers in which, as a teacher, she had treated me harshly. Why had she done that? She observed that her drawing of Dumbledore looked like a woman with a beard. I went back to our talk in which I had said there were important people missing. She responded quietly that it felt better not to talk about it and just let things happen. She said everyone was OK and that, after her father departed, they had spent the day with friends and had fun. She seemed to be able to tolerate her sadness and was not feeling overwhelmed.

In subsequent sessions she was angrier. She became fascinated with YouTube videos about two daughters who thought they were wizards and their mother was a Muggle. They refused to accept their mother's reality and continued to use their wands to practice magic spells. She also turned to a video of a Harry Potter doll getting revenge on the Draco doll. A sublimated form of sadism was evident. In continuing identification with her father, she often sported a T-shirt with a moustache. One day she said to me that, when puppies are born, the mother pushes them out of her vagina. Calmly she told me she had to go to the bathroom. As we walked down the hall, I asked her if she still held in her stool. She said she didn't. In the middle of the summer, Isabel said she would like to set a date for ending before school started, and we worked together in the remaining weeks.

SUMMARY

Isabel and I had worked together for 2 years 9 months; the first 2 years were in a 4-day-a-week analysis, with additional parental sessions. The last 9 months were a continuation of this work in attenuated form. Through her play in the analysis, we explored aspects of Isabel's inner world and her life experience. Early on her feelings and impulses overwhelmed her ego as she attempted to reveal and defend against her oedipal strivings. She relied primarily on silence, inhibition, and action defenses. Over time she was able through her play to show me how her oedipal development was derailed by her experience of physical injury and her exposure to the birth scene. Her use of silence as a defense required that much of the work continue in displacement. She would not or could not (especially in the first 6 months) verbalize her experiences and her feelings about it. In addition, she was highly controlling of my attempts to verbalize directly what I thought she might be experiencing. As Isabel became able to know her feelings and thoughts and to tolerate them, she was increasingly able to use her ego capacities and build on them. Her play became more integrated, symbolized, and sublimated. She became able to use her intellect and curiosity to explore the world and learn about procreation. She could let herself know about her female body while also enjoying her masculine identifications. There were structural changes as her harsh, punitive superego matured and softened; changes in self and object representations developed and freed her to have less conflictual relations with her mother and other important women in her life. Isabel made good progress in our work, despite the impact of tensions between her parents and her father's illness and subsequent injuries. In this Isabel demonstrated a fundamental resilience. She arrived at my office a silent, inhibited young girl, and she left our work with greater confidence and a greater ability to know her feelings and to choose when to reveal them. She loved school and was thriving academically. She had a group of girlfriends she was close to. Importantly, she traversed her parents' difficulties to maintain a close relationship with both of them. Puberty and adolescence loomed in the not-too-distant future for Isabel. These developmental milestones always present a young person with challenges; I would wonder if they won't challenge Isabel in a more significant and fundamental manner.

Chapter Two

Discussion of Isabel's Analysis

Edward I. Kohn

Oedipal development places a young mind amid phase-specific anxieties, passions, and emotions. Dread and terror regarding bodily mutilation, love, hate, sexual desire, overstimulation, curiosity, and an effort to understand the world are all at play. The child with an immature ego tries to cope with the overwhelming nature of these experiences, drawing on a mind with limited experience and cognitive capacity. The adults who try to help the child manage all this are also embroiled in the drama. Theories and fantasies about the sexual act, pregnancy, and birth of babies operate consciously and unconsciously, stirring powerful feelings that can bombard the child. The child's efforts to communicate her emotions and her behavior can leave the adults perplexed, off balance, and stirred up themselves.

Reality events, earlier in life or during the oedipal phase, inform, shape, stimulate, and intensify the child's oedipal experience. The child in Dr. Huddleston's presentation is not one who can calmly sit down and talk about the birds and the bees or imagine a quiet ambulance that visits during the night to deliver the baby or take someone's penis to the hospital. She was exposed to the birth of her sister in the midst of blood, screams, and sirens. She also suffered her own frightening physical injury during toilet training and contended with her father's serious injury during her analysis.

While reading this case, the listener gets to see and hear the overwhelmed little girl in full flower, the strains that this places on the analyst, and how the analyst tries to contain the action and maintain her own balance while helping the child understand her own experience. In this discussion I flesh out a picture of this child's internal world, her specific oedipal constellation, the relationship between traumatic events and oedipal development, the technical interventions informed by this understanding, and a vision of the therapeutic arc of this analysis.

The first session, when Dr. Huddleston met Isabel, was somewhat chaotic. Her play, controlled at first, became increasingly intense and active. We can see manifestations of Isabel's preoccupations in this active play, even though they were not pulled together in a cohesive whole. In this initial hour, we see the first evidence of themes that will continue through her analysis. As we immerse ourselves in Dr. Huddleston's presentation, I pay attention to themes that appear repeatedly and consider how they evolve, how they deepen, and how their portrayal becomes ever richer and more complex. This helps us to observe how the mode and process of communication changes as the analytic work progresses.

In the first session and early phase of the analysis, Isabel's theories and fantasies about birth and sex were, to a significant extent, expressed in action. Gradually, action between Isabel and Dr. Huddleston became less intense and direct, in favor of a move into the microcosm. Action was portrayed more in the play with puppets. The play itself transformed, as symbolic representation and verbal communication—dreams, books, and stories—took center stage. Toward the end of the analytic work, direct discussion was possible. Isabel asked her mother to explain the incident when she was attacked by the family dog, and she talked with Dr. Huddleston about her concerns about her father leaving the family.

By tracing themes, we also get to see how the content of Isabel's concerns or preoccupations evolved developmentally. We observe how her theories about the workings of the body became more organized and coherent in form, which allowed her to communicate their content with greater clarity. Initially, she described how babies are pooped out, but as the analysis approached its end, she noted that mothers push their babies out through their vaginas. Of course, this simple statement by itself does not capture the intensity associated with these ideas. The terror and violence of the birth and poop experience, stimulated by her exposure to the precipitous birth of her sister and the dog attack while she was on the potty, were overwhelming. The quality as well as the content of her fantasies and theories transformed over the course of analysis.

We can follow the theme of the nature of the parent–child and analyst–child relationships. Isabel's play revealed a view of mothers as demeaning inquisitors, while fathers were more nurturing and instructive. These images changed in the context of her relationship with Dr. Huddleston. Internal representations of mother figures became more patient and caring, and in her play, they provided needed guidance for children. Isabel not only dealt with the disappointing reality that her idealized father was simply human, but she also came to see him as a vulnerable and damaged figure. These views of mothers and fathers influenced another important theme: what it means to be a boy or a girl and the anatomical distinction between the sexes. We can observe Isabel's confusion, anxiety, and ambivalence as she moved toward a more consolidated sense of her femininity. All of these themes came together in a complex and rich, movie-like portrayal of the oedipal drama. From the *Wizard of Oz* to the wizards of Harry Potter, we see epic battles of good and evil in a world of witches, idealized and disappointing men, and the efforts of children to contend with the turmoil.

The oedipal experience is a product of a child's fantasy life and the realities in which she lives. Little girls, like Isabel, have baby sisters. Adults have powers and do things that children don't understand. Adults know the secrets of the body and the bedroom. We are able to trace Isabel's intense feelings about these secrets and her efforts to make sense of them through her work with Dr. Huddleston.

The animals in the opening session ate voraciously, and the doll that Isabel called "Troublesome Baby" penetrated aggressively inside the bodies of the puppets. Here, we see portrayal of Isabel's own aggressive oral hunger and a view of her baby sister as an aggressively intrusive feeder. In addition, we can infer a fantasy of how babies burrow their way into their mothers. Isabel felt driven to get inside the bodies of the puppets and compelled to figure out the secrets that went on in there. Bodily functions, like pee and poop, were in her mind, as well as the most perplexing parts: babies and conception.

Efforts to make sense of gender differences were reflected in her interest in the lion's bushy mane, her grandfather's bushy hair, and the squirrel's bushy tail. Isabel was filled with excitement and anxiety. The play with the puppets quickly intensified and got more aggressive. She moved from the microcosm of play into the realm of action, jumping from chair to chair, repeatedly approaching her analyst for "uppies." Isabel was overstimulated, and this presented a challenge to her analyst. How could she manage the child's physical activity in order to maintain a safe and contained environment conducive to analytic work? We observe how Dr. Huddleston and Isabel dealt with this, how the quality of this interaction evolved, and how it entered the content of their communication.

Six weeks into analysis, while dealing with her father's illness, Isabel reported a dream about fairies and monsters. While it is evident that she was interested in the dream, she also insisted that she didn't want to talk about it. Dr. Huddleston noted her curiosity but also commented that a part of Isabel says, "No way!" This moment elicited an emphatic "All parts say no!" from Isabel. She left the dream and turned her attention to Dr. Huddleston's books about the births of Athena and Aphrodite. While manifestly she had retreated from her dream, the work had deepened, and she exhibited a more organized, aim-inhibited effort to come to grips with the scary and exciting questions about where babies come from.

In a subsequent session, we see Isabel's effort to explore the many facets of the oedipal constellation in her story about Esther and Mordechai. Despite her overexcitement—jumping on the sofa—she told a coherent story and provided her own analysis of the tale. It is not Esther but Mordechai who is the hero. Beautiful women, nakedness, replacing the queen, power, evil, and different kinds of father figures, including the king, the murderous Haman, and the wise and protective Mordechai, were all involved. After telling the story, Isabel revealed that she had wet her pants. While we may think of this as regression, a retreat from the anxiety of oedipal sexuality, it is also important to remember that sexual excitement in young children causes and is confused with urethral stimulation. It is not a big leap to think of wet pants as a reference to genital sexual as well as urethral excitement.

The oedipal themes were again portrayed when patient and analyst talked about the *Wizard of Oz* (Fleming & LeRoy, 1939). Isabel reached for a happy resolution as she sang "Somewhere over the Rainbow." In the movie, Dorothy dreams of a magical place. She yearns to be free of the painful conflicts of the oedipal phase and real life, but her dream and her solution are not so simple. She has to deal with a wicked witch, as well as a good witch, and she eventually learns that the great wizard is a terrible disappointment. Yet, she comes to appreciate and value the flawed men in her life and that "there is no place like home." Young Isabel, however, had not yet achieved this resolution. The intensity of her feelings and her hostility toward her envied mother were not readily manageable. She burst into action mode, hitting Dr. Huddleston in the breasts, the same problematic behavior she had engaged in with her mother. She squished Dr. Huddleston's body with the inner office door, as if she was cutting off her breasts and belly, those parts of the woman's body essential to feeding and housing the baby.

Dr. Huddleston notes that Isabel had difficulty allowing herself to defecate; at school and in the analytic sessions, she would not ask to go to the bathroom. She had difficulty containing what was inside and asking for help to get it out. This included poop, pee, and her emotions. It is likely that her anxiety about going to the bathroom was influenced by the vicious attack she endured when she tried to push the dog away from her poop. As well, it seems credible to think that the precipitous birth of her younger sister was a scary and overwhelming instance of bodily violence, in which the head of this slimy, bloody creature created a wide opening in her mother's body and was pooped out. A giant, destructive, messy, and noisy poop seems like a good explanation for birth and a good metaphor for emotions.

Four months into the analysis, Isabel examined and compared the genitals of the boy and girl dolls. She reacted to this discovery by tossing the girl doll aside and played at cutting off limbs. In subsequent sessions, she went back to the issue of sexual differences in classroom play. No longer the dutiful student, she assumed the role of the demanding teacher who harshly questioned Dr. Huddleston about her knowledge of a boy's penis, demonstrating her analyst's ignorance. The themes of secrets, gender differences, and body parts were expressed within the context of the mother–child, teacher–child, and analyst–child relationships. Rather than warmly helping the child to learn about these matters, the teacher took pleasure in humiliating the little girl who lacked the knowledge. Isabel envied the secret powers of the adults and was endlessly frustrated that they knew the secrets and she did not.

As the work continued, Isabel became more active and provocative, and she precariously straddled her analyst's desk, exhibiting her underpants. Dr. Huddleston wondered about the many reverberations that contributed to this exhibitionistic moment and made a judgment in her effort to facilitate the unfolding of the process. She noted out loud that Isabel seemed to want to show her bottom. Isabel responded with a correction, explaining that her bottom was her rectum and her seat was her genitalia. Bringing to bear her excellent cognitive and verbal capacity, Isabel worked with Dr. Huddleston's seemingly simple observation and took charge, again teaching her analyst. Isabel was working, for both of their sakes, to make sense of her experience of a hot topic by giving names to these confusing and stimulating body parts.

While this teaching moment was likely influenced by Isabel's wish to demonstrate her superior knowledge, it seems that the hotness of the topic became the driving force. At first, she shifted to singing "Itsy Bitsy Teeny Weeny Yellow Polka Dot Bikini," but words and music were not sufficient to contain her sexual excitement and anxiety. Isabel moved from words and music to play-action. She pretended to break an egg on Dr. Huddleston's head, poke her with needles, and plunge a knife into her back. It became a scene that reflected her vision of sexual intercourse as a violent, bloody, sadomasochistic act.

Isabel had begun this sequence with relatively less modulated behavior, straddling her analyst's desk and exhibiting her underwear. Dr. Huddleston's intervention, putting Isabel's wish to show her underwear into words, brought her back from the edge (of the desk) to the song, but the power of sexual stimulation and anxiety led Isabel back toward action. When she play-acted the stabbing of her analyst, she was not very far from direct action. Despite this trend, Isabel did not cross that line, and her behavior was more contained and less precarious than it had been at the start of the session.

A few sessions later, Isabel described a dream about five chocolate turtles. While she had refused to discuss the earlier dream, Isabel not only talked about this dream but also provided her own analysis. She thought that one of the turtles was her sister. The chocolate turtles represent brown poop-babies delivered anally. In the history provided by Isabel's mother, we learned that Isabel would hug her mother and sister so hard that she would hurt them. We see this loving destructiveness in the dream when Isabel ate the chocolate baby/turtle. We might wonder, as well, if this was an expression of a fantasy of oral impregnation.

Using Kleenex and a pencil, Isabel created a flower with elements of male and female genitalia. Previously, when she examined the two naked dolls, she tossed the female doll away in shock. Now she was engaged in a more derivative exploration, and she tolerated it more comfortably than the accurately portrayed organs of the dolls. Isabel attentively watered her flower every day. She may have been yearning for a penis or a penis and a vagina, but it seemed likely that, with sufficient loving care, this flower with ambiguous genitalia would unfold its petals and transform into a beautiful vision of a vagina.

During the period when Dr. Huddleston and Isabel discussed the Harry Potter series, her father suffered a serious injury. When Isabel explained that she didn't know how her father was doing, Dr. Huddleston commiserated, noting how difficult it is when adults don't explain what is happening. She had put her finger on the distress of the moment. For Isabel, the knowledge of her father's condition was another one of those frightening, infuriating, and humiliating secrets that were kept from her, and she was very upset!

Isabel was a child who was driven to make sense of these mysterious and overpowering matters. The secrets, wizardry, and dangers of the Harry Potter novels were a fine setting to engage her concerns (Rowling, 1991, 1998, 2004). The adults in her life were like the teacher in her earlier play or the wizards of the novel: They have the knowledge but keep the secret powers to themselves, away from the Muggles. What goes on in the Chamber of Secrets, be it the bedroom or the inner sanctum of a woman's body? How unfair that only the adults get to know what goes on or are allowed entry to this chamber! Isabel was gleeful when Dr. Huddleston couldn't answer her questions about the novels. The narcissistic injury had been reversed.

With her increasing capacity to reflect, Isabel thought about her past interactions with Dr. Huddleston. Like us, with the advantage of hindsight, she could look back on earlier sessions with a perspective that was different from the one she had at the time. She wondered if her analyst remembered "Troublesome Baby" crawling in the nose and belly of the owl. She explained that owls are born from eggs in the mother's belly and she poops them out. Considering this theory, and in light of the attack where it seemed like the family dog would kill her on the potty or the precipitous birth of her sister, it is no wonder that asking to go to the bathroom was fraught for this child or that "Troublesome Baby" was so pressured to get inside the owl.

Isabel's mother informed her that she would be changing her sitter and school. In her session, Isabel seemed shutdown and hostile. Dr. Huddleston connected her attitude and mood with feelings of anger and guilt. Isabel laughed bitterly and drew a picture of Voldemort, writing, "I'm back." Her mother had reentered the scene again with bad news, and Isabel's angry feelings had returned. When Dr. Huddleston talked with her about feeling callously treated and vengeful, Isabelle introduced "Shiskapoo." Identified with Dr. Huddleston, Isabel spoke to "Shiskapoo" in a reassuring tone and provided him with a house, including a kitchen and a place to sleep. It is noteworthy that this sequence foreshadowed Isabel's later response to termination of the analysis.

As the session ended, Isabel whispered that her friend had gotten her period. In the next hour, Dr. Huddleston explored how it felt to have so much thrown at her before she felt ready. Isabel responded to this question and interpretation about the potential to be overwhelmed with further play involving "Shiskapoo." Isabel provided grooming items for "Shiskapoo" that would help him to manage the messiness.

When we compare this play to the activity when the teacher humiliated the child, we see how analyst and analysand continued to transform Isabel's internal representation of the mother–child relationship. In the previous hour, Isabel had let Dr. Huddleston know that a new source of stimulation and uncertainty—menstruation—had entered her experience, but she did more than allow Dr. Huddleston to view this development in her inner world. Her mind filled the room, and both child and analyst had become players on this stage. From the psychological perspective, Dr. Huddleston had sat with this messy (and now the mess included menstrual blood), angry child and warmly brushed her hair—an emblematic mother–child activity—helping her to learn to understand and care for her body, it's productions, and her emotions.

After their return from their August vacations, Isabel sang the song "Summer Nights," a tale of adolescent summer love. She loved the refrain, "Tell me more! Tell me more!" She was filled with feelings of love and sexuality and wanted to learn as much as she could. This continued in her subsequent play about Alvin and the Chipmunks. The boy and girl chipmunks went into one another's bathrooms at school. The teacher discovered them and took them to a private area in order to talk to them. This play reflects the further evolution of Isabel's capacity to deal with the intense and rich experience of sexuality. It is an age-appropriate, coherent, nonchaotic expression of heterosexual desire. We see that this includes the need for the adult to help manage the behavior of the children.

This story represents an important point on the arc of Isabel's analysis. Dr. Huddleston had brought the sexually excited, anxious, angry, and curious girl to a private room to talk about her feelings. Rather than getting angry, being overly permissive, or shaming the child, she limited the child's actions and also engaged her in a long discussion over a period of years. In this context, it actually is possible to talk about the birds and the bees.

Isabel's father's accident was hard to deal with. Not surprisingly, Isabel's play portrayed injury and castration, as well as efforts to build and repair structures. She drew a picture of a bloody, disembodied arm and insisted on showing it to her mother. Freer to wonder, with less of a sense that events must remain secret, Isabel was able to question her mother about the incident when she was attacked by the dog. Silence was no longer the predominant solution.

The important matters of secrets and the frustration of being the child rather than the adult continued when Isabel portrayed Hermione Granger and assigned Dr. Huddleston the role of a Muggle. She turned passive into active and played that she was the one with the powers of wizardry and Dr. Huddleston was the one on the outside. At the same time, she had created a place with Dr. Huddleston to explore and sort out her ideas and feelings, safe from the peering eyes of the other adults, like her mother. Isabel created a diary. While, in the play interaction, Dr. Huddleston was not privy to the secrets of Isabel's diary, in a fundamental way, the analytic relationship had become the secret diary, where Isabel could explore the workings of her heart.

While trying to come to grips with her father's injuries, Isabel's oedipal antagonisms and anxieties were intensified. Her stories about Harry Potter reveal complex versions of her unique oedipal struggles and help us to get inside the intermingling of reality events and her fantasies. Professor Umbridge is an evil witch allied with Voldemort. If we do a little homework and read *Harry Potter and the Order of the Phoenix* (Rowling, 2004), we learn that Umbridge is fundamentally a nasty inquisitor who torments the children. She is another portrayal of the mean teacher in the classroom, the Wicked Witch of the East, or the mean mother. Isabel's anger with her mother is further portrayed in the story about angry ants. The queen ant lounges around with an umbrella drink, surrounded by the little ants, who sing, dance, and fight in an unruly fashion. This child still needs the attentive, caring, and supportive figure who can help manage reality and help contain the excitable children. She blames her mother for this failure and perhaps for failing to protect her father.

More reality intruded into Isabel's world and her analysis. She learned that her parents were going to divorce. Her response was to dream that Dumbledore, the kind father figure, had died. The evil witch, Professor Umbridge, was telling Peeves what to do. It was distressing to Isabel that this nasty mother figure was bossing this small figure around. It is the kind woman, Professor McGonagall, who should be giving orders. Peeves is a male poltergeist, the embodiment of disorder. When Umbridge tried to take over the school, Peeves went on a rampage in an effort to thwart the evil usurper. In the character of Peeves, Isabel captured her own out-of-control behavior, her fury at her mother, and her effort to prevent her from taking over control of the family. For Isabel, the divorce was a coup by her mother, who threatened to displace the kind father whom she saw as more nurturing.

Isabel's efforts to contend with the divorce and her father's injuries were imbedded in her references to Professor Moody. He is a heroic figure who has battled many criminal wizards in the past. He is left with facial scars and has lost an eye, part of a leg, and part of his nose. Like the Wizard of Oz, her father was a bad wizard but a nice man, and she saw him as a heroic figure who had been damaged, like Professor Moody.

Isabel's mother again brought a harsh reality into the analytic world: termination! Isabel discussed the movie *Parental Guidance*, in which children are left with their grandparents who, like the queen ant, don't adequately supervise the children. While the children are excited to be free, the need for guidance dominates. Ending analysis meant that Isabel had to say goodbye to Dr. Huddleston, the kind, firm, and guiding teacher. Earlier in analysis Isabel had watered the tissue flower of genital sexuality every day. In response to the prospect of termination, she was distressed that Dr. Huddleston was making one of her plants wait too long for the water. How can this wonderful plant fully flower and bud without the precious nurturance of analysis?

Seeing Dr. Huddleston as the parent figure who leaves her with the inadequate grandparents or the queen ant who is not sufficiently attentive to the children, Isabel was angry! She pretended to come at Dr. Huddleston with a tack and later rushed at her with "Horsey." Despite her anger, she made a parachute to ensure a soft landing. While the intensity of her feelings was high and tsunami-like, Isabel and Dr. Huddleston could still talk about this.

Loss and change were worked over repeatedly, for the most part within an envelope of benevolence and guidance. Isabel was the teacher who helped Dr. Huddleston, the student, to adjust to her new school, and she developed a schedule for her. She made maps during sessions, and as the kind teacher, she explained to Dr. Huddleston how to find her bus. In the same way that they had cared for "Shiskapoo" after learning that Isabel was going to lose her sitter and her school, they now built a home for her pet rat and provided water and a bed.

Isabel's growing capacity to manage her intense feelings allowed her to talk directly with Dr. Huddleston about the departure of her father. She wrote him a letter. She continued her effort to sort out the emotional qualities of men and women as she noted that her drawing of Dumbledore looked like a woman with a beard. While her father had been the figure who represented kindness, it appears that Isabel was open to seeing kindness as a maternal quality, as well.

The analytic duo weathered storms of anger, resentment, and loss. Amid these painful emotions, Isabel's theories about sex and birth continued to evolve. She explained that, when puppies are born, their mother pushes them out through her vagina. She said this quite directly, but it remained a hot topic, and it had a physical impact on our young heroine. She had to go to the bathroom, but unlike the child who could not ask to leave the room early in analysis, she calmly explained that she had to go.

Over the course of this analysis, Isabel had gone from action to words. Her capacity to tolerate frustration and delay was enhanced. The parachute she made demonstrated the development of internal structure, the capacity to modulate affect. She explained to Dr. Huddleston that sometimes you can't have what you want. Anal theories about birth had become genital theories. Representation of the mother–child relationship had evolved from demeaning, critical, and withholding to benevolent teaching and provision of skills that help little girls manage their emotions and make themselves pretty. Isabel demonstrated that she could nurture "Shiskapoo" and herself. This little girl, anxious and confused about gender differences, was well on her way to becoming proud of her femininity.

Chapter Three

Ella

Adele Kaufman

"I say 'Mother,' not 'Mommy'!" These were the first words that Ella, a 4-year-10-month-old adopted girl, spoke in the waiting room as she stepped out from behind her mother. Her tone of voice was surprisingly aggressive and contemptuous. Because she was trembling and looked so scared, I said to her, "You don't know me yet. It could be scary to come with me to the playroom." Her mother handled her in an impatient, intolerant way, and Ella walked quickly ahead of me. She said, "I'm not scared at all!" in a tone of voice that suggested it was very silly of me to suggest such a thing. I felt concern and wondered to myself what lay beneath this pseudoadult presentation of a young child trying so hard to cover up her fear. In responding to her affect, I had unknowingly elicited a defense. This moment points to the complexity of beginnings, when we do not know what a child's words and actions really mean or what our words and actions mean to the child.

With this case study, I demonstrate how this young child's symptomatic aggressive behavior was multidetermined and embedded in her developing character structure. My emphasis is on the analytic process and ways in which we adapt analytic technique to be responsive to the changing developmental and intrapsychic phases of the child. Despite difficult circumstances and obstacles, conflicts from different developmental levels appeared in the transferences, and our work together resulted in significant change.

At the start of her analysis, Ella could not allow much play. Play is a natural mode of communication for children, but play and playfulness had become engaged in conflict and had taken on dangerous meaning for her. As I thought about the dysregulation and interferences in her capacity to play, it was difficult to distinguish primary developmental disturbances and imbalances in her development from disturbances brought about by conflicts at higher levels of development. We worked at the interface between the shifting levels of development and psychic conflict.

Ella's difficulty in playing or engaging in playful interaction was from both internal and external sources and required adaptations in technique to allow me to engage and communicate with her. Shifting levels of organization led to rapid shifts in Ella's functioning, which required rapid shifts in my functioning in turn. The analytic process was characterized by bursts of forward-moving analytic work, talking, and playing, interrupted by periods of impulsive, aggressive, chaotic, activity in which nothing I said or did was right. In the beginning Ella often required holding and physical management, which was sometimes difficult because of the intensity of her aggressive behavior. It was not until later in the analysis that she calmed in response to the emotional and physical holding that she craved. When she could play, her play most often represented themes of abandonment, aggression, good versus bad, and bodily damage.

WHO'S THE BOSS? THE DIAGNOSTIC HOURS

From the first diagnostic session, it was apparent that Ella believed that only one of us could be in charge and that it must be she. In the playroom she introduced me to her doll and insisted I admire the doll. She criticized the dollhouse, saying it was a "mess." She decided to rearrange it, and I complied with her exact instructions about how I was to participate. Partway through the session, Ella said to a doll, "You bad girl. You want the teacher to pay attention to you, not the other kids." She then said directly to me, "I want to do bad things I see other kids doing. I have to stop myself."

With this revelation, Ella became silent and unapproachable when I spoke either to the doll or directly to her, until close to the end of the session. I was suddenly shut out (an important pattern emerging), and she acted as though she did not hear me when I said to both Ella and the dolls, "How terrible this is for you to feel you are so bad." When Ella turned away, I said that maybe she was worried that I, too, would think she and her doll Rosie were bad. I tried unsuccessfully to enlist Ella to help understand the doll's feelings and to enlist the doll to help understand about Ella stopping herself from doing bad things. Finally, I concluded aloud that neither of them was ready to talk more about these things, but I was glad they told me what they did. I hoped that Ella's observation about herself reflected a nascent capacity for mastery.

Ella refused to leave until we arranged the toys precisely as she wanted them. As we did this, I reflected to myself on the depth of her need for control and said, "I have a hunch you feel better when you are the boss." Ella agreed readily with this observation as we arranged the toys together. I assumed that being controlling provided a sense of safety and made note to myself of her awareness of her feelings and capacity for self-observation at this young age.

Ella brought another doll to the second diagnostic session and this time introduced it to my dolls. We were on the road to getting acquainted and developing connection. She arranged the dollhouse with a bedroom for the children and a bedroom for the mother. There was no mention of a father. She added to her play "looking for the lost covers for the bed" and demanded I join the search, which I did. Her play soon broke down into frantic efforts at controlling me, shouting commands, and becoming physically wound up as she escalated toward increasingly aggressive chaotic action. My effort to learn more about the "upsetting lost covers" only increased the chaos. When I was able to make eye contact with her, I said, "I think you are being bossy with me to cover up worries." Ella stopped shouting and silently looked at me, and I said, "You don't know yet if I'm a grownup who can understand a kid's feelings." Ella remained silent, and I added, "You're probably not sure you want me to know you worry a lot about your parents." With these small incremental steps, I tried to convey to Ella that I was listening to her and was interested in understanding her feelings and what she required from me. I was quickly learning that, when her play broke down because her ego functioning was overwhelmed, I could not attempt continuing to communicate with her in the play metaphor. At those times, direct verbal communication, which provided acceptance of her highest-level defenses against overwhelming anxiety and supported her secondary process thinking, often helped her to recover.

Ella said in a complaining tone, "My mother works all the time. She works with lots of people. Now I have a brother. He cries all the time. He wakes me up. I have to play alone." I told Ella that she was helping me to understand another of her worries: how lonely she feels and how hard it is to share her mother with her brother and all those people. I said that, as I got to know her, I may be able to help her with these worries. Ella volunteered that she didn't have to miss her father because he was always home. I thought to myself that Ella was a child with awareness of her feelings but with limited ability to control them.

As we were arranging the dollhouse, again according to Ella's instructions, she suddenly laughed maliciously and crashed a toy car full of "baby boys" into the "mother's bedroom closet." Ella felt around the inside of the dollhouse closet and then looked inside. She shouted repeatedly in a panic-stricken voice, "It has shapes inside. I don't know where they came from." Play again turned to panic as she forcefully threw the contents of the dollhouse all over the room. I picked up the dollhouse closet and looked at it. I said I could see how worried she was about the shapes, and I wondered aloud if we could figure out a way to help her. She was unresponsive, and the frenzy continued. Her aggression did not seem directed at me but was chaotic and dysregulated. I wondered to myself what the scary shapes represented—babies, a baby brother, a pregnant mother, primal scene exposure or fantasy, a triadic configuration, or a transference that I did not yet understand? (This became more understandable later.) I believed that Ella was not "fantasy playing" in her dollhouse activity at this point but was enacting. Her activity was controlled and rigid, though these defenses were not completely successful, and she rapidly became overwhelmed and dysregulated. Qualities that we consider essential to play, such as externalization, symbolization, and displacement, were absent. Play, which occupies an intermediate space between fantasy and enactment, easily and quickly tipped into aggressive enactment. Terrified of her own affects, seeming to lack signal anxiety at these times, and without a useful repertoire of defenses, Ella could not play. The session descended toward chaos, as she became impulsive and increasingly aggressive.

In that instant between reflection and the need to act quickly, I searched within myself for something to reassure her and help reduce her panic. My initial attempts to respond in what I assumed was her play metaphor (being worried about the shapes) had increased her anxiety. This presented a technical dilemma given her young age and development, and I needed to find another way to try to make contact. Play was impossible, and this early in our work I was unsure of the meaning of her words or how she might receive my words. I made a rapid choice based on my initial assessment of her poor defenses against intolerable affects and her questionable capacity to distinguish fantasy and reality in the dysregulated state. I chose to offer a reality-based verbalization in an effort to support her secondary process. Given what I had already observed about her defenses, I thought that reality-based words might provide some containment by reducing the impact of the moment and moving us out of the heat of the here-and-now thinking when she was overwhelmed by intolerable emotion and conflict. I said, "I think, from what just happened in this playing, you want me to know you are confused and worried about your baby brother, where and who he came from." Ella began to calm and spoke tearfully. She said, "All I know is my parents went away to have a baby." Although the nature of Ella's fantasies about her birth and adoption and the adoption of a second child had yet to emerge, her anxiety and terror were evident. This somewhat-unusual choice of technique was repeatedly necessary in the early phases of Ella's analysis.

Beginning with the early sessions, I learned that what could help Ella at these times was direct verbal communication in a calm, accepting, understanding tone of voice, often accompanied by other necessary nonverbal interventions, such as holding during her aggressive outbursts. Even during this early phase, these interactions helped restore Ella's ego functioning and equilibrium, often gradually bringing her into a state of being able to play.

Ella was brought to the last diagnostic session by her father. The separation was easier. When I commented on this, she said it was because she saw her father more. Ella told me she was afraid of the dark. Sometimes it helped to put her head under the covers, and she demonstrated how she did this. In this way, our communication about her defensive hiding began to deepen.

Ella resumed playing: "This doll is all alone. Her mother went to the hospital to have a baby. They played a trick on her. They said they were going to work. They went to have a baby instead." With tears in her eyes, Ella became silent and then began to stomp around the room with increasing intensity. I was now keenly aware of how easily anxiety overwhelmed her ego functioning.

Although she was obviously talking about herself, I did not know to what extent this was conscious. I was faced with another dilemma. Trying to bridge these possibilities, I said, "This is very sad. I see how upset you are about *that* baby." Ella said very directly, "I don't know who is going to take care of me now. They don't know. I'm all alone." I agreed that this was a terrible worry and certainly one of the reasons she was so upset lately.

After these initial diagnostic sessions, I developed a clinical picture of a young child with deficits in affect regulation, signal anxiety, and impulse control; a limited repertoire of defenses; and a fragile narcissistic balance that interfered with fully engaging a separation-individuation process and higher-level conflicts, along with highly developed intellectual capacities and intellectual defenses. These aspects of psychic structure in a child so young presented dilemmas, but as they were her most adaptive defenses, they required respect and acceptance until her development proceeded enough to allow more flexibility. Ella also demonstrated a capacity for self-reflection and awareness of her feelings, although she was often not able to make use of these capacities. Although there appeared to be triadic conflict and anxieties, the subsequent process demonstrated that earlier developmental conflict was more prominent at that time. I viewed her as stuck in a rapprochement phase of separation-individuation shaped in large part by the hostility and ambivalence of her parents. Oral and anal sadistic trends competed with Ella's desire for nurturing, emotional freedom, self-agency, and safety. I tried in all of my verbal interventions to explain how I arrived at what I was thinking or saying in order to give her an opportunity to learn something about how my mind works and at the same time provide the opportunity for Ella to begin to think about how her mind works. This technique was part of the crucial nonverbal aspects of our communication. Given the need to address both development and conflict, it was challenging at times to follow Ella's rapidly shifting levels of mental organization.

BACKGROUND

Ella's parents sought help because of her increasingly provocative, aggressive, and controlling behavior. She insisted on being the focus of attention and could not allow her parents out of her sight without a struggle. When she did not get her way, she hit, kicked, bit, or screamed. Her parents felt exhausted by their daughter. During the preceding month, an infant boy was adopted, and the nanny who had cared for Ella since birth was replaced. Despite their concern, her parents were unaware of the impact of these events on Ella.

In their interactions with me, Ella's parents were cautious and aloof. One comment by Ella's mother was especially significant: She believed that Ella's behavior was inherited from the biological mother. Ella's parents were silent about their own difficulties and unable to face that Ella's problems were connected to their problems. However, their ongoing determination to find help for Ella helped me to feel hopeful that I could help them.

Unable to have biological children, Ella's parents had searched for and believed they found the perfect adoption. The adolescent birth mother lived with them, so they could be involved in her care and the delivery, and they knew the health history of the birth father. However, during their time together, tensions arose between the two women. Ella's adoptive mother came to view the birth mother as demanding, provocative, aggressive, and dishonest. (You can see later how this gets displaced to the child and becomes part of the child's self-representation.) The birth and delivery were without complications; the birth mother did not return to their home, and there had been no contact since then.

In the beginning, I thought about Ella's adoption experience; her parents' experience of her adoption; and the trauma of the abrupt, confusing, unpredictable shifts that took place as she became a toddler, as primary organizers of her personality. Her fantasy life, defensive organization, narcissistic balance, sense of self, and other and object relations all seemed to be organized around a personal self-hating and other-hating system of beliefs surrounding her adoption. Ella's adoptive parents also created a belief system about her adoption that had a crucial impact on her development and on their development as parents. As Ella's analysis progressed, we were able to understand how her adoption fantasies and beliefs demonstrated the underlying nature of the separation-individuation process and her efforts to gain autonomy and a sense of self-agency. They also served defensive purposes in managing conflict about her aggression and terror of the abandonment she believed she deserved, as well as being a source of emotional pain and conflict in reality.

Ella was described as a perfectly easy and satisfying baby to care for. She ate well, slept well, and was vigorous and alert. She was kept in a snuggly for most of the first year, and her parents described the first year as a happy time for them. I had a picture of a mostly passive infant who accepted the physical restraint and who was first overidealized by her parents and then abruptly deidealized. I speculated that Ella may have experienced her first year of life in the snuggly as one of constraint rather than security and that, once freed from those restraints, her innate potential to assert herself made its appearance.

Things changed abruptly and traumatically when Ella became an assertive toddler. Nurturing was withdrawn as her parents deidealized her; they experienced her activity and assertiveness (which appeared to be within an expectable range) as disruptive and attacking. Feeling increasingly helpless and out of control, they resorted to domineering and physical punishment. Ella's parents, too, had problems with autonomy and affect regulation. They could not help Ella during the rapprochement phase, when she faced struggles with separation and reunion, dependence and independence, power and control, and love and hate. Ella's mother was especially prone to splitting (good baby/bad toddler) and was unable to manage her own aggression. There was a standoff as Ella became increasingly aggressive, domineering, and demanding. A pattern evolved of chronic mishandling of her assertiveness by shaming and demands that she "grow up and behave." She was assigned chores far beyond her capacities to manage. This traumatic split in Ella's early life had a profound impact on her development. She became increasingly difficult, aggressive, defiant, and provocative. By the time she was 4, she had run away from home several times, across busy streets—a behavioral representation of a fragile and disturbed emotional connection and another way in which her parents demonstrated their inability to protect her and keep her safe. It was notable that there were no playful or pleasurable activities between Ella and her mother. Her father, more emotionally available, had a warmer relationship with her, but her mother was critical of their play. Although she made an initial good adjustment in preschool, by the time I met Ella, she was unable to get along with other children and could only respond to teachers whom she perceived as preferring her above others. She was bright and intellectually precocious but shied away from any school tasks that did not offer immediate success. Her parents felt pride in her precocious social, language, and motor skills and through these found ways to feel better about her.

ANALYSIS: WHY DIDN'T THEY KEEP ME?

During the second week of analysis, Ella created the first of many versions of a play theme in which a homeless, abandoned child came to live with me. This theme, the first of many barely disguised representations of self and other in the analytic relationship, had complex, multilevel determinants and occupied the early phases of the analysis. In her doll play, Ella said, "Can I live with you? I have no home. I have no family. I have to steal food or starve to death." Two hours later, she added, "I'm nobody. I have no name. Can I live with you? Then I will get a home and a name." During this interaction, Ella told me I was to say, in the tone of voice she demonstrated, "Yes. You can come to live with me." With any spontaneous variation on my part or failure to exactly comply with her instructions, the doll left abruptly or, at best, ignored me.

One day, after being rejected this way, I said, "This feels bad. I am getting to know what it feels like to have to do things exactly right or be left all alone." "That's right!" exclaimed Ella triumphantly. She continued the theme, relieved for the moment, at making me into the rejected one. Sequences like these became building blocks of our analytic work, as she allowed me to provide acceptance and containment of her affective experience. We were beginning to understand her coercion in the service of merger and the fantasy of omnipotent unity, as Ella came to grips with the core anxiety of abandonment.

At many other times, when play or words didn't work, Ella became so disorganized and aggressive that nothing I could say or do was right or helpful, and we just had to get through these chaotic times. When she could not process what she was feeling or what I tried to communicate verbally and nonverbally, I continued to search within myself for ways to help her feel safe and offer containment. My willingness to search, as well as my willingness to get through these times without the retaliation Ella so feared, laid a foundation for Ella to begin to develop more adaptive self-regulation.

In the second month, Ella expanded her play to include reparative versions of the doll's history. The homeless doll's parents died immediately after her birth. I was a woman who lived alone, and she came to live with me so I would have company. In her play, Ella created an unambivalent adoptive mother with whom she felt wanted, valued, and loved. I felt the pressure of her intense wish that I be that mother. Anything that reminded her that I was not the longed-for mother led to breakdown in her capacity to play, with aggressive, chaotic outbursts. The times that she tried to kick, bite, or hit me made it necessary to restrain her. In this way, she also could experience the holding that she longed for.

In this early phase, I felt what Ella required of me was acceptance, predictability, and containment, and I stayed as close to what was affectively tolerable to her as I could. As Ella felt more secure with me, a new phase was ushered in. The channeling of her aggression began to move more into fantasy play sequences, though these were easily disrupted. The face-saving version of her history (that her biological parents died, requiring that she be adopted) gradually gave way to more painful thoughts and feelings.

One day she announced, "We're going to play the people with no home. This time there is a husband and a wife. The wife is pregnant. They'll have a baby tomorrow. The mother has the baby and gets rid of it. It's a girl baby. They say it's a yucky, bad baby that has worms in its hair. It kicks and spits. The king came and said to the mother, 'I'll give you one more chance.' Another girl baby is born. They get rid of that baby, too. It's yucky and bad. They say, 'Give it to someone else. We don't want it.'" Ella moved next to me, sobbing. It seemed obvious that she was talking about herself and that this was not unconscious. Her conscious beliefs had taken over her play. I felt she needed me to respond directly to her deep sorrow and affectively charged, frightening fantasy. I said, "Your play today helps us to understand your worries. You seem to believe you are bad and yucky and so you were given away."

Ella was shaking as she cried with increasing intensity, "Why did they give me away? Why didn't they keep me?" She was overwhelmed yet still accessible. I was learning to anticipate her becoming out of control. At that moment, with the rapidly increasing intensity, physical tension, and gestures, I anticipated her becoming dysregulated and inaccessible. Based on my assessment of her vulnerability to traumatic regression, when she was unable to differentiate fantasy from reality and was affectively overwhelmed, I made a technical decision. I chose to offer a clarification based on what I knew about the circumstances of her adoption in an attempt to correct this distortion of reality. During this period of the analysis, reality clarifications were aimed at supporting her ego capacities and correcting her feelings of responsibility, based in magical thinking, for causing her biological parents to give her up and for causing the dangers with her adoptive parents and with me in the transference. She was able to process what I said and what she was feeling during this sequence rather than block me out or block out her own emotions with the aggressive action defense.

In response to these interventions, Ella played out various versions of revenge against both her biological and adoptive parents: "The king came and said, 'No more babies for you.'" "The king sent angry, growling, biting bears instead of babies." She growled and made clawing gestures, but this time she stopped herself from trying to hit, kick, or bite me and instead hid behind a chair. I said, "I think you are hiding because you are afraid I will send you away when you feel so yucky and bearish." After a brief silence, Ella emerged and sat next to me.

During subsequent hours, Ella began play enactments of various versions of her birth. She crawled into an emptied toy cabinet and pretended it was her mother's uterus and vagina. In the first version, her theories about her birth, based in sadomasochistic fantasies, were revealed: When the baby was ready to be born, she tore a hole in her mother's body to make the vaginal opening. Her mother was in terrible pain and was forced to submit to the powerful baby. Her mother was permanently damaged and came after the baby for revenge by physically punishing and then abandoning her. The terrifying, destructive aspects of her aggression, with consequent irreparable damage and punishment, were now in full view. This theme evoked dysregulation, panic, and aggression. It is notable that during these sequences she was beginning to take some responsibility for the consequences of her feelings and behavior, believing that her destructive aggression was a justified response to her mother's mistreatment.

One day, while we were playing "being born," a powerful enactment occurred. Ella suddenly tore at my clothing, growled, and tried to crawl between my legs—literally trying to tear her way inside me. I was startled and felt aggressively invaded. As I restrained her, I involuntarily flinched and pulled back. Ella was startled and upset by my action. Regaining my composure, I gently told her that I could see her feelings were hurt by my action but I wasn't used to being treated this way. Ella in pantomime repeated the gesture with a hostile fake laugh and then turned away. I said I could see, by her action, that she was afraid I wouldn't care about her anymore. Ella moved closer, and the session ended with Ella sitting quietly next to me in my chair.

Maintaining empathy with Ella's aloneness and self-hatred, in the face of her relentless attacks on me, was quite challenging. Her encroachment on both my physical comfort and psychological boundaries presented formidable technical and personal challenges. At times, when she was being relentlessly provocative, I felt anger, rejection, and guilt: feelings that she so feared and that were mobilized by her fear of abandonment. I found myself, in this way similar to Ella, struggling with a diminished stimulus barrier, so that being receptive to her communication sometimes meant my feeling overstimulated. Ella was aware of her impact, and this awareness increased her sense of danger—an awareness that required repeated interpretation, both direct and displaced. Being abandoned is the punishment for out-of-control aggression.

A SENSE OF SELF-AGENCY EMERGING

By this time, it was clear that Ella's behavior was also a way of punishing herself; she believed that she had been given away and that she was unlovable by anyone because she had damaged her birth mother. In subsequent sessions I made a decision to correct her distortions about birth because I felt this was necessary to provide conditions for her ongoing development. These cognitive distortions, like those around the adoption experience, were interfering with her capacity to tolerate emotion and were in turn distorting her sense of self. Ella was punishing herself for her destructive aggression by turning it against herself, one way in which she demonstrated the harshness of her superego development.

Relieved, Ella incorporated the corrections I offered into play. There was a softening of her aggressive attacks, which I assumed reflected a softening of the aggressive attacks on herself. She returned to looking in the dollhouse closet, this time filling it with as many small dolls as could fit. This time there was anxiety but not the panic that had accompanied the earlier "shapes inside" belief, and we played her fantasy that many babies were stored in the mother's body, waiting to be born and take her place, like her brother. The feared consequences did not occur, and this play, in itself, was mutative.

In a later version, the mother's vagina stayed open so the baby could venture out into the world and then return to the comfort and safety of her mother's body. We had reached an important turning point. Now the positive aspects of aggression made their appearance with signs of the development of a sense of agency in her ability to assert herself as she came and went in her play, no longer always victim or victimizer. This material suggested that she was beginning to rework this aspect of her beliefs about herself. Stalled developmental processes were underway as she reworked rapprochement-phase development. She was beginning to use play in a sublimatory way, with evidence of a developing capacity for affect regulation, and her sense of self as a more lovable girl who could have some pleasure in life was emerging.

Still, Ella appeared to feel continually threatened from within and without by her aggressive urges. Because of her ongoing conviction that I could not care about her and could only eventually reject her, Ella was compelled to continuously test my interest and care. The aim of her behavior seemed to be her need to reassure herself that I would provide acceptance and affective containment without retaliating or abandoning her during these moments of great vulnerability. Through processes of externalization and displacement, one of us still had to be defeated, controlled, and bad. The predominant theme of these sessions was abandonment, followed by violence and destruction.

As Ella increasingly revealed the defensive, protective aspects of her aggressive behavior, I could address it. I observed how her "feelings come smashing and crashing out all over the place." Later, Ella used those words: "My feelings are smashing and crashing out all over the place." As she took ownership of these words, they began to replace the actions that disguised her loneliness, sadness, thwarted longings, and hatreds.

By "being the boss," Ella could feel some control in the face of her sense of rejection and abandonment. Through her behavior, she enlisted my help to provide her with needed external support and control. At these times, she still often felt criticized, controlled, and attacked by me. At the same time, there were subtle affective shifts toward aggression in the service of agency as we played good versus bad, robber versus victim, and parent versus child.

QUEEN, DEVIL, BEAR, OR GIRL: THE NEED TO BELONG

In the sixth month, after my first vacation during this analysis, Ella introduced a new play theme: "I'm the queen. My mother was a queen, so I was born a princess. I married the prince. I sit on a throne, and I know all the answers." Ella went on to tell me that I was her servant and I needed to follow her orders. She startled when she "made a mistake" in her coloring, saying haughtily, "You made an even bigger mistake. I color better than you. I don't make mistakes. I'm queen, and queens don't make mistakes." Suddenly regressed, Ella flung herself at me and tried to tape me with the tape she was using to fasten her drawings together. As I stopped her, I said, "You want to tape me so I can't leave you again."

Denying her anxiety, Ella said, "I knew you would come back." I said, "This helps us to understand your need to be perfect. If you are perfect, you don't make mistakes, and then you don't have to worry about losing me." Ella burst into tears. Moving away from the transference intensity to externalization that was also a problem in reality, Ella said that while I was away, her mother gave her extra household chores. She had to dry dishes, and she broke one. Her mother got angry, broke another dish, and insisted that Ella clean it up. When we talked about this event and others like it, we clarified another dimension of the passive–active reversals that were such a prominent aspect of her defensive organization. What on one level appeared as passive–active reversals, on another level also represented her internalization of her mother's disapproval and rage.

It appeared that Ella knew, at least unconsciously, of her mother's "biological" fantasy (that Ella inherited her badness from her biological mother). In her play, Ella elaborated another version of her origins, one that closely matched her mother's version. She developed a play theme in which she was a devil and explained that baby devils were born from devil moms and dads. She grew up and married a devil, and together they made more baby devils. She explained, "That's how families are made, whether they are people or devils. When you are born a devil, you will always be that way." Ella gave a devilish laugh, spitting, clawing, and trying to hit and kick. As I held her, I told her, "You know I am going to hold you and stop you from hurting me or yourself." When I felt her begin to relax, I said, "You seem worried that neither you nor I believe you can be anything but a devil." It seemed to me that being a devil was linked with her identification with her mother's view and the impingement on her sense of self, her own sense of badness, and her thwarted needs to be close. She continued for several sessions to play the devil baby who hides and scares me. I would then reject the dangerous, unlovable devil baby. Gradually, this theme turned into a form of hide and seek, in which she was repeatedly lost and then found. In this way, I repeatedly demonstrated that I was not as afraid of her and her dangerous impulses as she was of herself. Ella was now using play to represent the dilemmas and conflicts created by her aggression and her wishes for an unconditionally accepting maternal environment, and she was trying out new solutions.

In the seventh month, Ella began an hour saying that she hated both her mother and her father because they fought all the time. She said she had a right to fight and hurt them, too. She set up a dollhouse scene: The parent dolls were close to each other but fighting in one room, while she was alone and apart in another room. Ella then tried to hit me. I restrained her (easily in comparison with earlier times). In an effort to encourage her to think with me about her state of mind, I said, "Now you are trying to fight with me. I wonder what you think about this." Ella cried that I was hurting her, although I was holding her gently. I said I thought she liked fighting because then she wasn't left out and then she was part of the excitement that she saw between her parents, which she tried to have with me. The oedipal aspects did not seem close to consciousness, and I did not address them directly. However, this session marked a turning point. Following this line of interpretation and clarification of affect, Ella's aggressive outbursts began to fade away. This work appeared to open new pathways to progressive development.

Ella's play themes expanded to include more age-appropriate sexual material, and she demonstrated an increasing capacity for self-regulation. In her doll play, she peeked at the boy dolls' belly buttons and bottoms. When she glanced anxiously to see my reaction, I said she seemed uncertain if it was alright with me for her to be curious about their bodies. She said she wasn't worried but "just wanted to be sure." Now the dollhouse contained a family of a mother, father, two children, and two dogs. There was a lot of quarreling and punishing. There were also some nice times with daddy.

THE EMERGENCE OF GRIEF

In subsequent sessions, there was clinical confirmation of the development of Ella's capacity to tolerate her feelings. She brought in a book and described a "scary story about sad horses who drowned." As we read and reread this story that illuminated her own story, Ella became openly sad, demonstrating development of a greater range in her affective life. In this way we worked on how she had submerged and drowned out vital aspects of herself to maintain contact with an unpredictable, depressed, and punitive maternal object.

By the end of our first year, Ella was experiencing symptomatic relief in her external life. Her parents reported that she got along better with other children. She was less coercive, clinging, and demanding. Competition with her brother for attention continued and was experienced by her parents as intrusive attacks. In the analysis there were fewer chaotic outbursts, with increasing tolerance for a range of feelings. Directly and in her play, Ella talked about how her feelings "come smashing and crashing out all over the place."

As we began the second year, the question emerged about whether Ella's mother would permit the analysis to continue. In our regularly scheduled sessions, I worked with her parents to stabilize support for the analysis. Ella's father was gratified by the changes in Ella and in their relationship. As he stopped colluding with the biological fantasy, he began to explore his feelings about the loss of the perfect adoption and his feelings about not having biological children. He began to provide support for his wife during this difficult time, even as the developing difference between them led to increased strain in the marriage. In our sessions, I worked to help Ella's mother, who was struggling with her feelings about her daughter's attachment to me and increasing closeness to her father. Evidence of Ella's improvement seemed to increase her mother's narcissistic vulnerability, as Ella was not as readily the active recipient of her mother's projections. Not only did she not have a biological child nor a perfect adoption, but she also had an adopted daughter who preferred others. She modified her behavior, but her beliefs about Ella remained fixed.

Ella was low key and on her best behavior with me during this time of threat to the analysis. She was unresponsive to any efforts, either in talking or playing, to consider the defensive aspects of her being "on best behavior with me." She elaborated various versions of the end of her analysis and fantasies of abandonment, in which she saw herself as unloved and unwanted. We worked on her view that ending analysis would be a broken promise. In this way her disappointment with me—that I could not control her parents—came into the analysis. She brought in a book, a poignant story of immigrants and their journeys and sacrifices. "They gave up so much," she quoted sadly. In the story the immigrants were separated from their families by great distances. "They didn't know if they would ever see each other again."

With these words, Ella collapsed on the floor, clutching her doll. It was painful to see her vulnerability as she cried. "This doll is falling apart. A part of it is missing. I won't leave until I find it. It will never be right." She tried to lick my foot and put her feet in my face. She yelled, "Smell my smelly feet." I said as I held her, "You want to be so close that we remember each others' taste and smell, even if we aren't together."

REPRIEVE

After a period of about a month, Ella's parents became convinced of potentially serious consequences if they were to actually stop the analysis. They were frightened by the return of Ella's impulsive, aggressive outbursts. At the same time, they observed an intensification of her pseudomaturity. Neither could recognize that Ella's pseudomaturity and conforming behavior was stereotyped and defensive. An important aspect of their interpersonal dynamics was clarified. Because they did not believe that Ella was unable to control herself, they waited until she fell apart before providing external limits, and limits were then provided in a punitive way. I was able to help them understand this interpersonal dynamic. Her father developed more sensitivity with her. Her mother gained more control of her own behavior but continued to cling to the belief that Ella's character and behavior were biologically based and unchangeable, despite awareness of her own inability to control her attacks on her daughter. This split in her mother's psyche, her inability to be aware of her impact, was still inaccessible. We agreed on a plan to reevaluate in a year because Ella's mother was unable to accept the idea of analysis as open-ended.

Ella expressed pleasure and relief, as well as ongoing anxiety about abandonment. "Play you're my mommy and I'm your daughter," said Ella. "You hunt in the forest for all the stuff I need." Over the next several days, Ella played out various versions of running away and being found, of being lost and being found. She built a wall around me with pillows and blocks so that I could not leave and played various versions of the always-available mother who never leaves her. Later, she changed the wall to a road. In her play, Ella traveled down the road, over increasingly long distances, and then returned to me suggesting forward movement in the stalled reapproachment phase. Her play was becoming more imaginative and pleasurable, suggesting processes of internalization, developing psychological structure, and the reestablishment of a capacity for symbolic communication. The "good mommy" transference took on a more "as if" quality.

THE OEDIPAL STORY

Ella's sadomasochistic view of sexual intercourse emerged, a frightening cloacal fantasy, in which the penis was trapped and injured in the vagina/anus. The man was weakened and overpowered by the woman's body. As this version of aggression as bodily damage emerged, Ella was affectively overwhelmed and again regressed to action. She suddenly grabbed a toy rolling pin from the kitchen toys and tried to jam it in her underpants. When we could talk and play about these fantasies, I clarified and corrected the distortions that were impeding her sexual development.

Ella's masturbatory fantasies emerged more directly. She reported fantasies of scaring away boys by showing her body. She brought in her favorite doll to show me how she damaged it by rubbing herself intensely with it. Her masturbation provided her stimulation, excitement, and comfort, but her fantasies of her body as a weapon left her once again totally alone.

Ella talked about how she tiptoes into her parents' room at night to get her father when she is scared. He stays with her all night, and her mother has to be alone and jealous. With this, Ella aggressively accused me of not remembering that she can swim and tread water without any help. I said she sounds worried that I, like her mother, will be jealous because she loves her father and wants him for herself at night.

The next day, Ella tentatively kissed her father goodbye in the waiting room. They hugged before Ella came with me to the playroom. It was the first time I had seen such open affection between them. Once in the playroom, Ella searched for my reaction. She worried that I would be jealous because she had a gift from her father. She wondered if the room was colder than usual. I said, "You sound worried that I won't like for you to be close and loving with Daddy." There was a turning point in Ella's play as she was relieved of the imbrication of pleasurable play, oedipal wishes, and anxieties colored by overwhelming aggression.

RAPUNZEL

Ella became interested in the story of Rapunzel. This story became the vehicle for our work on the ways in which oedipal-phase development was colored by the earlier developmental derailments and conflict.

Rapunzel's witch mother tricked her beautiful adopted daughter and locked her in the tower to keep her from marrying the prince. Ella drew a picture of herself as Rapunzel, holding hands with a boy. She got worried about what I would think of her interest in the boy and changed the story to Goldilocks "because there are no mothers in that story." With a witchlike laugh, Ella said, "I changed the story. I can trick you before you can trick me." Ella then burst out shouting, "I know you're not an evil witch!" I said I could see that she got worried that I, like Rapunzel's mother, would be jealous and trick her. Offering a differentiating observation, I said, "You seem mixed up between your feelings and mine about tricking." Ella then showed me the "engagement ring" she was wearing, given to her by a boy at school. With this disclosure, she again was worried and retreated behind the chair. I said I thought she was afraid to look at me because she expected to see me jealous and disapproving. She came out from behind the chair and remained next to me for the rest of the hour, talking and drawing. A place of safety had been created in the transference to play out the feared oedipal jealousy.

In the following days, Ella developed more versions of Rapunzel for us to play. Rapunzel was sent away by her evil witch mother, and she was lonely. In another hour, Rapunzel had two children, but there was no father. In yet another version, the king, the father alternately of Rapunzel or of Rapunzel's children, gave her a ring, and her mother took it away. Ella interrupted herself to criticize me. I pointed out that she had left her engagement ring on the play table the previous day and said it seemed she thought that I, too, didn't want her to be interested in the king, the prince, or being a mother someday.

Ella said, "Let's talk about this some more." Over several hours, there was exploration of her oedipal longings and anxieties and elaboration in fantasy play. She made a spontaneous link with her fantasy (perception?) of her mother's jealousy that she could, when she grows up, have biological children who would love her and belong to her. Thus, Ella surpasses her mother in this crucial way.

Ella elaborated these themes in her playing of the tooth fairy. In her play, Ella was a tooth fairy. She was born that way, and babies had no choices. She drew pictures of herself and me as tooth-fairy mother and daughter who look alike. The next day she drew herself and her mother, looking very different from each other. She drew a picture of her mother flying in and attacking me for claiming Ella for my own. In the end, Ella said she was locked out of my house and her own house, injured and alone. Again suddenly aggressive, Ella crumpled and tore up her pictures and then frantically began to try to put them back together. I suggested this was a job for two, and we spent the rest of the hour restoring the images as best we could. In this way, we worked on Ella's imagined aggression and rivalry between her adoptive and birth mothers, between her adoptive mother and transference mother, and her longing for the mother by whom she felt rejected. Despite the ongoing work with Ella's parents, her adoptive mother's attitudes and beliefs lent support and reality to Ella's fears.

There was a long outburst of hatred toward her mother. She said rageful-ly, "I want Mom dead. I'll kill her, cut off her head. I only love Daddy. Mom is a bully." Ella then began to bully me and to yell that she liked being a bully. In an effort to promote her developing sense of agency and respon-sibility for her actions, I suggested we try to figure out how she got to be a bully, too, and what we could do to help her with this problem. Ella made mean, bullying faces that she said were like her mother's mean faces. She recalled that, when she first came to see me, she tried to hit, kick, and run away but that I always caught her and stopped her.

We entered a period of vigorous work on the dilemma of Ella's desperate need for her mother and wish to be like her mother, even though she ended up feeling like a mean bully, and her need for me, which made her fearful of losing her mother. Ella said that, when she was scared of being alone at night, she called me on her toy telephone and told me about it. In sessions, Ella taught me how to make friendship bracelets. Sometimes we wore them separately and sometimes she linked them so that we were chained together.

During this time of making friendship bracelets, there was a turning point. Ella had what she described as a bad dream but not a nightmare. She and a friend were chased by a scary figure who was trying to steal her dolls. Her friend, who was not afraid, helped her. Ella reviewed other dreams of being chased by something dangerous and dreams of being lost or losing her favorite dolls. This dream, although frightening, was less disturbing than other dreams. In this dream she had a helper. She was no longer alone with her displaced aggression but belonged with another. We played out these dreams, which demonstrated her sense of greater stability and self-control over powerful affect-laden fantasies.

TERMINATION

In the thirtieth month of Ella's analysis, her mother insisted on making a plan to stop. Her parents reported significant improvement in her external life: Her moods were more even; she was less irritable and restless; and her cruelty to her brother had subsided, and she was more thoughtful and considerate of him and them. They were convinced there was nothing more to be gained. Although they noted her improvement, as well as problems that remained, they were convinced that Ella was insatiable and that the analysis would be endless. This represented a dilemma that could not be worked through.

It was only then that Ella's mother began to indirectly acknowledge my importance to her. She talked with me in more depth about her own loneliness as a child and how controlling, cold, and harsh her mother was. She spoke of ways she was like her mother and her efforts to be different. This awareness and her deepening ability to be more open with me and reflective did not change her beliefs about Ella. I offered support and recognition of her efforts. For Ella's mother, this included supporting the need to control the ending of the analysis and our relationship. Ella's father, who was depressed and withdrawn, went along with his wife's views as he had earlier in our work together.

Ella's parents agreed to allow Ella to choose the date of the final session in 5 months, with the idea of giving her some sense of control of the ending. They told her that evening. She chose a date that was 3 years and 1 day after our first session, a date that extended the analysis by an additional month and gave her some sense of control. Although again faced with a decision about separation over which in reality she had no control, Ella did not fall apart. Her response, with a wide array of affect and capacity to mourn the loss, demonstrated the impact of the analytic work.

In the next hour, Ella played "funeral." Beginning to feel her grief about ending, she told a story of a baby who was born in a car, saying that "it came out too soon." A passive-active reversal emerged as she played that she was in charge and knew what would happen to the baby. For several days, Ella played that cars were taken to a "smashing machine" after they were in car crashes. They got smashed into chunks to make new cars. The airplanes were scared because they did not know what was going to happen to them. "We'll show them how it can be done," she said but then turned her back on me to play alone. I was reminded of the earlier metaphor of "smashing and crashing feelings." This play sequence informed my decision to first express my understanding that the airplanes were scared about crashing but they knew what to do, which led her to invite me back into the play. In an attempt to support her growing capacities, I chose to comment at this manifest level of self and other. Ella said, "These other guys aren't scared because they are together in a team. They go into the smashing machine together." We continued playing various versions of going into the smashing machine together. Ella continued to use various designs on a small Oriental carpet for different parts of the smashing machine. "This rug always comes in handy for something," she said. "It's been a house, a zoo, a world, a place to find missing things, and now a smashing machine." I said I knew she was already missing me and my rug, and the smashing machine was a way to tell me about her feelings. I made note to myself that, in her play, separation was still a destructive act, but it was no longer hidden. We talked about this. "It hurts, but we both survive and go on living." These words became a songlike refrain at the start of the smashing machine play sequences. Despite the intensity of feelings, Ella did not fall apart. Real capacities had replaced omnipotence and magical control of the object. The reworking of the stalled and distorted separation-individuation process seemed stable.

Three months before the end of her analysis, Ella began many sessions by checking for evidence of other children. She wished to be my only child and feared that her brother would take over her relationship with me. She cried when she thought about anyone taking her place with me.

As we talked about the loss of our relationship and being remembered, Ella had occasional, brief, mildly aggressive outbursts. I said I could see she wanted me to stop her so we could be close in the old way. Ella couldn't believe I cared about her because I didn't stop her from leaving. She was deeply in touch with previously split-off affects. I encouraged her to think with me about when she was able to face the thoughts and feelings about ending and when she got so angry she was afraid she couldn't control herself.

Every session came around to her wish to be remembered in a positive way. At times, she was deeply sad. In other hours, she could not face the sadness directly, despite her behavioral and symptomatic communication of her pain. She brought small items into the playroom and hid them. She told me not to look for them until after her last session. In this concrete way, Ella reassured herself that I would remember her.

Her last reported dream suggested developmental progression with a stronger ego, diminished narcissistic vulnerability, diminished conflict, and modification in her defenses. In this dream, she tried to play soccer with one arm and one leg tied behind her back. She realized she needed both arms and legs to play well, and she had that needed strength. She untied her arm and leg and scored the winning goal.

Ella could still be a difficult child, but she was able to maintain a forward-moving developmental momentum, despite symptomatic flare-ups. She tried to take small items of mine without me knowing it. Ella made messes, as she had done earlier in the analysis, in efforts to provoke me to control her: an externalization of her superego and her guilt over her wishes to steal from me to cope with the impending loss of our relationship.

In the last hours, Ella explored the office and its contents. As she touched various items, she said, repeatedly, "I remember this. I remember that." There was a deep sense of sadness in the room. There was also a sense of satisfaction, despite recognition that our work was incomplete. Ella had a brief attacking outburst. I reminded her of how often she had behaved that way before, and she was doing it again, to try to provoke a fight, which brought us close so she didn't have to miss me. We talked about how she kept her parents and me involved in fights that were sometimes exciting, sometimes painful, and hard to give up. Ella said, with a sense of pride, satisfaction, and humor, "I love playing with my friends. I love swimming. I love soccer. I still love to fight."

CONCLUSION

This case study presents the unconscious psychodynamic meanings of symptomatic aggressive behavior in a 4-year-10-month-old girl. When I first met them, Ella, who was adopted at birth, and her adoptive parents had created adoption myths that dominated their lives. Ella's preoccupation with rejection and inferiority because she was adopted appeared to be the organizer of her fantasy life, object relations, sense of self and other, and defensive organization. By the end of her first year of life, her parents were faced with the loss of their myth of having a perfect adoption, as Ella became an assertive and aggressive toddler. The failed perfect adoption haunted their lives and dominated their functioning as parents. The collision of these mythologies led to breakdowns in Ella's development and in parental functioning.

At the start of her analysis, one of the outstanding features of Ella's development was that she could not play. Play and playful interaction had become engaged in conflict and had taken on dangerous meaning for her that led to chaotic dysregulated states. Due to extreme imbalances in her development, it was difficult to distinguish primary developmental disturbances from disturbances brought about by conflicts at higher levels of development. Her shifting levels of organization and difficulty in playing or engaging in playful interaction were from both internal and external sources and required adaptations in technique to allow me to engage and communicate with her. I discovered another unusual feature of her development: that verbal communication offered in a calm, quiet, friendly tone often helped her to recover from the dysregulated state. Given her young age, this was an unusual choice of technique but one that respected her need for her intellectual defenses until she developed more flexibility; it also took the heat out of the here-and-now interaction when it was overwhelming for her. My focus was on creating a place of safety in which Ella could more openly express herself. As Ella felt safer with me, the analytic work revealed an inner life dominated by her belief that she was dangerous, had destroyed her birth mother in the process of being born, and was deserving of the punishment and rejection she experienced with her parents and that she tried to provoke with me. She lived in a state of continuous anxiety, which she attempted to manage with defenses that left her vulnerable and at risk. The trauma of the split in her early life (perfect baby/bad toddler) and on-going painful sense of self and other, left Ella trapped in a desperate situation, being so terrified of aspects of herself and of those she needed. I stayed as close to her affective state as possible, whether she was experiencing the unbearable feelings of being bad and destructive and when she gradually began to trust the experience of herself as accepted, valued, and deserving of some pleasure and playfulness as her psychological structure strengthened and her capacities to tolerate ambivalence and self-regulation developed.

As our analytic work proceeded, I came to view the adoption mythologies as external manifestations of the stalled rapprochement phase of separation-individuation, shaped in large part by the early trauma and the ambivalence of her mother and internalized by Ella. While constructing or reconstructing aspects of her history were important, the underlying developmental psychopatholoy was the primary focus of much of this analysis. Oral and anal sadistic trends were competing with Ella's desire for nurturing, emotional freedom, self-agency, and safety. As a toddler, Ella did not have experience with initiating separations in manageable ways. The analysis demonstrated how her developmental history predisposed her to a core anxiety of abandonment and conflict around ambivalence and autonomous strivings. Later in the analytic process, we worked on the ways in which oedipal-phase longing and conflict were colored by the earlier developmental derailments.

The termination process suggested the possibility that Ella's forward-moving developmental momentum and her rich fantasy life that increasingly facilitated the analytic work could continue to aid her negotiation of life experiences.

Chapter Four

Discussion of Ella's Analysis

Edward I. Kohn

In her case presentation, Mrs. Kaufman draws our attention to two kinds of interventions. The first is a direct verbal explanation of the patient's immediate emotional concerns. For example, she said to Ella that she (Ella) was confused and worried about the baby. I intentionally use the word *explanation* rather than *interpretation* because Mrs. Kaufman raises the possibility that her intervention did not bring into consciousness a concern that was out of awareness. Rather, these distressing thoughts were conscious, and Mrs. Kaufman's intervention had some other therapeutic effect. The second type of intervention was a clarification with the aim of correcting a distortion. In one instance, Ella play-acted a birth in which she, the baby, tore a hole in her mother's body to make the vaginal opening. Mrs. Kaufman educated Ella about the way a baby emerges from the birth canal, with the hope of easing the guilt and self-hate associated with the belief that her birth was a hostile, sadistic assault on her mother's body.

I imagine, in the early years of child psychoanalysis, child analysts would have assumed that the first kind of intervention was beneficial because it was an interpretation that made the unconscious conscious. The model for child analysis at that time was adult analysis. Making the unconscious conscious was the curative factor. The behavior of children who would act or play rather than free-associate was a problem that raised concerns of whether child analysis was really analysis (A. Freud, 1945). As child analysts learned more about intensive work with children, they saw play as a fundamental activity of childhood, one that was exceedingly useful in the analytic situation (Neubauer, 1994). Like the dream in adults, if you knew how to unpack its meaning and work with play, it provided remarkable access to the inner world.

Play is important precisely because it is not real. The child is free to imagine all sorts of scenarios, working over her life experiences and internal preoccupations without the threat of reality consequences (Cohen & Solnit, 1993; Solnit, 1998). Remarkably, the child analyst can enter into the play, stay within the metaphors, and intervene as part of the play, and internal change can occur even when the child does not consciously recognize that these metaphors apply to her (Fonagy & Target, 1998; Mayes & Cohen, 1993a; Sugarman, 2003b). An interpretation to a boy, such as "The prince really wants to sit on the king's thrown, but he is afraid the king will be angry" might be more readily digested than "You like it when Daddy is away at work so that you can get in bed with Mommy." Displaced into the universe of imaginative play, the theme is more safely engaged, but it often succeeds in deepening the work, yielding a therapeutic effect that can be understood by attending to the unfolding play themes. The child might respond, "If the prince does what the king wants, he will give him a new little sword with jewels, but if he angers the king, he will never get a sword."

Mrs. Kaufman points out to us that she attempted these latter kinds of interpretations that stayed close to the play metaphor, but they were unsuccessful. We might expect, if the child was frightened by her thoughts and fantasies, that the direct explanations would frighten her more and that the displaced references to her play would allow a more dosed approach to the overwhelming material. This was not the case with Ella. Therefore, this intriguing case compels us to think about what we do as child analysts that is therapeutic. Do we bring the unconscious into awareness? Do we interpret resistance and free up the associative process? Do we disabuse distortion and lessen the development-impeding impact of these terrifying fantasies or beliefs? Do we reestablish reality, help to organize chaotic fantasy, or help to integrate unmodulated affects (Miller, 2013)? Are we new objects who engage with the child in such a way that fixations can be freed up, allowing development to move forward (Baker, 1993; Bollas, 1979; Ornstein, 1974; Tolpin, 2002)? Are we adults whom children naturally turn to for emotional sustenance, comfort, reassurance, support, empathy, or learning? Are we therapeutic simply because we are there or because we survive (Winnicott, 1965)?

I think we have our hands full trying to answer these questions in terms of Ella's treatment, let alone trying to come up with a universal answer. I'd suggest we start with a consideration of the structure of Ella's mind and draw on Sandler and Rosenblatt's (1962) paper "The Concept of the Representational World." The mind is a theater in which the self and object representations play out their dramas. The shapes of the representations and the plots of the dramas are the stuff of analytic work. Mrs. Kaufman certainly paid attention to the action on the stage, but she was also alert to the state of the stage and the theater. Can this stage contain the performance or hold up under its power? Is the theater about to collapse? The stage and theater are metaphors for the child's ego, self, internal structure, or defense constellation. Whatever the plot or whichever play is being performed, it is going to influence and be influenced by the state of the stage and theater, and the impact of the analyst's interventions will be affected, as well. If you can rely on or even ignore the stage, you might devote your attention to the drama in one way, but if the boards of the stage start to crack, if the performers are knocked off their feet or fall through the floor, or if the roof of the theater is in danger of crumbling on the performers and viewers, then the analyst has to be prepared to embrace different kinds of activity.

I suggest that Ella had deficits in her psychological structure that made her vulnerable to feeling overcome by experience and her own affects. At times, the theater remained intact, but it was readily shaken. When Ella felt the tremors of the pending earthquake, she would desperately try to shore things up. At these moments, she could not bear the messy dollhouse or desperately insisted that Mrs. Kaufman do things in exactly the right way. Her psyche was a house of cards, and any deviation was the potential tipping point that threw her into a state of chaos. When the tremors would begin, there was at times potential, with the right intervention, to help Ella stabilize the crumbling theater before it totally collapsed. Then she would regain control and actually be able to communicate in a more direct and meaningful way.

When Ella felt inside the dollhouse closet, she panicked and shouted, "It has shapes inside. I don't know where they came from." The theater and her capacity to modulate herself began to crumble, and she threw the contents of the dollhouse about the office. When Mrs. Kaufman explained that Ella was worried about her baby brother, where and who it came from, she calmed down. She spoke tearfully, tolerating this emotion, and confirmed the interpretation by adding that all she knew was that her parents went away to have a baby. At other times Ella was beyond the tipping point, and the best that Mrs. Kaufman could do was to survive the explosion, trying to protect the child, the office, and herself until the dust and debris had settled.

Mrs. Kaufman points out that Ella's parents tended to assume that she was more capable of gaining control of herself than she was, and they would wait too long to set limits. In the analysis, we see the child's vulnerability, her desperate need for adult intervention, and her capacity to respond when the adult is able to effectively intervene before it is too late.

The history and much of the imagery and stories put forth by Ella point toward her adoption as a defining experience. I suggest, however, that the transition from infancy to toddlerhood was the developmental step that went significantly awry. According to the parents' history, the first year was a happy time for them, and Ella was an easy and satisfying baby to care for. Things changed when she became an assertive toddler.

Otto Rank (1929) wrote about the birth trauma, and this image is very meaningful as we examine the experience of separation. I think, however, that the work of Margaret Mahler and her book with Fred Pine and Anni Bergman, *The Psychological Birth of the Human Infant* (1975), provides a different slant to the story. The transition from infancy to toddlerhood is a major development in the separation and individuation of the child. This begins the period when fundamental psychological structure is laid down. The literal birth trauma is a metaphor for this psychological birth.

Ella began treatment shortly after losing her nanny and being displaced by a baby brother. Feelings of abandonment with regression to oral anxieties like starving were intense. The adoption history had shaped a belief system in the family that included the idea that Ella had inherited her biological mother's bad behavior. The narratives about the adoption provided content for the expression of Ella's fantasies and fueled her concerns that parents really do get rid of their children and that she was a devil who could not be loved by her mother.

Ella's fantasy about the sadistic and destructive birth process can be understood as a vision of the struggle with her mother as she moved from being a lap baby to a young child with her own will and with heightened capacity to function independently. In order to achieve this independence, the baby portrayed in the play must force the mother to submit by inflicting permanent damage on her. Of course, the baby still needs her mother, even as she tries to separate. The injured mother can easily and readily retaliate with the threat of abandonment, pulling the floor out from under the child. The play theater could not contain this threat, Ella crumbled, the play interrupted, and she literally tried to crawl inside her analyst's uterus. Mrs. Kaufman was under assault and lived through the experience of Ella's parents and the way that Ella's behavior contributed to the very abandonment she most dreadfully feared.

When Mrs. Kaufman offered a more realistic view of the birth process, she also metaphorically offered a different view of separation and individuation. While this was a direct explanation of the birth process, it was also an interpretation within the displaced metaphor about the separation-individuation process. Leaving your mother's lap does not have to be a violent assault. It can be a natural move into the outside world. Ella responded with relief and a story where the mother's vagina remained open so that the child could venture out and return as needed to the comfort and safety of her mother.

We see this kind of venturing out and returning with toddlers all the time. Ella yearned desperately for a mother who would allow her to be her own person, someone with her own name, a mother who would still love her and welcome her back with open arms rather than abandon her in response to this bad-girl behavior. Like a toddler's tantrums, Ella's outbursts, panic, impulsive behavior, and chaotic activity were the result of affective storms that her psychological theater could not contain. Mrs. Kaufman's explanation helped Ella with her efforts to separate, and the child had a new experience. The adult could participate with her as she ventured out from the mother's orbit. With this support, her psychological resources were not overwhelmed, she could function within a play space that reflected her developmental task, and she could be a pleasant child rather than the desperately frightened and enraged devil who re-creates abandonment.

It was not primarily the content of Ella's stories that determined Mrs. Kaufman's mode of intervention. It was Ella's affective states and her responses to these interventions that led Mrs. Kaufman to alter her approach of staying within the play metaphor in order to shift to reality-based verbalization, where she spoke directly to the child about her concerns and worries. In Ella's play, the doll was all alone. Her parents had tricked her, saying they were going to work, when they really went to have a baby. Ella then became tearful and began to stomp around the room. The painful affect led to a play interruption, and the tremors of an impending collapse had begun. Before the distress reached the tipping point, Mrs. Kaufman said that she saw how upset Ella was about that baby. Ella did not escalate and directly replied, "I don't know who is going to take care of me now. I'm all alone." Whatever our theory of technique might tell us about the impact of such an interpretation, Ella responded in a calmer, more integrated way and could talk directly about her concerns.

What clues do we have that might help us understand why these kinds of interventions were effective and others were not? In a relatively calm moment, Ella explained that she was afraid of the dark. Sometimes it helped to put her head under the covers. Without light and the usual visual clues of daytime reality to orient a child, her imagination is let loose, and she is afraid of the monsters in the closet or under the bed, the burglar at the window, or the strange noises coming from the house. It is the loving adult who has the power to comfort the child, reassure her that she is safe, and show her that the closet has her clothes and not a dangerous monster. Perhaps this is the function that Mrs. Kaufman served for Ella. When Ella reached inside the doll-house closet, she panicked about the shapes inside, not knowing where they came from. Talking about the worry or even offering to help did not provide any relief. When Mrs. Kaufman left the play and defined the shapes—they were babies, including her new baby brother—Ella calmed down and talked about the birth of the new baby.

When Mrs. Kaufman made direct verbal interpretations, she brought a flashlight into the closet and showed the terrified child what was in there. Sometimes this was enough to calm her. At other times, what she imagined was so terrifying that Mrs. Kaufman had to look carefully in the closet and explain that what Ella saw was not real. This is the second kind of intervention. Then Ella could be reassured that her fantasies were not true or would not come true, and she was able to communicate in a more direct and less frantic way. Her capacity to respond to such interventions demonstrates that her psychological structure, though fragile, was resilient, and it allowed her to mobilize her other resources and abilities when she got the help she needed.

Now, drawing on the ideas I have just put forth, I examine a series of analytic moments to assess the progressive consolidation of structure within Ella's mind. I believe this illustrates aspects of the therapeutic action of Ella's analysis.

In the first diagnostic session, Ella insisted that Mrs. Kaufman admire her doll. She told the doll that it was bad because it wanted the teacher to pay attention only to her. Ella wanted attention and to be admired but experienced anxiety because this was bad behavior. Then, Ella stopped playing and became silent and unapproachable. Play interruptions in response to anxiety are typical with children, but her anxiety was overwhelming. She could not manage her disordered internal state and felt compelled to make sure the toys were precisely arranged. Mrs. Kaufman was pressed to comply with this effort to shore up the fragmenting psychological theater.

In the next session, Ella demanded help looking for "lost covers" and "scary shapes." She had not yet explained her fear of the dark and her solution of hiding her head under the covers, but this new place and this unfamiliar doctor were frightening, like the dark. Worse yet was the threat that this adult would take away her one coping mechanism, her covers, leaving her alone and exposed to the scary, amorphous shapes of her fantasies. She dealt with this fear by desperately insisting that Mrs. Kaufman help find the covers and the shapes. When Mrs. Kaufman said that Ella didn't know whether she could understand a kid's feelings, I think this addressed Ella's fear that she would make things worse rather than better. When Mrs. Kaufman then brought up Ella's parents, she gave form to the shapes, and she did not leave the child alone. Ella settled down and did not need to hide under the covers; she complained about her mother and brother, explaining that at home she has to play alone.

We see familiar behavior 6 months into the analysis, when Mrs. Kaufman returned from her vacation. Everything had to be done exactly according to Ella's dictates. Everything needed to be exactly right. When Ella made a mistake, her psychological house of cards began to crumble. She tried to shore it up with words: "I color better than you. I don't make mistakes." But this failed, and Ella flew into action. She tried to tape her analyst with the same tape she had used to fasten her drawings together.

The cohesion of herself and the reliability of her internal structures remained vulnerable to collapse, but there are signs that progress had been made during these 6 months. First, she was attached to her analyst and did not maintain the haughty barriers we first observed. Second, the action of taping Mrs. Kaufman seems more modulated and organized than the kinds of activity we saw earlier in treatment. She was not throwing things around in a frenzied, chaotic state. Ella's effort to tape her analyst, though impulsive, driven, and concrete, seems less aggressive, less intrusive, and less primitive than her earlier effort to crawl into her uterus.

Despite the physical and concrete nature of the taping, symbolism and the capacity for communication were not lost. Mrs. Kaufman saw that Ella was trying to control her and to keep her from leaving. The tape was also a way to fasten things together. Ella was dealing with the threat of coming unglued, and she was looking for a way to repair herself. The overpowering and dreadful experience of fragmentation and Ella's effort to compensate for it had been represented symbolically. She enacted the task of gluing her fragmenting self back together as she applied the tape to the body of her analyst.

When Ella felt that she could consistently rely on Mrs. Kaufman, the changes were dramatic. Their relationship was a kind of glue that firmed up the structure of her psychic theater, and then her foundation was genuinely stronger and more flexible. Seven months into treatment, her angry outbursts were more easily restrained, and she began to venture into a new developmental arena: sexuality. She could tolerate affect more reliably, and the play space was less vulnerable to disruption. Over and over they read the story about sad horses. Ella was openly sad yet did not fall apart. The analytic pair could more consistently work within the microcosm of stories and play metaphors.

Even when the analysis was threatened with premature interruption in the second year, the child's psychological structure showed more resilience. Ella was on her best behavior in order to stave off the loss. Though she did not respond to efforts to understand the defensive aspects of this behavior, her capacity to mobilize this defense was quite an achievement. This is a relatively adaptive defense and serves her much better than the driven, controlling behaviors or the chaos of her crumbling psyche. Structure had been created.

Ella related a range of fantasies about separation and loss. She talked directly with her analyst about broken promises. Then, when they spoke of the migrant family members who might never see one another again, Ella collapsed on the floor. But this action was not chaotic. It was more modulated than her previous outbursts, and it served a successful communicative function. Rather than feeling under attack, Mrs. Kaufman felt Ella's vulnerability, sadness, and pain.

Ella's play, ever more clearly, portrayed the experience of her crumbling internal theater: "The doll is falling apart." Her relationship with Mrs. Kaufman had become part of her psychic structure: "A part of it is missing. I won't leave until I find it." As Kohut (1968, 1971; Kohut & Wolf, 1978) describes, the analyst had become a selfobject. Ella was not just losing another person. She was losing a relationship that provided essential functions that served as part of her mind. When it was finally established that the analysis would continue, Ella play-acted various versions of a theme of being lost and being found. This was her way of working over the threat of loss and separation.

Ella showed much greater capacity to contain her concerns in the microcosm. They told stories about Rapunzel, Ella pretended to be the tooth fairy, and they could talk these things over. Oedipal, sexual, and triangular themes emerged, including Ella's rivalry with her mother and her worry that her mother would be jealous of her biological mother or Mrs. Kaufman. There were many anxiety-laden moments and play interruptions, but they were less disruptive.

Mrs. Kaufman provides one vignette during this phase, when Ella got overwhelmed and the psychic stage started to go to pieces. Ella drew a picture of her mother flying in and attacking Mrs. Kaufman for claiming Ella as her own. Ella abruptly became aggressive and tore up her pictures and then frantically tried to put them back together. She readily responded when Mrs. Kaufman suggested that this was a job for two. Manifestly, they were repairing her drawings, but unspoken, amid the intense turmoil of her conflicted feelings, Ella allowed her analyst to help soothe her feelings and glue her pieces back together.

As the analysis progressed, Ella internalized these functions, building psychic structure. This process is described in Marian Tolpin's paper, "On the Beginnings of a Cohesive Self" (1971). Ella's capacity to use her analyst's functions as her own is poignantly portrayed in two vignettes. She dreamed of a scary figure. Her friend, who was not afraid, helped her. She had achieved a more reliable state of object and self-constancy. When facing frightening circumstances, she did not feel totally alone because she could mobilize Mrs. Kaufman in her dreaming mind. On another occasion, she was scared to be alone at night, and she pretended to call her analyst. During the initial sessions, Ella could not sustain her play, and Mrs. Kaufman was another frightening presence in the dark. On this night, Mrs. Kaufman was a longed-for source of comfort. Rather than breaking down, Ella's play sustained her. She created an imaginary space where she could draw on the resources of her analyst, and then Ella was able to soothe herself.

During the termination phase, she grieved the loss of Mrs. Kaufman but was much less apt to fall apart, and her outbursts were less frequent, milder, and briefer. Losing her analyst was sad and upsetting in many ways, but she did not feel like she was losing essential structures of her own mind. With this developmental achievement, the loss could be worked out as a drama on her psychological stage without feeling that the foundation was pulled out from under her.

Along with the pain, the grief, the defensive efforts, and regression, there was a process of reminiscing with her analyst about their experience together: "This rug always comes in handy for something. It's been a house, a zoo, a world, a place to find missing things, and now a smashing machine." She had had an amazing experience with Mrs. Kaufman, and she could reflect on it. She could construct a historical narrative that strengthened her biographical self and facilitated her taking into herself the functions and memories of her analyst. This was a rug that she could take into her mind, that could be part of her own mind, separate from her relationship with her analyst, and she would be less vulnerable to having it pulled out from under her in the future.

Chapter Five

Psychic Structure and Models of the Mind

Edward I. Kohn

Sigmund Freud develops and explains his models of the mind with metaphors and visual images. In the topographic model, the mind is composed of three systems arranged in layers: The system unconscious is the deepest, followed by the system preconscious, and then the system conscious at the surface (S. Freud, 1915/1953–1974o). He compares the work of psychoanalysis to an archaeological dig in which deeper and deeper layers of the psyche are explored. In *The Ego and the Id*, he reorganizes his model, identifying the structures of the mind in the tripartite model as id, ego, and superego (S. Freud, 1923/1953–1974d). This allows him to account for unconscious defenses and guilt, while it maintains the importance of the layers of unconscious and conscious processes. His visual image of the mind changes, and his diagrams illustrate that his understanding changed as well.

Freud explains that the child's experience with external reality facilitates the transition from the mode of operation dictated by the pleasure principle to one dictated by the reality principle. The early ego forms as the id bumps up against reality. In response to optimal frustration, the child's mind copes with the disappointments of reality and creates regulatory structures, including defenses. Lack of frustration can lead to fixation and interferes with development, while excessive frustration is overwhelming and also interferes with development.

David Rapaport (1960) places the structural model of the mind under the microscope, in an effort to make the underlying assumptions explicit, clarify the concepts, and pursue their implications to their logical conclusions. He notes that "drives do not unequivocally determine behavior in general, nor symptom formation in particular" (53). This leads him to think in great detail about the structure of the mind, the psychological entities that transform those biological and psychological drives into thoughts and goal-directed actions. Hierarchically layered structures (defenses and controls) serve as channels and dikes that delay, prevent, or redirect the flow of psychic energy. These intricate series of flows, channels, and dikes modulate the energic flow, leading to neutralization and sublimation, and direct the flow in ways that allow for more adaptive and effective satisfaction of desires. Rapaport summarizes his understanding of psychological structure in *The Structure of Psychoanalytic Theory*:

1. The structural determiners of behavior were introduced as intervening variables to account for the observation that motivations do not determine behavior in a one-to-one fashion.
2. Structural determiners differ from motivational determiners in that they are relatively permanent: their rate of change is relatively slow.
3. There are inborn structures and acquired structures: apparatuses of primary and secondary autonomy.
4. Structure-building transforms motivations and thus gives rise to new (more neutralized) motivations. (56–57)

Analysts with different visions of the working of the mind draw on different concepts and develop different vocabularies to explain their theories. Each of these writers puts forth, either explicitly or implicitly, a model of the mind. It is my belief that, despite their differences, there are similar psychological phenomena with which each of these investigators is trying to come to grips. There is some fundamental structure to the mind, and each theorist must grapple with this.

In this chapter, I explore a number of psychoanalytic visions of the mind in order to clarify what we mean by psychological structure. There are relatively enduring ways in which the human mind functions that must be considered in order to understand the human experience and the psychoanalytic process. These relatively enduring functions are manifestations of psychological structure. This chapter demonstrates that each theorist, within his or her own model of the mind, describes a point of transition in the development of the mind in which the functioning of the mind changes in a fundamental way. The achievement of this fundamentally important way of functioning— whether we call it a cohesive self (Kohut & Wolf, 1978), the depressive position (Klein, 1975), the capacity for object constancy (Mahler, Pine, & Bergman, 1975), capacity for alpha function (Bion, 1963; Brown, 2011), or capacity for reflective thinking (Fonagy & Target, 1998)—is an essential consideration in our understanding of psychological structure and our understanding of a difference between Isabel and Ella.

I explained in chapter 4 that one way to portray the structure of the mind, for either children or adults, is to draw on Sandler and Rosenblatt's (1962) paper "The Concept of the Representational World." The mind is a theater, and its stage is the representational world on which the self and object representations play out their dramas. The shapes and colors of the representations and the plots of the dramas are often the stuff of analytic work. The state of the stage, not only the performance, must be considered. Can this stage contain the performance or hold up under its power? Is the theater about to collapse?

The theater serves as a metaphor for the child's ego, self, or internal structure, and the stage, the representational world, is one of the ego's substructures that serves an essential function. Whatever the plot or whichever play is being performed, it will influence and be influenced by the state of the stage and theater. This will have an impact on the experience of the child and the analyst, shape the impact of the analyst's interventions on the child, and affect the analytic process. If you can rely on or feel free to ignore the stage, you might devote your attention to the drama in one way, but if the boards of the stage start to crack, if the performers are knocked off their feet or fall through the floor, or if the roof of the theater is in danger of crumbling on the performers and viewers, the child's state of mind, affective experience, and functioning capacities are very different, and the analyst has to be prepared to think in a different way or embrace different kinds of activity or both. The fragmentation of a child's mind becomes the overriding experience. The original drama is disrupted or totally lost.

KOHUT: SELF PSYCHOLOGY

When Kohut (1971, 1977; Kohut & Wolf, 1978) talks about the self, he refers to a structure of the mind that is central to our sense of who we are and what we experience; our sense of purpose and agency; and our sense that we are the same person despite changes in our mood, passage of time, or changes in location. It is more than a vague term that points toward identity or the person. For Kohut, there is a structure in the mind called the self, and the functions of this structure determine the functioning of the individual. In his model, the self is supraordinate to the structures of id, ego, and superego. This structure is the centerpiece of his theorizing:

> If we keep in mind the processes by which the self is created, we realize that, however primitive by comparison with the self of the adult the nuclear self may be, it is already at its very inception a complex structure, arising at the end-point of a developmental process which may be said to have its virtual beginnings with the formation of specific hopes, dreams and expectations concerning the future child in the minds of the parents, especially the mother. When the baby is born, the encounter with the child's actual structural and functional biological equipment will, of course, influence the imagery about its

future personality that had been formed by the parents. But the parental expectations will, from birth onward, exert a considerable influence on the baby's
developing self. The self arises thus as the result of the interplay between the
newborn's innate equipment and the selective responses of the selfobjects
through which certain potentialities are encouraged in their development while
others remain unencouraged or are even actively discouraged. Out of this
selective process there emerges, probably during the second year of life, a
nuclear self, which, as stated earlier, is currently conceptualized as a bipolar
structure; archaic nuclear ambitions form one pole, archaic nuclear ideals the
other. The tension arc between these two poles enhances the development of
the child's nuclear skills and talents—rudimentary skills and talents that will
gradually develop into those that the adult employs in the service of the pro-
ductivity and creativity of his mature self. (Kohut & Wolf, 1978, 416–417)

Moore and Fine (1990) define the self in this way:

> a depth-psychological concept referring to the nuclear core of the personal-
> ity . . . various constituents emerge into a coherent and enduring configura-
> tion . . . and the enduring unity of the self develops in the lawful gradual
> manner of a psychological structure. The self is the center of initiative, the
> recipient of impressions, and the depository of the individual's constellation of
> nuclear ambitions, ideals, talents and skills. These motivate and permit the self
> to function as a self-propelling, self-directed, self-aware, and self-sustaining
> unit, providing a central purpose to the personality and yielding a sense of
> meaning to the person's life . . . all experienced as continuous in space and
> time, and they give the person a sense of selfhood . . . a sense that he or she is
> an independent center of initiative and impressions. (177)

For my purposes in this book, Kohut's (1971, 1977; Kohut & Wolf, 1978)
vision of the self as a psychological structure is of central importance. When
I discuss Isabel and Ella's development, I consider the evolution of the
structures of their minds. Kohut's view of the developmental line of narcissism (Kohut, 1966), the development of the self, its cohesion or lack of
cohesion, and the role of the selfobject in maintaining cohesion and facilitating development informs my comparisons of the structure of each girl's
psyche, her potential for fragmentation, how her structure changes over the
course of her analysis, and how the analytic work facilitated therapeutic
change.

MAYES AND COHEN, A THEORY OF MIND, AND FONAGY AND TARGET, MENTALIZATION

For Fonagy and Target (1998), the fundamental transition in the mind occurs
with the achievement of reflective functioning or the capacity for mentalization. *Mentalization* is defined as the ability to consider that the other person's

actions and words are influenced by his or her own internal world. This recognition—that others are influenced and motivated by their personal ideas, beliefs, observations, feelings, desires, and wishes—is intimately related to the capacity to recognize one's own inner world. Mayes and Cohen (1996) describe the same phenomenon and refer to it as the child's development of a theory of mind.

In terms of the framework that I provide in this chapter, Mayes and Cohen (1996) and Fonagy and Target (1996) explore the construction of the representational world described by Sandler and Rosenblatt (1962). The mind functions differently when the performance on the stage can be observed and when it is recognized as distinct from the external world. Fonagy and Target explain that, prior to this development, the child's mind functions in two insufficiently integrated modes. In pretend mode, the child can be immersed in play with no recognition that her imagination reflects anything real about herself or her life. In psychic-equivalence mode, the child assumes that what is in her mind concretely reflects that which is real in the outer world. There is a split in the mind that must be integrated before a representational world is cohesive and reliable. With the achievement of a theory of mind or reflective functioning and an imagination that can play on a secure stage, the child's capacity to deal with her own thoughts, feelings, and actions and those of others is dramatically enhanced.

MODELS OF PSYCHIC STRUCTURE

Fonagy and colleagues (1993) developed two models for the development of psychic structure: the mental-representation model and the mental-process model. According to the mental-representation model, procedures or patterns of action rather than individual experiences are retained from infant–caregiver interactions, and these procedures come to organize later behavior. These intrinsically interlinked sequences of events, when taken together, amount to a representation of a relationship. Mental schemata are formed in which expectations of a particular person toward the self are aggregated and working models of representations of self and others are formed. The mental-representation model illustrates how interaction with the external world creates and progressively expands internal structure. The aggregation of working models of representations of self and others provides an interesting slant on a process I discuss later in this chapter: the process described by Kohut (1968) and Tolpin (1971) in which selfobject functions become internalized.

Links between component features of representations store our past experience and guide our perceptions. We construct mental models that integrate numerous attributes based on experience, wishes, fantasies, fears, or other affective structures. Internal models and their links between component features of representations are the basis for the organization and interpretation of experience, especially relationships with others. Repeated activation strengthens the links among features such that subsequent activation of features is more likely to activate the entire representation. While this process serves to integrate mental representations, there is also the potential to impose a representation on a variety of experiences. In the analytic situation, this can be manifested as transference.

Transference is an instantiation of the current structure of the mind and the representational world, and elucidation of the transference is an essential part of the process by which we revise old, enduring connections and create new connections and structures. This, then, allows the individual to develop new and more flexible models for engaging internal and external reality. Such a picture of the mind, with layer upon layer of connections, including connections that feed back to the original models, is very helpful when we think about transference interpretation, working through, deepening the analytic process, and the therapeutic action of psychoanalysis. In the analytic situation, we find a way to trace back the series of interconnections and establish new connections.

The second model of the mind devised by Fonagy and his collaborators (1993) to explain the development of psychic structure is the mental-process model. They illustrate this model by discussing memory, describing it as an autonomous mental process. The process of memory constructs and operates on the psychological phenomena that we call memories. This model fits with Sandler and Rosenblatt's (1962) elucidation of the representational world. Memories are contents of the mind or images on the psychic stage. The process of memory is the ego apparatus that photoshops and choreographs these images. This vision also fits with, and provides new ways to think about, Hartmann's (1939, 1950) and Rapaport's (1960) models of structure. Mental processes, such as memory, are autonomous ego functions that evolve over the course of development. The child's relationship with a healthy environment can facilitate or enhance the development of these autonomous ego functions, while an adverse environment can interfere with their development, leading them to become embroiled in conflict, inhibited, or fixated.

LYONS-RUTH: IMPLICIT OR PROCEDURAL KNOWING

Lyons-Ruth (1999), like Fonagy et. al (1993), addresses mental processes and psychological functions:

> New research is now pressing psychoanalytically oriented scholars to expand accounts of how meaning systems are organized to include implicit or proced-

ural forms of knowing. Procedural knowing refers to knowing how to do something and how to behave adaptively, rather than knowing information or images that can be consciously recalled and recounted (Cohen and Squire, 1980). The organization of memory and meaning in the implicit or enactive domain only becomes manifest in the doing. . . . Much of our relational experience is represented in an implicit procedural or enactive form that is unconscious, though not necessarily dynamically unconscious. . . . In both development and psychoanalysis, the increasing integration and articulation of new enactive "procedures for being with" destabilize existing enactive organization and serve as a primary engine of change. . . . Enactive procedures become more articulated and integrated through participation in more coherent and collaborative forms of intersubjective interaction. Put another way, at the level of unconscious enactive procedures, the medium is the message; that is, the organization of meaning is implicit in the organization of the enacted relational dialogue and does not require reflective thought or verbalization to be, in some sense, known. (578)

Significantly, Lyons-Ruth adds to the discussion an understanding of nonconscious as opposed to dynamically unconscious mental processes. The knowing is in the doing rather than in mental representations that are consciously in awareness. This kind of process and this procedural way of knowing is relevant in chapter 9, when I discuss the therapeutic nature of psychoanalysis; in chapter 10, when I examine the therapeutic value of play; and in chapter 11, when I explore the continuum from action to words as an expression of a child's mind.

BROMBERG: THE ILLUSION OF THE SELF

Bromberg (1996) explains that the self is not an actual entity but an illusion created by the increasing integration of dissociated self states. This is a model that organizes the mind or the self in a way that is different from Freud's structural model. Rather than visualizing water running through a series of dikes, we can picture a large circle surrounding many smaller circles. The smaller circles are the distinct and split-off or dissociated self states. As the interconnections grow among the smaller circles (the split-off self states), the complexity of the interior of the larger circle increases. As the split-off states become integrated, the mind or illusion of self achieves greater structure.

Bromberg's (1996) view that the self is an illusion might sound ominous. Freud has already taught us that we are not the conscious masters of our houses but are influenced by unconscious processes. Is Bromberg now telling us that we are not even an individual self? Let's not despair too quickly. The illusion of a self reflects a very important achievement in the structuring of the mind: a high level of integration of the varied self states that may be compared to Kohut's (1971, 1977; Kohut & Wolf, 1978) vision of the cohesive self.

If we think of the larger circle from my explanation as the map of a political community and the smaller circles as population centers, we have at hand another analogy that can help us consider the development of psychic structure according to Bromberg's (1996) model. When the roads between population centers are too narrow to bear the traffic, too poorly built to hold up, or too few to get people where they need to go, the community can't function adequately. A certain amount and quality of infrastructure is needed to have a cohesive community. The more integrated the successive networks, the more flexible and cohesive the mind. Additional infrastructure and the capacity to repair infrastructure when needed add to the capabilities of the cohesive community. Roadways can be reliable even when the weather is adverse. Multiple routes are possible, and additional subsidiary arteries can get people to more places because travel is not limited to the essentials. People have a wider range of options and opportunities for more varied and more subtle experiences. An individual with fewer connections or a less reliable integration will either have a more limited range of options, a more fragile structure, or both. Such an individual is more apt to find that the slats in the bridge are too far apart and to feel more vulnerable to falling into the chasm beneath the bridge that has failed to maintain a secure and reliable support. The cohesive community, with a more intact and robust infrastructure, will be more reliable but is not totally free of disruptions. Catastrophic failures may be less frequent, but smaller gaps in the infrastructure still have notable consequences.

The process of remembering serves as an example of a psychological process, and the creation of memories may also serve as a model for the development and construction of psychological structure. Memories are not passive imprints on the magic tablet. They are constructions. Memory is a process of integrating bits and pieces of information and different aspects and qualities of an experience (Bonanno, 1990a; Bromberg, 1993). The original sense impressions are discontinuous bits of data that the brain integrates into the phenomena we experience in our minds. Individual memories are then integrated into patterns that are further integrated into larger, more complex, and more subtle patterns. This way of considering the developing organization of the mind suggests that there is much in common between Bromberg's view of the integration of split-off self states and Fonagy and colleagues' (1993) vision of the development of psychological structure.

We might consider that discontinuities always remain in all human beings. In more disturbed patients, the breadth of the discontinuities or the frequency of the disruptive discontinuities is greater than we see in healthier patients, whose internal structure is more cohesive. We can understand psychological structure as the creation of internal maps. This view serves as a metaphor to consider the ways in which interconnections bridge discontinuities and facilitate (or fail to facilitate) a more cohesive mind. In the analyses in this book, Isabel draws maps, and Ella makes a road. While the girls are busily at play with their constructions, I understand these maps and the road as reflections of the internal structures of their minds. As Isabel's analysis progressed, she drew different maps and told different tales about her maps. Ella, before the analysis started, would run away from home across busy streets. Later, during the analysis, she built a wall that she changed to a road over which she could travel increasingly long distances and then return. We get to observe the changes within their minds.

INTEGRATION VERSUS DISINTEGRATION

Thinking of the mind as an integration of networks, self states, mental processes, or modes of functioning is helpful when we consider the increasing capacities of the mind and its structural reliability. When Bromberg's (1996) illusion of an integrated self is reliable, the state of mind is comparable to Kohut's (1971, 1977; Kohut & Wolf, 1978) cohesive self. With sufficient integration of the subselves or self states, a new state is reached in which the psyche functions more reliably than less integrated states. Bromberg's model is very informative when we think about how the self, the ego, or the mind becomes more structured. Greater connections among the varied subselves provide a compelling and clear visual image that fits very well with neuro-psychoanalytic studies of the brain in which the mind grows in complexity as connections among networks of neurons increase. Bromberg's model also provides a straightforward picture when we contemplate fragmentation. The illusion of the self is lost when the connections among the subselves are disrupted. Then, the self and the mind begin to function in a demonstrably less integrated way.

When we try to understand exactly what we mean by fragmentation, the image of an integration of networks is helpful. Loss of connections between or within the networks of the mental-representation model or the modes of functioning of the mental-process model has potentially the same consequences as splitting off or dissociating the self states in Bromberg's model. Disintegration means the loss of cohesion, the loss of the illusion of a self, and the loss of a reliable theater within the mind. Return to an earlier mode of functioning, like the split between pretend mode and psychic-equivalence mode, occurs. The consequences for the functioning of the mind are striking and demonstrable.

There are other ways to picture vulnerable psychological structure or lack of cohesion. Michael Balint (1979) writes about the basic fault, a defect in the structure of the mind. It is as if the I-beam of a house has a structural defect, leaving the entirety of the house vulnerable to unnatural shifting, cracking, or collapse. Analysis of patients with such vulnerabilities could be problematic because analysis, like other experiences that might send tremors through the house, has the potential to strain the I-beam beyond its capabilities. When surrounding structures and defenses have compensated for the basic fault, their analysis could leave the entire mind vulnerable.

Pine (1994) uses the word *deficit* to describe developmental failures of the environment, and he chooses the word *defect* to describe the internal lack of structure caused by the environmental deficit. Kohut (1968; Kohut & Wolf 1978) refers to deficits of structure and initially believed that narcissistic disorders were fundamentally different from the transference neuroses. He explains that individuals with narcissistic disorders suffer with a deficit in psychological structure. Establishment of a selfobject transference and analysis of this transference facilitates healing of the deficits in the psyche. Later, he suggests that neurotic disorders, as well, are fundamentally the result of empathic failures, leading to more subtle deficits in the structure of the self. The normal and healthy conflicts in life are not resolved because, in the mind of the child, her parents—her oedipal selfobjects, for example—do not provide the pride in or mirroring of her new strivings while comfortably helping her to contain the power of her feelings, including rivalry, jealousy, wishes to murder, and fears of retaliation. The neurotic symptoms, then, are not simply the result of conflict but are an effort to contend with the structural deficit caused by the lack of internalization of developmentally appropriate parental functions.

DEVELOPMENT OF PSYCHIC STRUCTURE

Throughout this book, I look carefully at the child's capacity to soothe herself and modulate her affects. I see these capacities as indications of the development of psychological structures. Consideration of the vicissitudes of the child's capacity to soothe her anxiety or modulate other affects helps me to define psychic structure and helps us examine the shifts in the reliability of psychic structure.

Tolpin (1971) examines in detail how the child at first relies on the selfobject parents for their capacity to soothe her. During toddlerhood, she creates an intermediate space, a way station, where her transitional object, such as a teddy bear or blanket, provides comfort. Her developing mental capacities allow her to imbue this inanimate object with the comforting power of her parents. Her imagination is at play, but it feels very real, and her capacity to create and believe in the transitional object allows her to begin the process of taking possession of or internalizing the soothing or modulating functions of her parents. With further maturity, the little girl's capacity to comfort herself resides more securely within her, and she loses interest in her transitional objects.

Tolpin's (1971) view requires that we position ourselves inside the mind of the child in order to capture the way she experiences the presence of the parent as part of her self. The parent does not live outside the child and fortify a stimulus barrier. The parent is not an auxiliary ego that supports or interferes with development of mental processes and structures from the outside. The child experiences the support on the inside. With time, she takes full possession of this capacity, and it becomes an enduring part of her self.

Wilson and Weinstein (1996) build on Vygotsky's study of the process of learning. The zone of proximal development (ZPD) is a concept to formulate the ways in which linguistic mediation between child and adult facilitates internalization:

> Being in the ZPD "calls to life in the child, awakens and puts in motion an entire series of internal processes of development. These processes are at the time possible only in the sphere of interaction with those surrounding the child and in collaboration with companions, but in the internal course of development they eventually become the internal property of the child." (Vygotsky, 1956, 450, cited by Wertsch, 1985, 71, cited by Wilson and Weinstein, 1996, 170)

The ZPD exists in the space between self and object and is proximal to "those functions that have not yet matured but are in the process of maturation" (Vygotsky, 1978, 86, cited by Wilson and Weinstein, 1996, 170). The concept of ZPD provides a way to understand how the more highly organized mind (Loewald, 1960) facilitates the reorganization of the less organized mind and how the selfobject facilitates development of the self. The parents' engagement with the child in the ZPD provides an "entrance into an internalization community" (Weinstein and Wilson, 1996, 183). This provides a scaffold that supports the unfolding development of the child and allows the child to take possession of the evolving processes.

Mayes and Cohen (1993b) trace the modulation of aggression through the early years of development: "What comes to be symbolized and represented in the human mind as predatory or dangerous, what kinds of events are perceived as threatening, . . . is defined and refined in the context of the child's earliest experiences" (153). Development of a theory of mind, according to Mayes and Cohen (1996), or development of the capacity to mentalize, according to Fonagy and Target (1998), is a transition that provides the child with mental capabilities that greatly enhance her capacity to modulate and manage her emotional states as exemplified by anger and aggression.

The mental-process perspective, the selfobject perspective, the concept of the ZPD, and ego psychology have some very important concepts in common. Each of these theoretical points of view posits that immature or perhaps

virtual processes develop in the context of the child's relationship and interactions with the object. These processes, capacities, or autonomous ego functions develop in a good-enough environment, while conflict or failures of the
environment are apt to interfere with this development.

For Fonagy and Target (1998), mentalization is enhanced when the child
sees her experience as it is reflected in the minds of her parents. This can be
compared to the mirroring function of the parent as described by Kohut
(Kohut, 1968; Kohut & Wolf, 1978). Both perspectives address the structure
and workings of the psychological theater in addition to the performance on
the stage or the contents of the mind. The theater is reliable when the little
girl is mirrored by the love and empathy of her mother and when the mother's strength serves as an I-beam for the structure. The child's engagement
with her mother facilitates the process of mentalization and the process of
memory. The memories or relationships that are contents of the mind can be
more effectively integrated and more reliably and complexly portrayed on
the stage.

We see the development of psychic structure with Ella as her analysis
progressed. When she first met Mrs. Kaufman, she dealt with her fear by
insisting that she was a big girl and was not afraid. By the end of her analysis,
she dreamed of a friend who was not afraid and who helped her with a scary
situation. When she pretended to call Mrs. Kaufman during the night, she had
created a transitional space in which she began to take ownership of the
comforting function of her analyst. She was not at sea without the actual
presence of her analyst. On the stage of her dreaming and imagining mind,
she was the director and playwright, and she conjured up a performance in
which her analyst helped her feel more secure. Here, we see evidence that
Ella's developing capacity to imagine (Mayes & Cohen, 1992) and to mentalize (Sugarman, 2003b, 2006) facilitated her ability to modulate a potentially overwhelming emotion: anxiety.

Lyons-Ruth (1999), Fonagy and colleagues (1993), Mayes & Cohen
(1996), and Tolpin (1971) all address psychological functions. They look
around the theater of the mind, examine the apparatuses, and try to explain
them. They help us to understand how the mind operates, how it is structured,
and how it changes. All of their ideas inform our understanding of the development of psychic structure. Lyons-Ruth's perspective is particularly helpful
when we consider the role of action in the therapeutic process. Isabel and
Ella were action-oriented, and their actions had meaning. Relational experience, represented in an implicit procedural or enactive form, was important
in their analyses. The children's actions and the analysts' responses brought
into the room these nonconscious modes of functioning. In chapter 11, I look
at the analyses of the two girls and examine how consideration of action and
enactment help us understand the girls and the ways in which their relationships with their analysts led to internal change.

In chapter 9, I look at the ways in which the meeting of two minds in analysis facilitates a reorganization of the analysand's mind (Loewald, 1960) and how the analyst's openness to the mind of a child or adult (Lyons-Ruth, 1999) provides a scaffold (Wilson & Weintstein, 1996) between them that allows new forms of organization of implicit relational procedures, as well as other mental processes. The models of the minds and theories of development presented by Bion (1963); Bromberg (1996); Anna Freud (1965); Sigmund Freud (1953–1974c, 1953–1974d, 1953–1974o); Fonagy and colleagues (1993); Klein (1975); Kohut (1971, 1977; Kohut & Wolf, 1978); Lyons-Ruth (1999); Mahler, Pine, and Bergman (1975); and Mayes and Cohen (1996) are all relevant to the consideration of structure formation, the developmental object, fragmentation, trauma, and therapeutic action.

Chapter Six

Trauma and Fragile Psychic Structure

Edward I. Kohn

Both Ella and Isabel had to deal with the arrival of a younger sibling, and both portrayed persistent preoccupation with their mothers' bodies and pregnancy. The manifest similarity of such material might suggest that the two children were grappling with similar emotional concerns at comparable developmental levels. However, we need to consider the latent meaning of the surface expressions in order to enter into the internal world of each child, and we need to consider her unique psychic fingerprint and family situation in order to understand her response to a seemingly similar life event. By examining the meaning of birth and mother's body to Ella and Isabel, we can achieve a better understanding of how they experienced their worlds. The process of each analysis and the analytic material associated with each girl's references to women's bodies provide insight into the developmental factors that shaped their visions. Isabel began analysis amid oedipal development, while Ella predominantly dealt with concerns about separation-individuation and abandonment. As I trace the arc of these two analyses, we also get a close-up view of the process in which a content of the mind changes in meaning and significance as a child moves from one phase of development to another.

Sandler and Rosenblatt's (1962) representational world is the stage within the theater of the mind. Ella was prone to fragmentation because the foundation of her theater lacked sufficient stability. Toddlerhood, the transition through the stages of separation and individuation, creates important internal structures. Ella's developmental struggles left her with an incomplete foundation, and we can give a variety of names to this vulnerability of her psychic structure: ego deficits, lack of a cohesive self, a basic fault, failure to achieve the mode of reflective functioning, failure to achieve the depressive position, and failure to achieve object constancy.

Isabel's theater, in contrast, had a more flexible and enduring foundation. She did not fragment, and the theater of her mind did not collapse when the wolf of life huffed and puffed. However, when oedipal development led her to reexperience traumatic events, she was overwhelmed, the characters on the stage were blown about, and the theater vibrated. These differences between Ella and Isabel allow us, or perhaps demand of us, to consider further the concepts of psychological structure, trauma, and fragmentation. What do we really mean by these terms, how do they help us understand these two girls and their analyses, and how can our observations and inferences about them help to illustrate these concepts?

TRAUMA

Trauma can occur at any stage of development. The severity of an external experience, its particular meaning to an individual, the preexisting personality structure and resilience of the individual, and the nature and availability of emotional support all contribute to the greater or lesser likelihood of being traumatized. Large numbers of war veterans immersed in violent battle that is foreign to their normal daily lives return home with PTSD. Children, with their immature psyches, are highly vulnerable to being traumatized. They rely on their parents to buffer them from internal and external experiences. Anna Freud's and Dorothy Burlingham's (1943) study of British children during the London blitz reveals that the state of mind of the child's mother was a significant determinant of whether the child was traumatized by the bombing.

What is different and the same about an experience we call trauma and one we call fragmentation? What is the difference between an individual we view as neurotic, who feels overwhelmed by a traumatic experience, and an individual whose psychological structure is not as reliable, is more fragile, and is vulnerable to fragmentation? In trauma, the ego is overwhelmed, passively helpless in the face of a consuming experience. In fragmentation, we hypothesize that the structure of the psyche has crumbled.

When discussing trauma, Sigmund Freud describes experiences that present the mind with stimuli that cannot be managed. The mental apparatus, whose purpose is to manage stimuli from within and without, in effect is flooded and cannot master the stimuli in the usual way (S. Freud, 1920/1953–1974a). He explains that automatic anxiety is a response to this unmanageable situation. In "Inhibitions, Symptoms and Anxiety" (1926/1953–1974g) and "The Ego and the Id" (1923/1953–1974d), Freud describes his second theory of anxiety. Anxiety is no longer seen as the result of restrained libido that transforms into anxiety. Instead, it is a function of the ego, and signal anxiety is a response of the ego to a threat of danger. With development, assuming the presence of a protective and comforting mother, the overwhelming nature of automatic anxiety—a primal biologically based state—gets drawn into the realm of the ego. The ego is able to tap into a little bit of the automatic anxiety and use it as a signal. We might think of a fire alarm at an elementary school. The sound of the bell of signal anxiety leads to an orderly retreat from the building, while unrestrained clanging that itself overwhelms the children increases the likelihood of a panicky response and disorder. Especially when the student body is not familiar with the routine of exiting the building, when ego functions are not in place, terror and chaos are apt to result in response to the signal itself.

The word *overwhelming* or similar terms, like *shattering* or *devastating*, are central to Sigmund Freud's and Anna Freud's (1964/1967) definitions of *trauma*. Almost every writer who considers trauma uses the word *over-whelming*. What exactly does it mean to be overwhelmed? What is the internal state of the psyche under such a circumstance? In the study of trauma since the time of Freud, we can identify a persistent effort to enhance our understanding of what it means to be overwhelmed. Over the years, scholars who have written about trauma have given us a variety of tools to assess, appreciate, or get inside this state of mind. What does the subject experience? What is happening inside the mind of an individual who is in a traumatic state? How is this similar or how is this different from a fragmented state of mind? How does the mind function at such a time compared to more normal circumstances? What enduring consequences remain after an episode of fragmentation or a traumatic event?

KRYSTAL'S VIEW OF TRAUMA

Henry Krystal (1985) begins with the ego-psychological perspective and gives us additional tools to consider traumatic states, their impact, and the internal developments associated with such states. One way that he approaches the concept of trauma is by expanding on the concept of affect (Krystal, 1978, 1985). A young child lacks the capacities to differentiate one affect from another or to verbalize or symbolically represent affects, and for a child of this age, the experience of affect is primarily somatic. The immaturity of the child's ego functions and defenses make the infantile form of trauma qualitatively different from the adult form. The adult's greater affect tolerance and defensive armamentarium enable her to deal with adversity more effectively, and the experience of being overwhelmed is different for the adult than for the child.

Krystal (1978) explains that

two different types of psychoanalytic emergencies can be observed. One is related to the cognitive aspect of the emotion as illustrated by the fear that

> aggressive wishes may get out of hand and magically cause great destruction.
> The other is an "affect storm," which represents quite a different problem. In
> this situation, the patient experiences himself as "flooded" by emotion and
> dreads that the emotion not only will be "endlessly" violent, but will go on to
> destroy him. (92)

Krystal draws a distinction between the flood—the experience of being over-whelmed—and "catastrophic trauma." It is when the subject feels helpless and surrenders to the dangerous situation that the full-blown traumatic state, the "catatonoid" reaction, has occurred: "In the catatonoid state, we are deal-ing with the very moment of the self being overwhelmed with a phylogenet-ically determined surrender pattern" (93). Automatic anxiety is the experi-ence when the childhood version of trauma, a global unregulated flooding, has occurred. This is the state he describes as overwhelming of the ego.

Krystal (1978) goes on to describe the phenomenological picture of a traumatized individual:

> a paralyzed, overwhelmed state, with immobilization, withdrawal, possible
> depersonalization, and evidence of disorganization. There may be a regression
> in any and all spheres and aspects of mental function and affect expression.
> This regression is followed by characteristic recuperative attempts through
> repetition, typical dreams, and eventually by long-term neurotic, character-
> ological, psychosomatic, or other syndromes. The so-called traumatic neurosis
> is just one of many possible sequelae of traumatization. (90)

THE IMPORTANCE OF CLARIFYING OUR TERMS

In her work with children, Anna Freud (1964/1967) began to be more specif-ic about what she meant when she used the term *trauma*:

> Like everyone else, I have tended to use the term "trauma" rather loosely up to
> now, but I shall find it easier to avoid this in the future. Whenever I am
> tempted to call an event in a child's or adult's life "traumatic," I shall ask
> myself some further questions. Do I mean that the event was upsetting: that it
> was significant for altering the course of further development; that it was
> pathogenic? Or do I really mean traumatic in the strict sense of the word, i.e.,
> shattering, devastating, (and) causing internal disruption by putting ego func-
> tioning and ego mediation out of action? (237–238)

These questions are relevant when we think about Isabel. She suffered three events that we loosely call traumatic: breaking her collarbone, being attacked by the family dog, and witnessing the precipitous birth of her sister. Looking more closely at the cases, we see how the thinking of Anna Freud (1964/ 1967) and Krystal (1978) enable us to be more precise in our understanding. I portray the impact of these events on Isabel's development from the inside of her experience of the traumas and see how this impact unfolded into her oedipal phase.

CUMULATIVE TRAUMA, STRAIN TRAUMA, AND RETROSPECTIVE TRAUMA

Khan's (1963) cumulative trauma or Ernst Kris's (1956b) strain trauma are chronically repetitive experiences that adversely affect development and the unfolding of the ego or self. Yet, individually these experiences don't trigger the overwhelmed response described by Krystal (1978) or the shattering internal disruption that Anna Freud (1964/1967) describes. We might think of these influences as impingements on the developing ego or self. Winnicott (1960) describes the development of a false self that enables the infant to adapt to the impingements of a misattuned mother while preserving her true self, though at great cost. From the perspective of self psychology, if the child must adapt to the narcissistic needs of the parents rather than the parents responding to the vital and natural unfolding of the child's nuclear self (Kohut & Wolf, 1978), her self becomes misshapen. When light cannot satisfactorily reach a young tree because it is overshadowed by the larger surrounding trees, its growth may be stunted or its direction of growth might bend in order to reach the sustaining light. An ego or self that has been stressed and strained in this way is less flexible, less resilient, and more vulnerable to the effects of later experiences. This child is more at risk of being overwhelmed or traumatized by experiences that occur later in her life.

Ella did not experience the singular, circumscribed overwhelming incidents that were suffered by Isabel. She dealt with a different kind of major disruptive event: She was adopted! She also endured a toddlerhood filled with conflict with her mother. When we move inside Ella's mind, we see how these experiences influenced her. Would we consider these events traumatic? If so, how do we understand the traumatic impact? Or, do we require a different kind of explanation?

Kris (1956b) states, "The problem is further complicated by the fact that the further course of life seems to determine which experience may gain significance as a traumatic event" (73). He is referring to a kind of retrospective trauma. The meaning of an experience is an essential piece of its traumatic nature. There are experiences that appear traumatic only in retrospect. As the child's development moves forward, meanings change for her. She views the present moment differently than she would have viewed the same moment if it had occurred 2 years earlier, and the present meanings of past experiences change for her, as well. Freud (1918/1953–1974f) uses the term *Nachträglichkeit* to describe this phenomenon, referring to the ways in which a past event is reinterpreted as development progresses. *Nachtraglichkeit* has been translated as *après coup* in French and "deferred action" in English. These words provide a name for a phenomenon that an earlier experience may not be traumatic at the time but the meaning it acquires and the interpretation applied to it under different developmental circumstances gives it a power that can make it traumatic at the later time.

Experiences that felt overwhelming or potentially overwhelming early in childhood but did not trigger a fully traumatic response might be managed by early defensive maneuvers. This establishes a fragile equilibrium, where infantile affects are precariously stabilized by an immature ego. As later development tips the equilibrium that has been established, the earlier defensive structures are no longer sufficient. A new experience that throws this equilibrium out of balance, like a rising river bearing down on an already-compromised dam, will at the minimum intensify the affective state of the new experience and has the potential to unleash a traumatic state. For Isabel, the early frightening experiences influenced her oedipal development, and the related affects were too much for her to contain.

GROTSTEIN'S VIEW OF TRAUMA AND FRAGMENTATION

Grotstein (1990a) states that the traumatic state is one of organismic, annihilation anxiety. Nothingness and meaninglessness are the most dreaded states of mind. He draws on physics for a metaphor to describe the collapse of the self:

> It is the traumatic state itself which approximates the experience of randomness and approaches cataclysmic meaninglessness (the "black hole"). This cataclysmic, disorganizing, traumatic state is psychological and biological and precipitates a series of events which are understandable according to chaos theory and self-regulation theory. These events are as follows: The onset of the traumatic state bespeaks the dissolution (and therefore functional disappearance) of the holding-containing matrix of the internal world (the background presence of primary identification) with a dissolution of figure-ground distinction and, with the dissolution of this internal structuring map, there is experienced a violent, implosive pull into a "black hole," one which is experienced as spaceless, bottomless, timeless and yet, paradoxically, condensed, compact, and immediate, yielding suffocation anxiety. A manic variant of this "black hole" experience is that of explosive expansion or even of splintering. (281)

Grotstein (1990a) applies this description, not only to the state of trauma, but also to the crumbling of the mind into psychosis. As strange and disordered as the symptoms and signs of psychosis are, he sees these as the mind's most fundamental effort to organize and give meaning to experience as the it enters the black hole. The inability to give personal meaning and realistic significance to an event is the descent into randomness. The observable signs and symptoms of psychosis are the mind's desperate claw-hold on some kind of organization outside the black hole.

There is a dizzying series of words and concepts packed into Grotstein's (1990a) description of the collapse of the self. A first and casual reading might itself create the feeling of being pulled into a black hole, where words fly around and seem incomprehensible. Fortunately, on further consideration, this is not the case, and the unpacking of this dense quote provides the reader with many concepts with which to consider the workings of the collapsing mind. In addition, the images that emerge enable the reader to better imagine himself inside that collapsing mind.

Grotstein (1990a) suggests that our usual ways of thinking about the mind are not able to explain the underlying rules of organization within the fragmented or traumatic state. He offers the possibility of chaos theory or self-regulation theory as alternative paradigms. This further emphasizes that something different is happening here. Like Krystal (1978) and Freud (1964/1967), he explains that this state is both biological or organismic and psychological. He is attempting to get inside the collapsing mind as our illusion of a self disappears and we live within a body that is unable to generate meaning.

The metaphor of the black hole can be taken further. In physics, the black hole is a singularity, where the force of gravity is infinite. Einstein's theory of general relativity cannot function in the black hole; the laws of nature as we know them break down. Yet, we can make observations from a vantage point outside the black hole as we observe its effect on matter, energy, and space. The event horizon is the point of no return. Nothing that crosses the event horizon, the point outside the black hole where its gravitational field is so intense that its pull is insurmountable, can return to the universe outside the black hole. There is no communication and no meaningful data to be extracted from the black hole. Information is lost! This can be compared to the fragmenting mind and loss of the capacity to symbolize, verbalize, or represent.

Freud's (1900/1953–1974i) insights into dream formation and the workings of the unconscious mind reveal to us that the mind operates in more than one way. Many latent dream thoughts can be condensed into one image, and many different images may represent or have embedded within them one dream thought. He notes that, when you enter the navel of the dream, the condensed representations that come together are so rich that you cannot determine an ultimate or irreducible meaning of the dream.

The mind's capacity to work in a primary process way, its remarkable ability to think in metaphor, symbolize, displace, and represent things, makes human beings unique in their ability to communicate with themselves and others. Yet, there are times when it seems like meanings are so densely packed that they cannot be unpacked. As the gravity of the black hole compresses the mind, reflective functioning and the capacity for mentalization are lost. There is no longer space to experience or contemplate a state of mind versus concrete and actual reality. As the mind succumbs to the deeper and stronger gravitational forces, reality and fantasy increasingly merge and may become indistinguishable. Rather than functioning creatively or as communication, it is as if the unregulated and uncontrolled capacity of the mind for condensation packs so much meaning within itself that it becomes infinitely dense and eventually unavailable to comprehension. Meanings have moved beyond the event horizon of the black hole and are so intensely compacted that the subject cannot represent and the object cannot receive communication in a meaningful way.

Grotstein (1990a) describes, as does Boulanger (2002), the dissolution of figure and ground and the loss of the holding and containing matrix of the mind. In our everyday experience, space is the container of the universe. In his theory of special relativity, Einstein explains that it is not so simple. Space is not simply a container that exists in time. Space and time are one continuum, one matrix. More complicated yet, he explains in the theory of general relativity that matter and forces do not operate within a simple container of space and time. Matter bends the space–time continuum. Therefore, within a black hole, the matrix of the universe—the space–time continuum—gets infinitely bent. When there is no matrix to the mind, there is no experience. Sandler and Rosenblatt's (1962) representational world has shrunk so small, there is no space.

BOULANGER'S VIEW OF TRAUMA

Memory under normal circumstances, according to Boulanger (2002), helps to integrate experience. Perception, affect, and action form a whole. Bartlett (1932) and Bonanno (1990) explain that memory is a process involving bits and pieces of information that are continually integrated and reconstructed during the course of remembering, dependent on the manner in which the memories are accessed. For a traumatized child, Boulanger suggests that memories are unformulated and stored in dissociated self-states. The connections between the dissociated states are not disguised or unavailable; they are simply obliterated. Paradoxically, this dissociation, splitting, or fragmentation of memory makes memory indelible because it prevents the memories from being integrated with the passage of time.

Like Krystal (1978), Boulanger (2002) draws a distinction between the child and adult versions of trauma. The adult self is catastrophically altered by trauma. The sense of a collapsed self permeates every aspect of the adult survivor's psyche. The sense of the self as singular and constant is lost. Everything that had been psychically familiar is called into question. She describes the phenomenological sense of the traumatic experience in much the same way that Krystal does. She refers to a feeling of paralysis, fear of physical fragmentation, loss of affectivity, disruption of continuity, and fear of annihilation. This calls up for Boulanger the primitive agonies described by Winnicott (1974).

TRAUMA AND FRAGMENTATION MAY BE DIFFICULT TO DISTINGUISH

Bromberg (1993) states that the illusion of unity of the self is a necessary condition for psychic function. When the illusion is threatened by an unavoidable disruption, in jeopardy of being overwhelmed by input that it cannot process, the sense of unity and cohesion becomes a liability. Dissociation interrupts the sense of cohesion so that data that are incompatible with a continuing sense of self are denied simultaneous access to consciousness. Concreteness supersedes the capacity to symbolize, and the immediate subjective experience is seen as the one and only true reality. Other possibilities are unthinkable. This sounds like Ella when she threw the contents of the dollhouse around the room or scrambled to find her way into her analyst's body. For Bromberg, the traumatic state is the pathological use of dissociation in response to Winnicott's (1960) impingement. Fragmentation is not the ultimate catastrophe; it is the desperate attempt to prevent the ultimate catastrophe.

Brown (2005) similarly explains that the unbearable emotions of massive psychic trauma cannot be experienced in a meaningful way. Defensive concretization and retreat from alpha function (the capacity for symbolic thinking) to beta elements (the raw sensory affective experiences that can't be mentally digested or thought), comparable to Freud's (1953–1974j) increments of stimuli, occurs. This compares, as well, to Krystal's (1978) catatonoid state. The beta screen, like Grotstein's (1990a) psychotic symptoms or the paranoid/schizoid functioning described by Klein (1975), is an effort to organize beta elements into a semblance of cohesion. Otherwise, trauma and catastrophe explode the psyche and disarticulate its organization. Brown's description draws a less clear distinction between fragmentation as a way to avoid the dreaded traumatic state and fragmentation as part of or the result of the traumatic state.

The more we get inside the mind during the catastrophic traumatic state, the more difficult it seems to distinguish it from the state of the mind while fragmenting. When we take a position deep inside the experience of the moment of catastrophic trauma or fragmentation, the consequences of the efforts to contend with the psychic event and the impact of the event itself become difficult to distinguish, as well. Is there an essence to the traumatic state or the experience of fragmentation? Can we distinguish the inflammatory response of the mind from the injury? Is fragmentation a defense against an unbearable traumatic state, or is it the unbearable state itself? Are there different kinds of fragmentation or traumatic states?

ISABEL'S TRAUMAS

Isabel's sister was born precipitously when she was 2½ years old. Exposure to the frightening scene and sense of chaos (mother giving birth to the baby on the toilet), the sounds of sirens and screams, and the sight of blood influenced her experience of and fantasies about the birth process.

When we talk loosely about the trauma of witnessing the birth of her sister or being brutally attacked by her dog, which of Anna Freud's (1964/1967) meanings do we have in mind for Isabel? That the event was upsetting? Yes. That it altered her course of development? That it was pathogenic? Yes, and yes. Was it traumatic, in the sense of being devastating and causing internal disruption by disabling ego mediation? That's harder to say. While her father assumed that Isabel must have been upset, an assumption that I share, her parents don't describe observable reactions at the time that point in an obvious way to a shattering impact. We don't see a child in a catatonoid post-traumatic state or see re-creations of ego collapse in the analytic sessions. What we do see is a girl who developed symptomatic behavior after the event, and, in the analytic sessions, we see a girl who gets overstimulated and can't contain herself. I infer that she was dealing with intense anxiety and sexual excitement.

We see indications of an enduring effect on her development and her functioning that I attribute, at least in part, to these individual, frightening events. Her mother described symptoms of selective mutism, demanding and controlling behaviors, and difficulty dealing with bowel movements at school. Her parents brought her to treatment when her inhibitions worsened, and she would not ride her bicycle or go to the park with the family. She told her mother she did not know if she could go on in life. It seems that her symptoms worsened as she faced oedipal-phase concerns. The new balance of forces made it more difficult for Isabel to contain her affective state.

Nachträglichkeit, retrospective trauma, or *après coup* are concepts that are relevant to Isabel's analysis, in that earlier experiences took on new meaning in this later developmental phase. It is not the case, however, that the trauma and its effects appeared anew during the oedipal phase. Isabel was affected by these early upsetting experiences prior to the oedipal phase of development. Kris (1956b) and Khan (1964), in their discussions of strain or cumulative trauma, worked to explain the impact of chronically active experiences that—over time—cause damage without the immediately overwhelming evidence of trauma. While we can assume that the earlier experiences affected Isabel's ego development and made her more vulnerable to being overwhelmed by later events, we also see that these earlier events were circumscribed in time rather than subclinical and chronic and that they left an enduring effect because they overwhelmed her coping mechanisms. This is more typical of what we generally refer to as a traumatic event rather than the more persistent, less obvious, and chronic misattunements or impingements due to strain trauma or subtle failures in the parent–child relationship.

A FUNDAMENTAL TRANSITION IN THE STRUCTURING OF THE MIND

Erik H. Erikson (1968) explains that development proceeds epigenetically. Earlier phases of development are not replaced by later phases but are transformed into later phases, and the earlier phases are never gone. Freud (1916/1953–1974j) compares libidinal development to the migration of a people into new territory, explaining that—as the group moves forward—some of the people remain behind and occupy the territory in the rear. Depending on the state of the child's psychological landscape, a greater or lesser number of the population is left behind. The child who leaves more resources (libido) at the earlier developmental position (fixation) has less capacity to deal with frustration or duress as she moves forward developmentally. Therefore, she is more likely to feel overcome as she moves forward, more vulnerable to regression, and more likely to retreat to the earlier established setting.

As a child's development progresses, certain emotional preoccupations and abilities take center stage. We call this phase specificity. Manifestations of earlier phases remain and may temporarily fill the screen, but for the most part, they remain in the background. Depending on the child's developmental progression, earlier stages of development may be on the stage of the representational world in a more enduring way, or they might temporarily come to prominence. With successful analytic work or successful parenting, the later developmental phase normally becomes dominant, and the earlier phases can be seen in the shapes and colorings of the dominant phase. We see with Isabel, who was 6½ when she began analysis, that oedipal concerns about birth and bodies were highly visible from the start, though mixed with anal concerns and fantasies of anal birth. When Ella began analysis at the age of 4 years 10 months, she displayed more concerns about abandonment, separation, and caretaking. Oedipal concerns emerged as the analysis progressed, and in some of her oedipal fantasies, we can see the patterns of separation and individuation from which they evolved.

Freud's (1905/1953–1974b) libidinal stages of development—oral, anal, phallic, oedipal, latency, and genital—are familiar. His developmental sequence of anxiety—loss of the object, loss of love, castration, and guilt

(1926/1953–1974g)—fit the libidinal stages very neatly and provides an exceptional tool for understanding the psychological experience of the adult and—even more directly—that of the child during different stages of development.

Mahler, Pine, and Bergman (1975) introduce a developmental line for object relations and the evolution of the capacities for separation and individuation. The achievement of object constancy, the capacity to keep the object in mind during periods of absence or frustration, is a pivotal developmental accomplishment. The quality of a child's experience and the child's resilience under duress or in the face of distressing affects is very different once a substantial degree of object constancy has been achieved.

Rapprochement, a subphase of separation and individuation, has often been seen as crucial in the development of borderline personality disorders. Fixations at this point, or at other points prior to the achievement of the capacity to maintain object constancy, leave the child with insufficient internal representations of the parents. The enduring intrapsychic representations of self and object and the affects associated with their interactions are the bricks and mortar of psychic structure (Kernberg, 1976). When the sustaining functions of the parent–child relationship, the child's internal structure, or both are faulty, the foundation for further development is unstable and unreliable, and the child's capacity to negotiate new developmental tasks is undermined.

Many analytic theorists, each in their own way, describe this fundamental transition in the functioning of the mind that occurs as the child develops. Achievement of this new mode of functioning is an enormous accomplishment; it allows the child to function more independently and more adaptively. Like water changing to ice, the mind becomes organized in a new way with new properties and capabilities. When water undergoes a phase transition, the molecules are still the same substance, but they interact differently. The properties of the substance have changed, and the equations that describe their interaction are different.

The mind, too, undergoes phase transitions, and different states of the mind exhibit different properties. If the higher mode of organization, which Kohut (1971) calls the cohesive self, is not achieved or is lost, the mind functions according to different rules and exhibits different properties. It operates in a less reliable way than a cohesive self. When Kohut considers the cohesive self in contrast to a self that is fragmented or not yet cohesive, he grapples with the same changes in the stability of the mind that Mahler, Pine, and Bergman (1975) refer to in the achievement of object constancy. I have pointed out a number of times that Klein (1975) addresses this shift in the capabilities of the mind with her consideration of the paranoid/schizoid position and the depressive position, while Bion (1962/1977a, 1965/1977b) discusses alpha function versus beta function (Brown, 2005).

Fonagy and Target (1996) point out that a young child, who functions in psychic-equivalence mode, expects her internal world or that of others to correspond to external reality. She distorts her subjective experience to match the outside world. In contrast to this—when a young child is at play and functioning in pretend mode—she recognizes no relationship between her activity and the outside world. It is when these alternative modes are integrated that the child achieves the reflective mode of functioning and the capacity to mentalize. Mental states can be experienced as representations of inner and outer reality. They are linked and no longer dissociated, but they are no longer equated, either. These capacities are properties of the cohesive state of the self or mind. We see in the case of Ella how functioning in the psychic-equivalence mode led her behavior to be more rigid and controlling. Ideas or feelings were experienced with the intensity of external events. When she felt her state of mind going to pieces, she desperately tried to keep the pieces of her play in place. When functioning in psychic-equivalence mode, a child is intolerant of alternative perspectives. Everything must be the way the child thinks it is or needs it to be.

For Boulanger (2002), the capacity to distinguish figure and ground is an essential organizing capacity of the mind. A fragmented self is one in which the ground/figure distinction is no longer viable and is disrupted. She points out that Mitchell (1993) explains that the "experience of the self as singular and constant serves an important adaptive psychological purpose. A sense of self independent of shifts over time, connected with the function of self-reflection, provides continuity from one subjective state to another. Even when I am not myself, I experience a continuity with previous subjective states" (107).

All of these developmental perspectives address a phase transition in which the structure of the mind takes on a new organization. When we consider the achievement of the depressive position, alpha function, object constancy, reflective function, or self-cohesion, we are using concepts that identify qualities of this phase transition. In Freud's (1953–1974b, 1953–1974d) line of psychosexual development, the oedipal phase is not just the result or manifestation of particular psychic contents, concerns, or preoccupations that have come to the fore. The achievement of the oedipal phase, in Freud's scheme, is enormously significant because it represents the consolidation of psychological structure. He points to internalization of the superego as the clearest evidence of a successful transition. Consolidation of psychic structure, the capacity to be classically neurotic, is a signal achievement in the psychosexual line of development.

Isabel is a child whose mind had achieved this kind of structure. The content of her play, thoughts, and actions predominantly depicted concerns about the oedipal stage of development. More importantly, for this section of the book, the structure of her psyche was more cohesive than that of Ella.

When I compare the two cases, there is evidence of fragmentation in Ella's sense of self that did not occur within Isabel, and I examine how their respective capacities to represent and communicate their inner worlds differed at the start of their analyses and became more similar as the analytic work progressed.

With the consolidation of the mind, mental processes that facilitate communication within the individual's mind or between her and the other are more reliable. The alpha function of the dreaming mind, as described by Bion (1965), allows more meaningful communication than a mind that is limited to beta elements. Psychic-equivalence and pretend mode are integrated, and reflective functioning has been achieved. The theater of the psyche is more reliably intact and less apt to crumble, and the drama on the stage can be considered with less worry about the viability of the stage or theater. Mitchell (1993) refers to the "capacity to take oneself for granted" (114). The characters on the stage have minds of their own. Their thoughts, feelings, and motives can be considered, and the author of the play can experiment with all sorts of scenarios. Mind as a playground has been established. Thoughts, feelings, and fantasies are experienced as different from concrete realities. They can be played with rather than desperately contended with. Meaning is alive.

A LOOK AT COHESIVE STRUCTURE AND FRAGMENTATION

When we talk of the cohesive self or intact ego, we are trying to conceptualize the sense of an enduring internal structure. Fragmentation occurs when the psychic structure collapses. This was a central concept in Kohut's (1968; Kohut & Wolf, 1978) ideas about self psychology. He sees the self as the fundamental psychological structure, and its cohesiveness—or lack of cohesiveness—has enormous influence on psychic experience and functioning. He describes a separate line of development for narcissism throughout the life cycle, intimately related to the cohesiveness of the self. Patients diagnosed with narcissistic personality disorders are, by definition, individuals who failed to establish a cohesive self and are vulnerable to fragmentation.

When the state of the psyche or cohesion of the self has not reached this reliable stage, fragmentation can occur. Patients capable of developing narcissistic transferences are able to develop a relationship with the analyst in which the analyst becomes a selfobject, providing the needed psychological functions that are usually provided by the parent during childhood or by the individual herself later in life. These are capacities that the child has not yet developed, but in the context of the self–selfobject relationship, she feels that these functions are hers. Virtual functions become real. When the analysand feels that the selfobject/analyst is sufficiently empathic, the individual's self *is* stronger, and the patient functions better. The child who goes to school knowing that her mother cares about her day and thinks about her will feel more resilient and stronger than the child who lacks that emotional support.

Disruptions in this self–selfobject relationship can precipitate fragmentation. We hope in analysis that this is a temporary circumstance. Reexamination of the disruption of the self–selfobject analytic relationship (often when the analysand has perceived an empathic failure on the part of the analyst) and reestablishment of the empathic immersion in the self–selfobject relationship is fundamental to the curative aspect of analytic treatment. For Kohut (1968; Kohut & Wolf, 1978), patients who have the capacity to form this kind of self–selfobject bond are treatable by the psychoanalytic method, while patients who cannot form this bond or whose fragmentations are not manageable are less likely to be successfully treated by psychoanalysis.

Manifestations of psychic fragmentation may be physical or behavioral. Precisely because the structure of the mind is breaking down, the individual's capacity to represent psychological phenomena, including the self state, in images or words will be variably impaired. The affective state of fragmentation can be unbearable, a living death. Narcissistic rage may occur in response: a vengeful fury that a person's mind is not theirs to control and a belief that the world has either caused this or not prevented it. Actions that serve to shore up the crumbling self can be implemented with desperate repetition in order to try to preclude this unendurable experience. Until a cohesive state has been reachieved, the consequences of these desperate actions may seem irrelevant. Relief is paramount.

Structures that we call defenses are part of the overall structure of the self or ego. Substructures can grow and contribute to the larger structures of the psyche, they can change and modify the psyche, or they can crumble. A dream about a leaking dam might capture a person's fear of a shift in defenses. The image of a bursting dam and the resulting flood that devastates the town below could be understood to be a fear or manifestation of the fragmentation of the self. The bursting dam might also reflect the experience of trauma when defenses have failed and the ego is flooded. This raises a now-familiar question: In what ways are the concepts of trauma and fragmentation overlapping, and in what ways do they capture different psychic phenomena?

ELLA: SEPARATION, INDIVIDUATION, AND PSYCHIC STRUCTURE

Ella did not experience birth in the same way that Isabel did. She was adopted, and when she was 4 years of age, her younger brother was adopted. She knew that she had been adopted, and Mrs. Kaufman looked for the meaning of this reality in the analytic material. We learned that, during infancy, Ella was a delightful child who spent much of her time in a snuggly attached to her parents. Once she emerged from the snuggly and functioned more independently, walking and talking, the mother–child bond became highly conflicted. Ella became the misbehaving child who had inherited devilish traits from her biological mother.

Ella seemed to have had difficulty as she emerged from the snuggly of infancy into the autonomy of toddlerhood. Her newfound independence led to persistent conflict with her mother. Ella's manifest story about how babies are born had meaning beyond the actual reality of the birth process. Her particular story could be a fantasy depicting her adoption. It was also a tale that, as a metaphor, reflected Ella's version of *The Psychological Birth of the Human Infant* (Mahler, Pine, & Bergman, 1975). In her story she explained that the baby tore a hole in the mother's body in order to get out. The mother, who was permanently damaged, submitted to the power of the baby but got revenge by punishing and abandoning her. Babies must tear themselves from their mothers in order to leave the maternal closet or snuggly and strive for independence and individuality. This is a highly destructive process that inflicts irreparable harm on the mother and forever damages the relationship between mother and daughter.

This description of the process of separation-individuation portrays an unreliable foundation for the internalization of psychological structure. The child needs a loving, responsive, and firm relationship with her mother in order to internalize parental functions and make them her own and to freely allow her individual capabilities to emerge. When the parent–child relationship is good enough, it provides a holding environment that becomes the little girl's firm psychological foundation. When the child feels punished and attacked or abandoned, when this environment feels fraught and embattled, the ground beneath her feet crumbles, and her world collapses around her. The child must manage this calamity immediately, and she rigidly mobilizes limited and immature defenses in order to cope and survive rather than having the leisure to gradually develop truly flexible and reliable psychological structures.

Ella's later story about the baby who can repeatedly leave and then return to her mother's womb depicted the more normal developmental process in which the child moves away from her mother, confident in her ability to return as needed for refueling. The analytic work, the consistency of the child–analyst relationship, and the new experience with a developmental object allowed this normal developmental need and this different view of the mother–daughter relationship to emerge and engage.

The closet in mother's bedroom, into which the boys crashed their car, represented the mother's body and the maternal space. It was an intense, aggressive, and destructive vision of the manner in which babies, especially younger brothers, get inside Mommy. Whether this was her vagina and uterus or her lap and snuggly, this was the space where the baby should be warm and secure and then can feel free to wander off and return. Ella had ventured away from this secure place and felt unable to return. The adoption of her brother (the boys crashing their car into the space she wished to occupy) intensified the angst of her situation. She already understood that her birth mother had abandoned her. Worse, she felt like an orphan in her adoptive home. Then her brother came barreling into her old space, exquisitely exacerbating her desperation. She felt alone and uncared for, the stranger with devilish traits who hurt and antagonized her mother, and then she was replaced.

Ella told stories about homeless, abandoned, and starving children. Repeatedly she wanted to play that Mrs. Kaufman was the kind mother who took these children in and cared for them. This was not the baby with the oedipal mother but the mother of the child whose anxiety centered on the threatened or experienced loss of the object. When Mrs. Kaufman interpreted that she was upset about the baby, Ella explained that she did not know who would take care of her. It was abandonment, not sexual curiosity or triangular competition, that preoccupied her.

OVERWHELMING AFFECT AND PSYCHOLOGICAL STRUCTURE

In early sessions, both children were excitable, intrusive, and physical. At times each physically attacked her analyst. Ella tried to crawl between Dr. Kaufman's legs and enter her body. Isabel squished Dr. Huddleston between the office doors and struck her breasts and belly. Isabel insisted that she have "uppies," in which she would hug Dr. Huddleston, bringing their bodies close together in what seemed to be a sexually stimulating way. She often jumped around the office in a state of excitement. Ella exhibited a desperate need to keep things exactly the way that she needed them to be. The dolls and furniture had to be in exactly the right positions in the dollhouse. Mrs. Kaufman had to enact Ella's story with the dolls in exactly the right way. When Ella felt that Mrs. Kaufman failed at this, she blamed her and became furious and frantic. These moments would precipitate assaults on Mrs. Kaufman or behavior in which Ella would throw things around the room.

In play that was driven and aggressive, Isabel took "Troublesome Baby" and had her crawl inside the other puppets. Ella played that a car full of baby boys crashed into the mother's bedroom closet. After the crash, Ella searched inside the dollhouse in a panicky state: "It has shapes inside. I don't know where they come from." She then took the contents of the dollhouse and threw them around the room. While both girls could be driven and aggressive and both resorted at times to direct action, there are differences in the quality of their actions that are relevant to an understanding of their psychological structures and capacities to modulate affect. Isabel was more apt than Ella to maintain the frame of the microcosm and stay within the play. When she left the microcosm and moved to action, her behavior seemed more coherent, directed, and revealing of meaning. Ella's play early on was harder to establish and more apt to break down into frenetic, aggressive action. Ella's actions at these times could be less organized, more concrete, and more difficult to recognize as meaningful communication.

Isabel had to contend with overexcitement that was difficult for a little girl to contain. In addition, she had to deal with the fear of physical injury that is phase-specific for the oedipal child but intensified—for her—by the traumatic impact of her sister's precipitous birth, her own physical injuries, and those of her father. Yet, Isabel's psychological theater and the play space of her analysis were more firmly grounded and intact than that of Ella. While the characters on the stage could be swept away by waves of anxiety or excitement, it did not seem that the whole stage would crumble. The crumbling stage was more Ella's experience, and this created a different kind of panic and desperation. Efforts to shore up the timbers of the theater were evident when Ella ordered Mrs. Kaufman to keep everything exactly in place. The earthquake of the crumbling self, surviving it or not surviving it, superseded the child's concerns about what happens in a mother's body. Mrs. Kaufman had to keep everything in exactly the right place, or it would all come tumbling down. It would be Humpty Dumpty all over again.

Because psychological structure had not been reliably established, Ella's tolerance of anxiety or other distressing affects was limited. Depressive affect (Brenner, 1982) in response to the feeling that abandonment had actually occurred was intolerable, as well. Ella's need to control her analyst, to make her be the way Ella needed her to be, was desperate and driven. If the dolls and furniture could be in exactly the right place, if Mrs. Kaufman could play with the dolls in exactly the right way, if Ella could color without making a mistake, then her fragile internal world could remain standing. Failure to accomplish this led to the crumbling of the sticks that supported her psychological building. This fragmentation then led to loss of recent developmental gains, and the affective experience was unbearable. Krystal (1978) describes regression in the realm of affects. Tantrums, meltdowns, chaotic action, or concrete behavior result when a child's internal structure cannot be maintained. For Ella at these times, representation and communication were prone to fail. She regressed from representational thinking to concrete action as she literally tried to crawl between Mrs. Kaufman's legs to get inside her womb.

The loss of representational thinking and the retreat to concrete thinking and action are described by many of the authors we have considered. In the terms put forth by Fonagy and Target (1996), Ella was functioning in psychic-equivalence mode. The urgent quality of her internal experience was as real and immediate as external reality. The capacity to use affects as signals was lost, and automatic anxiety prevailed. Her insistence that the toys remain in exactly the spots she had established were her effort to prevent the crossing of the event horizon into Grotstein's (1990a) black hole and chaos. When that failed, she became desperate and enraged. This fury is one example of Kohut's (1968, 1972; Kohut & Wolf, 1978) narcissistic rage, a manifestation of her fragmenting self. At the edge of Grotstein's black hole, facing chaos, her rage and growing inner disorganization led her to throw things around the room. This created more chaos. Without some intervention from an adult, and perhaps despite an adult's effort, the chaos fed on itself, and the gravitational pull toward deeper chaos intensified. Boulanger (2002) suggests that, under these circumstances, alternative associative connections are not only obscured, they are also obliterated.

Isabel's psychological structure was more intact, and she had, to a significant degree, achieved oedipal-phase specificity. Her interest in, preoccupation with, and anxieties about her mother's body were not primarily organized around abandonment. They were organized around the oedipal child's concerns about how babies are made, questions about what this has to do with what mother and father do in the privacy of their bedroom, confusion about what goes on in the mother's body during pregnancy, wishes to understand exactly how these babies get delivered into the world, and fantasies about bodily injury. Even though the new baby was a great rival for parental love and attention, abandonment was not the catastrophe that filled the analytic space. Castration fears and anxiety about bodily integrity were predominant, along with feelings of sexual excitement. The sensory and emotional overstimulation and the panic associated with the physical and psychological damage to her father, her own physical injuries, and the precipitous birth of her sister heightened her fears of bodily mutilation and added a great deal of anxiety to her speculations about the baby-making process. Isabel's psyche had sufficient structure that it did not crumble, but she did get overwhelmed. The frightening exposure to the birth of her sister and her own early injuries were more than she could tolerate, and her father's injuries during the analysis intensified this distress. Her oedipal experience was harder to integrate because these early experiences were the combustible material onto which the Molotov cocktails of oedipal events were thrown or vice versa.

OVERWHELMED BY CASTRATION ANXIETY

Isabel reacted strongly to her father's injuries. When information about his accident was kept secret from her, she was angry. When she learned of his injuries, they stirred fantasies of body parts being cut off, as well as fantasies of repair. She recalled her own injury on the toilet when she was attacked by the dog. Better able to face bodily damage at this point in her analysis, Isabel resolved to discuss this with her mother in order to learn more about the secret of her injuries. By following the thread of castration anxiety through Isabel's analysis, we see the evolution of this young girl's capacity to modulate and tolerate affect.

The sight of the two anatomically correct dolls startled Isabel. She threw the female doll to the side when she saw two bumps rather than a penis. To Isabel, castration seemed to be a frightening reality. She had to get rid of the sight of the castrated doll and interrupt her play in order to contend with this intense fear. Subsequently, using Kleenex and a pencil, she made a beautiful flower with elements of male and female genitalia. In this play, she tolerated the exploration of anatomical differences and bisexuality much more comfortably. The vagina-like petals of the flower coexisted with the penis-like stamen. This flower was a nodal point that reflected her growing ability to deal with the puzzling and frightening awareness of the anatomical distinction between the sexes. She lovingly watered this flower every day. With tender, loving care, this flower had the potential to transform from a bisexual organ into a representation of a beautiful vagina. Less overwhelmed by the threat of bodily damage, Isabel was beginning the process of integrating her feminine identity.

Isabel was confronted with the blood of menstruation and the threat of castration when she learned that a friend had begun menstruating. She spent a sleepless night and, in a subsequent session, made a costume for "Horsey" that seemed like a diaper. Poop and menstrual blood are both messy body products that come from somewhere down there. This diaper and sanitary napkin were part of her first effort to contend with this new kind of mess. It is striking to note that Isabel was developmentally ready for a more sophisticated solution to this potentially scary and certainly messy development. She portrayed "Shiskapoo" being taught to groom himself. The adult who responds as the oedipal-level developmental selfobject teaches the little girl how to make herself pretty. The experience of mother helping her daughter to brush and style her hair was more than a way to undo the mess, and it was more than a loving wipe of her bottom and taping of her diaper. It was part of the move to a new stage of development, where the girl and her mother work together to help her to integrate the changes in her mind and body, share the pleasure of making her pretty, and facilitate her progression toward new experiences.

SUMMARY

Isabel's development was affected by events early in her life. She was attacked by the family dog after she pushed him away from her potty seat, and her mother gave birth to her sister while sitting on the toilet at home. I call these events traumatic because they stirred feelings that were more than she could tolerate and manage, and we can see an enduring effect on her functioning after these events. Later, as she entered the oedipal phase of development, these events took on new significance, and her emotions were again too much to bear or contain. Her symptoms worsened, and we can see in her analysis how she was overwhelmed by anxiety and sexual stimulation. The defenses that Isabel used to cope with the earlier overwhelming experiences were less than fully successful, and they were yet less able to help her through the oedipal phase. Playing with Freud's (1953–1974j) metaphor, she had left too many libidinal countrymen defending the earlier developmental position.

Ella had not successfully negotiated the developmental tasks of separation-individuation. She was vulnerable and not equipped to satisfactorily manage further demands of development, but her vulnerability was different from that of Isabel. Rather than getting overstimulated or overwhelmed, Ella's psychic theater would temporarily crumble. A successful phase transition of the mind crystalizes a psychological structure that endures in a predominantly stable manner. Ella had not achieved this transition, and a cohesive self could not be maintained under duress. When the reflective mode of functioning gave way, there was a fault line in her psyche: Pretend mode and psychic-equivalence mode were ways of functioning that could not be integrated. At these times, like ice melting to water, her psyche assumed a looser and less structured functional organization. For Ella, these fragmentations were time-limited. With help from her analyst or with distance from the duress that triggered disorganization, Ella's self could reconsolidate to its baseline functioning.

Trauma and fragmentation are not the same, but there are important ways in which they are related. Catastrophic trauma, as described by Krystal (1978), leads to helplessness, triggers the phylogenetic surrender pattern, and has enduring consequences. Descriptions that capture this experience from the inside, like Grotstein's (1990a) black hole, suggest a state of mind that is similar to or includes fragmentation. At times, fragmentation serves as a last-ditch defense against unbearable catastrophe, though it is a defense with its own potentially devastating consequences. There are times, as with Ella, when fragmentation is a transient development, and there are times when the psyche of the individual does not return to baseline, as in persistent psychosis. It is not always clear when fragmentation is the catastrophe, the desperate effort to prevent catastrophe, or both.

Events can be more or less traumatic. There are degrees of trauma. For Krystal (1978), the ultimate degree of trauma is the catatonoid state, as much a biological as a psychological phenomenon. There are different phenomena that can be considered types of fragmentation. These include merger, loss of the ability to differentiate affects, depletion depression, and disorganization of thought processes. Fragmentation is a psychological phenomenon, but when the degree of disorganization is such that communication is lost, when the self has become a black hole, its psychological nature seems inaccessible. In chapter 8, I again explore fragmentation and the associated loss of meaning or the capacity to symbolize.

In the next chapter, I consider the ways in which the object helps to provide and develop structure within the self. The developmental object's role in helping the child to modulate affects and internalize the capacity to do so is my prime example of this process. Examination of the child's capacity to modulate affects and the consequences of her inability to do so sheds further light on an understanding of overstimulation, trauma, and fragmentation.

Chapter Seven

The Developmental Object

Edward I. Kohn

Parents serve as developmental objects through all phases of a child's life. The developmental need is different at each phase; each child puts her own unique fingerprint on the parent–child relationship; and the structure of the child's mind comes into being, evolves, and takes shape in the context of that relationship. While the child's phase of development and pressing developmental needs may challenge the analyst, the developmental aspects of child psychoanalysis provide remarkably direct access to the mind of the child and heighten the analyst's capacity to influence the structure of that mind.

At the start of her analysis, Ella's psychological structure was less reliable than that of Isabel. She was more vulnerable to fragmentation, and her developmental needs were those of a child in the separation-individuation phase of development. Isabel's psychological structure was cohesive, although she could be overwhelmed, and she was buffeted by the anxieties and the passions associated with the oedipal phase of development. Each girl brought her developmental needs into her analysis, and of necessity, she imposed a developmental object function on her analyst. The analyst was a part of that developmental relationship, and each analyst worked from within that developmental relationship because it shaped the child's experience of their interactions.

Different theorists use different terms: *selfobject, transformational object, new object,* or *developmental object*. However, they all recognize the power of the relationship and strive to describe the ways in which the parent or analyst influences the development of the child and the creation, shaping, or reshaping of psychological structure. In this chapter I examine this process.

Child analysts have examined the ways in which a child's developmental needs engage their parents or analysts. They have compared and contrasted this process with that of the classical vision of psychoanalysis, where interpretation is the mutative element. Children are naturally inclined to turn to adults and have an inherent capacity to draw emotional support from them in ways that enhance development. This inborn capacity of a child shapes her relationships with her parents and becomes a part of the relationship between the child and the analyst. Anna Freud (1965) points out, "The nature of the child's disturbance reveals itself via the specific therapeutic elements which he selects for therapeutic use" (229). Edgcumbe (1995) explains that Anna Freud is also saying "that whatever the analyst might mean to be doing, the child takes what he wants" (31). This is not only a repetition of the parent–child relationship: The child has a significant relationship with her analyst, who becomes an important part of her life, and it is important to recognize this when we try to understand the therapeutic effect of analysis. These developmental needs are also engaged in adult analysis, but they are overlaid with years of developmental change, defense structures, and character formation (Dahl, 1996). With a child, the relational needs are more obvious, direct, and immediate, and they are developmentally alive.

It is not unusual to see a child who is missing this developmental support—either due to failure of the parent, the complex psychology of the child, life circumstances, or a combination of all of these. The child may wish for this developmental support, demand it in direct or disguised ways, or insist that she has no such needs. Mrs. Kaufman explains in her case presentation that Ella's parents assigned chores to their daughter that were beyond her ability. They expected her to be able to handle her emotions or control her own actions in ways that she could not. Despite her young age, they did not prevent her from "running away" across the busy street. When she failed to handle things as her parents expected, they would angrily set limits on her. Ella's desire and ability to function autonomously became embroiled in conflict, and the development of her capacity to manage her impulses was interfered with. In important ways, a successful analysis allows these developmental needs to emerge in a less disguised or conflicted manner, facilitating not only their ability to be recognized but also their capacity to be satisfied. Whether the analyst intends to serve as a developmental object or recognizes that the child responds to her as a developmental object—or not—she *will be* a developmental object for the child.

DEVELOPMENTAL OBJECT FUNCTIONS IN OTHER GUISES

Winnnicott (1965) discusses the relationship between mother and child in depth and sees parallels between this relationship and the analytic relationship. He refers to the mother–child relationship as a holding or facilitating environment. The immaturity of the infant's ego requires that the mother manage her child's immersion in the environment. Many analysts have used the term *auxiliary ego* or Winnicott's *holding environment* in their efforts to understand the nature of the analytic relationship. Khan (1963), when discussing the impact of cumulative trauma, describes the mother as an auxiliary ego. He refers particularly to the mother's capacity to serve as a stimulus barrier. The mother must protect the child from stimuli that might overwhelm or impinge on her.

Drawing on the work of Spitz (1956), who wrote of the analyst's diatrophic function—the development-promoting aspect of the analyst's countertransference—Gitelson (1962) talks of the analyst's

> healing intention to "maintain and support" the patient. This is countertransference in its affirmative sense. . . . The diatrophic attitude arises as a response to the patient's need for help even as the parent responds to the anaclitic situation of the child. According to Spitz it derives in the analyst from the stage of secondary identification in the second trimester of life when the passivity of the infant begins its movement towards the mimicry of the feeding activity of the mother. In its ego-controlled form, that is, as a form of regression in the service of the ego, it is the basis for analytic empathy. It converges with the patient's need for ego-support and in this context the analyst, like the mother, has the function of an auxiliary ego. . . . The mother is the target for the child's drives and, in her capacity as auxiliary ego, guides their form and function, thus introducing the operation of the reality principle. . . . [Similarly, the analyst] in his diatrophic function, provides the irrupting instincts and revived developmental drive with direction and purpose. (198)

Jill Miller (2013) states that the analyst, in her role as developmental object, does more than serve auxiliary ego functions. The analytic relationship is not simply a reflection of the early mother–child relationship. The adult, as analyst or parent, is a developmental object through all phases of development: "She works to promote the conditions for development to occur and structuralization to take place, and provides an opportunity for change through a relationship fine tuned to the patient's developmental needs" (313). Miller lists many ways that child analysts have described the developmental aspect of the analytic relationship:

> to promote interactions, to address primitive defenses, to contain the transference (Hueves, 2003), to grow capacities for self-reflection and mentalization (Fonagy & Target, 1998), to give meaning to thoughts and actions, to provide language to describe states of mind, to differentiate cause and effect (Sandler, 1996), to be a container, to provide safety, to be there to be left, to provide controls and limits, to facilitate hope (Hurry, 1998), to regulate affects (Olesker, 1999; Sugarman, 2003a), to build a narrative (Knight, 2003), and to not be used as a projection (Horne, 2006). (314)

Bollas (1979) coined the term *transformational object*:

as the infant's other self, the mother, continually transforms the infant's internal and external environment. . . . The mother integrates the infant's being. . . . The mother is not yet identified as an object but is experienced as a process of transformation that remains in the traces of this object seeking in adult life . . . and manifests itself in the person's search for an object that promises to transform the self. (97)

THE SELFOBJECT

Kohut (1959) defines *empathy* with a surprisingly simple but powerful phrase: "vicarious introspection" (459). In everyday parlance, we talk about walking in the other person's shoes. For Kohut, empathy is a vantage point for observation: imagining one's self inside the mind of the other and looking out. The observer places his self at the imaginary center of the other person's psyche, looking from the center through her mind into the outer world. Many analysts seem to misunderstand Kohut's view of empathy: It is not sympathy or agreement with the person's perspective, and it is not a statement of "I feel your pain." It is a deep recognition of the experience and perspective of the other person. A sociopath may have excellent skills at recognizing the experience or perspective of the other but might choose to use this perspective in a manipulative and self-serving matter. The analyst's task is to use the empathic observational stance in a therapeutic manner, and his technical responses must be informed by this observational stance, not dictated by it.

When Kohut (1968) describes the parents' roles as empathic selfobjects, the distinction between observational stance and the adult's response may seem blurry. Yet, we can think of the parents' capacity for empathy as their ability, both consciously and unconsciously, to see the child and her world through her own eyes. We can distinguish this empathic stance from the empathic response, which is informed by and responsive to awareness of the child's developmental needs and state of mind as appreciated through the empathic observational stance. A father may decide to say no to a child or expect her to do something that she does not want to do. His capacity to have an empathic stance and his ability to appreciate the child's frustration might enable him to more comfortably tolerate her resentment and whining or be less shaken by guilt or anxiety when she says that she won't love him anymore.

THE DEVELOPMENTAL LINE OF NARCISSISM

In the libido theory, narcissistic libido is an earlier form of libido than object libido. Within this framework, the task is to shift the limited amount of libido from the self to the object. It is as if there is a finite amount of libido contained in a U-tube. You can tilt the tube so that more libido resides in the end directed inward, or you can tilt it toward the object. Rather than view narcissism as a precursor to object libido, Kohut (1966) dispenses with the U-tube conception of libido and describes narcissism, à la Anna Freud (1963), according to its own line of development. This allows a more sophisticated view of the transformations of narcissism throughout the life cycle. For example, rather than seeing the early grandiosity and exhibitionism of the child as a primitive precursor to object relations or as a defense against true object relations, he sees it as a developmentally appropriate stage that evolves into more mature and flexible narcissistic positions and becomes the source of ambition and pride.

When Ella began her analysis, she insisted that Mrs. Kaufman admire her doll, and then she scolded her doll, accusing her of wanting all of the attention. Ella yearned to be the center of attention and to be admired, but this wish was in conflict with a prohibition against wanting attention. It is not hard to imagine painful moments between Ella and her mother in which her demands were met with admonitions. Her developmental need for attention was embroiled in conflict, and during the doll play, it had to be disowned. Because of the conflict with her mother and the internal conflict, this yearning remained fixated at an earlier developmental phase. Therefore, the manifestation of her yearning—her demanding behavior—was more imperative and less manageable. This, in turn, increased the likelihood of conflict with the environment and reinforcement of the prohibition.

In the context of the analytic situation and Mrs. Kaufman's analytic attitude (her capacity to be open to Ella's yearning to be the admired little girl and to contain its disruptive manifestations), Mrs. Kaufman served as a selfobject, developmental object, transformational object, diatrophic object, or new object. Loewald (1971) explains that we can't separate the instinctual yearning and the object. In the same way, Ella's developmental need and Mrs. Kaufman's selfobject functions became one interwoven fabric. Their relationship sustained or, in some ways became, the theater of Ella's internal world. This allowed development to move forward and allowed the performances of her representational world to evolve. Over the course of her analysis, Ella had more access to her wishes; their depiction in her representational world became more subtle and complex, and the urgency of her needs became more modulated.

The early need to idealize the parents develops into ideals, the capacity to feel safe in the world, the capacity for trust and optimism, and the capacity to modulate affect (Kohut, 1966; Tolpin, 1971). When Ella first met Mrs. Kaufman, she was afraid of her, but her view of Mrs. Kaufman transformed over the course of the analysis. Mrs. Kaufman became an idealized selfobject whose presence was a source of comfort and security. Late in the analysis, when she was lying in bed afraid, Ella called up a representation of her analyst in her mind and pretended to call her on the phone. She could calm herself by drawing on her capacity for fantasy and did not need the actual presence of her analyst. She did not turn to the physical comfort of a transitional object but play-acted a telephone call and was able to soothe herself.

Isabel's sexual feelings, anxieties, and curiosity were a source of pain and conflict when she began analysis. When she played the role of a teacher who grilled Dr. Huddleston about boys' penises, we can see the shame and ridicule she associated with lack of knowledge. In her mind, the adult relished her own ability to demean Isabel for her ignorance. Over the course of her analysis, Isabel's image of the adult transformed. The teacher of the chipmunks brought them out of the bathroom and took them to a place where they could talk. The developmental need for an oedipal developmental object or selfobject emerged from the haze of conflict, and Dr. Huddleston became the adult who kindly but firmly set limits and followed through with discussion. In the context of this evolving developmental object or selfobject relationship, Isabel could better handle her sexual feelings and anxieties.

The teacher–student play enacted by Isabel portrayed her vision of her relationship with adults and her analyst. In the narrow sense of transference, it reflected her earlier experience of her relationship with her mother. It was also a reflection of her contemporaneous view of her mother. In analysis, the child's current relationships with the significant people in her life enter the work and the analytic relationship in a way that is more direct than is the case with adults. When we consider a broader sense of transference, the total relationship with the analyst, we are not limited to an examination of a repetition of the past. We can include the developmental needs of the child that are active and alive in the present moment. Freeing these developmental needs from conflict and allowing them to emerge in the relationship of the analysand and analyst is an integral part of the therapeutic action of psychoanalysis. We see this with adults, as well, but we have the opportunity to see it more clearly when we work with children. I look closely at this phenomenon in chapters 9, 10, and 11.

THE ADULT PROVIDES PSYCHOLOGICAL FUNCTIONS FOR THE CHILD

Instead of talking about developmental objects, Kohut (1971, 1977; Kohut & Wolf, 1978) uses the concept selfobject to describe the ways a child experiences the significant adults in her life. His understanding is that parents—either as mirroring selfobjects or idealized parent imagoes—provide psychological functions for the child. The child's immersion in her relationship with her parents, assuming sufficient empathic attunement, allows her to feel that these parental functions are her own. Much like Winnicott's (1953) assertion that we should not ask if the transitional object is real, the child in Kohut's vision does not have to think about whether these functions are actually hers or borrowed from her parents. She simply feels stronger and more capable.

We can see the power of these parental functions in children's typical day-to-day behaviors. When the little girl jumps off the diving board, repeatedly insisting that her mother watch her jump, the experience is quite different from jumping by herself. When she sees herself mirrored in the eyes of her mother, the exhibitionistic pole of her self is engaged, her sense of self is affirmed, and the experience of the jump is more real and indelible. The child who comes home from school and tells her mother about her fight with a classmate is strengthened and better able to face the ups and downs of daily life. When she is confident that her experience matters to her mother and when she has had repeated encounters in which she felt valued, appreciated, recognized, or comforted, she can take that confidence with her into the outside world.

The child's capacity to idealize her parents allows her to feel safe in the world despite the myriad ways that events are beyond her control. Whether we see the parents as containers, a holding environment, selfobjects, or developmental objects, they are the essential element of the background of safety (Sandler, 1960). When frightening or distressing events occur, engagement with the parents makes these difficult situations more manageable and facilitates a return to the equilibrium of the background of safety.

When a mother comforts her child by placing a Band-Aid on her skinned knee, more is at play than a medical intervention to prevent bleeding. The oedipal-age child, terrified of bodily injury, may be reassured when the Band-Aid covers the red scrape, but there is an enormously important additional quality associated with mother's touch. This quality is magical but very real for the young mind. The touch of her mother's hands, the Band-Aid, or the kiss of her lips soothes the pain and anxiety. The capacity of the child to imbue her mother or father with this idealized and magical power is an important developmental accomplishment. The young child who does not yet have the emotional resources to soothe herself when injured or frightened has a virtual capacity to soothe herself that comes alive when immersed in the parent–child relationship.

The child in whom this virtual capacity is impaired or whose parents can't adequately adapt to her or both is at a great disadvantage in the development of the capacity to comfort herself, to tolerate anxiety, or to contain other affects. With a breach in the child's experience of an empathic immersion in the self–selfobject relationship, these self-functions are diminished or lost. The child may crumble because her immature self is not sufficiently cohesive to endure the rupture. She may be deflated or simply feel weaker, more vulnerable, or less resilient. Anxiety may overwhelm her, or she might respond with an outburst of rage or a tantrum. When this healthy merging of minds fails, the child feels as if aspects of her self and capacities of her own that she usually takes for granted have been degraded or lost.

Throughout development the child's needs change, and the role of the parent as a developmental object or selfobject changes accordingly. Parents' abilities to adjust to these changes vary, and a parent may more successfully provide the needed functions during one stage of development than another. Parents reexperience, consciously and unconsciously, all of the developmental phases of life with each of their children. The changing developmental constellations influence the analytic relationship, as well.

Often, concepts like auxiliary ego, holding environment, or container are associated with the earliest phases of life, especially infancy, but the need for holding, containing, or support does not go away after infancy. Children need these parental supports at every stage of development but in different ways. When Mrs. Kaufman offered to help Ella tape her drawings back together, she was enacting a container that could help Ella to maintain an intact self. In contrast, Isabel's story of the teacher who responded to the chipmunks depicted an oedipal kind of holding or containing. She helped the chipmunks contain their sexual impulses, and then they would look at the contents of the container together.

OEDIPAL AND ADOLESCENT DEVELOPMENTAL OBJECTS

I have repeatedly referred to the mother's role as developmental object or selfobject for a young child like Ella, who moves from mother's lap to the wider world of the toddler. A latency-age child who has felt close to her mother may feel apprehensive about moving out into the world of adolescence, and both mother and child have to adjust to this change. If the girl feels her mother's longing to keep her a child, the step across the line into this foreign country can seem more ominous: You can either stay with mother and feel safe and loved, or you can venture into the excitement of the new land and leave her behind. The girl's conflicts and anxiety about sexuality get heightened if her parents have trouble setting limits or if they themselves find the new world of puberty and sexuality to be filled with danger. If the girl feels that her mother remains with her in a new way interpersonally and intrapsychically—interested in and proud of her activity—and there for her when she gets knocked down, feels overwhelmed, or is frightened of what she has to contend with, then her psychic ship will have more ballast and a more reliable rudder.

The fairy godmother of Cinderella represents the developmental object of the child in the oedipal phase of development and resonates with the child's need for emotional support as she enters adolescence. The oedipal-age girl's newly emerging sexual desires and desires for her father create new conflicts and new situations for her to contend with and master. Her mother has become her rival, and she must deal with her jealousy of and hostility toward the same person whom she relies on, gets so much from, and dearly loves. Her conflict is represented by the antithetical figures of the wicked stepmother and the fairy godmother. The defensive function of this split is necessary because it is so difficult for a little girl to deal with conflicting feelings of such intensity. The magical quality of the fairy godmother is necessary because the little girl has no idea how to manage this transition. The fairy godmother is drawn from the idealized qualities of the mother and the magical power that a mother has to comfort, help to manage the unmanageable, and facilitate developmental progression. While the fairy godmother is magical, she is not primarily a denial of the realities of life. She is a portrayal of the reality of an "illusion," the real and necessary development-enhancing aspect of the parent, analyst, or developmental object.

Up to this point in this chapter, I have, to a large extent, drawn on Kohut's concept of the selfobject in an effort to understand the development-enhancing function of the developmental object. The parent or analyst, as the mirroring selfobject or idealized parent imago, empathically engages the child, creating an intersubjective matrix in which the child and adult are inextricably immersed. The child's unique capacities emerge in the context of the relationship with the developmental object or selfobject. We cannot neatly separate the child from the adult, but we look to the adult to maintain an attitude that allows the child's capacities and her developmental needs to predominate in the shaping of the nature of this relationship. The object has the capacity to transform the child's self.

DIFFERENT LANGUAGES FOR SIMILAR CONCEPTS

While Kohut has his own theoretical constructs and his own language, we see that he is not the only psychoanalytic thinker to address these issues. We can turn to some of the other writers I discussed in chapter 1 in order to point out how their thinking addresses the concept of developmental object and how, even when their languages are very different, we can trace a similar idea through all of them. They all examine the engagement of self and object and the ways in which this engagement between adult and child or analyst and analysand transforms the mind of the child or analysand.

Kohut (1968, 1971, 1977; Kohut & Wolf, 1978) talks about empathy, the gleam in a mother's eye, and a merger with the strength of the idealized object. Wilson and Weinstein (1996) suggest that Kohut's contributions regarding empathy are explained by the object's capacity to tune into the zone of proximal development (ZPD). The concept of the ZPD explains the way the object influences the acquisition of language. Because the ZPD exists in proximity to the buds of language, it also exists in proximity to the buds of development. The parents' or analyst's engagement with the child in this zone acts as a scaffold that stabilizes the transformation of buds of language and development to flowers. The mother uses language in a way that is slightly ahead of the child. When the baby says, "Up!" her mother says, "You want me to pick you up," as she bends toward the child. The mother's dialogic interchange with her child does more than provide the meanings of words: It also engages the organizing power of language and gives shape to the child's inchoate experience. Wilson and Weinstein refer to this repeated and evolving interaction between parent and child as an internalization community. This is a specific and interesting way to think about Kohut's selfobject, Bion's (1963, 1977a, 1977b) container, Winnicott's (1960) holding environment, or Gitelson's (1962) auxiliary ego.

Winnicott (1960) explains that the child looks into her mother's face and sees what she herself is like. Rather than empathy, he refers to attunement. The mother's attunement to the child enables the child to see herself. If she sees her mother instead, this becomes an impingement. If there is a lack of modulated synchrony—if the mother's defenses interfere with her capacity to represent the child's emotional experience coherently—the child's self is then constructed around a false representation.

Fonagy and Target (1998) explain that children develop awareness of their own psychic experience by seeing their intentions, desires, and beliefs in the minds of their parents. Sugarman (2006) refers to insightfulness, and he says that the child analyst's capacity to facilitate the child's interest in and awareness of her own mind is more important than the content of particular insights. Insightfulness, like mentalization, is a process, and this is, for him, the essential therapeutic factor in child analysis.

Mayes and Cohen (1993) explain that aggression is first experienced in the context of loving relations. The quality of these relationships, with the caregivers' interpretations of and responses to the child's affect and behavior, shapes the child's aggressive strivings. When the nursing baby bites, the mother's interpretation of and response to the baby's action—as an aggressive attack or a momentarily painful notification of the baby's assertiveness—influences how her child experiences such moments in the future. The child who runs off to explore and then looks back will have her sense of mastery enhanced if her mother seems pleased, or it will be dampened if she faces her mother's fear, anger, or absence. The furious child who receives a beating may stop her behavior, but her capacity to modulate her rage will be interfered with.

Isabel repeatedly tried to squish Dr. Huddleston's breasts and abdomen between the doors. Her analyst prevented the door from hurting her but participated in the action, though in a restrained way. The aggressive action became play-action that served the analytic process. Ella ran away from home across a busy street. Her parents did not successfully contain her behavior. Her anger and negativity were interpreted as evidence that she had inherited devilish qualities. Ella's view of herself when angry was altered, and her capacity to modulate her feelings and actions was inhibited.

Lyons-Ruth (1999) emphasizes the parents' openness to the state of mind of the child. This allows the child's affective or emotional state to remain open and develop. Failure to be open to the mind of the child causes her mind to be overtaken and foreclosed. As a result of this failure, discontinuities in implicit, nonconscious procedures result, leading to segregated and fragmented functioning, with little opportunity to update and revise these procedures.

Bion (1965/1977b) suggests that the experience of finding one's own mind in the mind of the object makes inner experience real. This is one function of containment. Additionally, the containment of projective identifications and their processing by the parent's more mature mind allows them to be reinternalized by the child in a more modulated and integrated fashion (Bion, 1965/1977b; Brown, 2011).

The capacity of the parent or the analyst to give the child back to herself (Winnicott, 1960) is not a wish or yearning that gets interpreted and goes away. It is a real psychological phenomenon that remains alive throughout development. The little girl who draws a picture has a compelling experience when she shows it to her mother. When Ella reviewed the history of the rug in Mrs. Kaufman's office or when Isabel played school with Dr. Huddleston, the experience was transforming in a way that is different from engaging in these activities alone.

STRUCTURE DEVELOPMENT, THE CAPACITY TO TOLERATE AFFECT, AND THE DEVELOPMENTAL OBJECT

Modulation of affect is a fundamentally important mental process or ego function. The manner in which psychoanalysis facilitates a patient's capacity to tolerate and modulate affects illustrates an essential aspect of therapeutic action. From the vantage point of this book, this growing capacity is evidence of developing psychic structure. Study of the manner in which the relationship and interactions (including verbal insight) between child and adult influence this psychological function enables us to watch the mental apparatus in operation and understand the ways in which change occurs.

The developmental needs and conflicts of the analysand determine the nature of the object that the analyst represents and the potential for the analyst to provide developmental functions. The relationship with the analyst interacts with the structure of the analysand's mind, and through their intersubjective immersion, they coinhabit her mind. This facilitates internalization or growth of these capacities, such as affect tolerance. The concept of selfobject is of particular value when we consider not just the interaction between the two minds but also the ways in which the analytic relationship comes to function as a part of the patient's mind. The therapeutic impact is not then a moving of something from the outside to the inside but a taking possession of something that is already inside. In this section I consider the concept of the developmental object, its role in the development of psychological structure, and the evolving nature of the developmental object as the analysand, either child or adult, changes.

Ella imagined that Mrs. Kaufman was the tooth fairy and she was her daughter. This was a scenario that foreshadowed potential resolution of the oedipal drama. The girl identifies with her mother and selectively inherits her real and her magical powers. The tooth fairy is a figure who responds to a developmental moment in the child's life. Losing your tooth can be painful, bloody, and scary. The tooth fairy comes during the night and leaves some money for your tooth. She is part of the process of turning this physical experience, which could be alarming, into a milestone, something to be proud of and rewarded for. Like the fairy godmother of Cinderella, who helps the girl find her way to the ball, the tooth fairy is part of the real magic of the parent–child or analyst–child relationship captured in fairy tales and stories. The magic of the fairy godmother is not a simple withdrawal from reality or fantasy of wish fulfillment. Fairy godmothers and tooth fairies watch over us, protect us, and help us feel less afraid of new developmental steps or life experiences. The adult, be it the parent or the analyst, has real magical powers that serve to facilitate the child's transitions even when shaken by frightening experiences. They enable us to feel less undone by obstacles to development in our daily lives.

When we have the tooth fairies, fairy godmothers, good witches, and great wizards in our lives, we are freed up to inhabit the transitional, transactional play space. The line between our parents' objectively real capacity to take care of things and that of the magical, idealized view of them is indistinct. Our capacity for idealization creates a real phenomenon in which our parents can do magical things for us. It is not just that parents are bigger, know more, and can do things the child cannot yet do. They have magical influence. The laying on of parental hands transforms the frightening or painful experience. In the comfortable relationship with the selfobject, developmental object, or new object, the child *is truly* stronger and more resilient.

Bollas's (1979) transformational object is the source of hope in childhood and throughout life. Fortunately, we never fully lose this belief in magic. We might find it in our god, mentors, humanity, art, or families. We are genetically programmed to look for ourselves in our parents' responses or to feel safe in their embraces. The writer of the most profound novel is sharing herself with her readers, and the reader of the novel might find himself in the words of the author as they formulate unformulated or not-yet-articulated experience.

Our parents are our guardian angels through childhood, and gradually we take those functions over for ourselves. These abilities traverse a path through our transitional objects, toys, play, fantasies, thoughts, religions, and ideals. Eventually, they become a part of us in ways that we may not even notice. At the beginning of her analysis, Ella had not yet achieved such a cohesive internal psychological structure. These functions were not reliably her own. Identification with her analyst was complicated. She had to undo her identification with her representation of her mother. In the closet or under the bed of her mind were visions of the wicked stepmother who saw her as a devil child. Initially, she was frightened and threatened by Mrs. Kaufman. Yet, she needed help dealing with the strange and scary shapes in the closet. Her relationship and her work with her analyst allowed her to feel less afraid. She came to rely on Mrs. Kaufman for these functions and wished to be like her. Her internal representation of a mother figure changed; in her mind Mrs. Kaufman was someone who provided love and care for her, and the capacity to soothe herself became internalized.

Ella's fantasies and the real-life conflict with her mother rattled her world and destabilized her internal structures. She drew a picture of her mother flying in and attacking Mrs. Kaufman for claiming Ella as her own. Ella said that she was locked out of her own house, as well as Mrs. Kaufman's house, injured and alone. She crumpled and tore up her drawings and then wanted to piece them back together. At that moment, without the belief that she could experience a consistently loving, supportive, and empathic mother figure, and in the face of her own anger and jealousy, there was no solid ground for this child to rely on. She could not comfortably internalize the mother's or analyst's magic and couldn't venture forward developmentally. The mother–child or analyst–child relationship serves as a foundation, but when it crumbles from within or due to an attack from without, the child's foundation crumbles, too. Ella's rage and desperation led her to tear up the drawings. In the act of destroying these drawings, she represented her internal fragmentation.

When Mrs. Kaufman calmly suggested that repairing the drawings was a job for two, the magical, healing power of the fairy godmother or tooth fairy was successfully reestablished. As they worked together repairing the drawings, they talked about the painful emotional experiences that contributed to her meltdown. This interaction helped to untangle the intense conflicts of the moment and those with which Ella lived in an ongoing way. When the developmental object or selfobject, the fairy godmother or the tooth fairy, steps in to help stabilize the crumbling moment, the child can communicate, think, and begin to understand. For Ella, it became a moment when the healing power of the analyst was felt and further internalized. Later in the analysis, when Ella dreamed of the friend who helped her with the frightening situation and got her play phone and pretended to call Mrs. Kaufman on a scary night, she showed further evidence that she was making this magic her own.

Ella's preponderant need during the early periods of her analysis was for a parent or analyst who could strengthen her psychological structure and help her prevent fragmentation or cushion or repair the collapse when it began. She needed from the adult a secure attachment that could support her interest in the awareness of her internal world. Without secure attachment, she could not sustain her representational world. She needed a parent who could feel present for her when she moved away or when they were in conflict. Ella needed a parent who could tolerate her having control of the separation process, one who could be attentive and proud of the little girl as she wandered off or asserted herself and then could welcome her back when the child felt the need. Later in the analysis, she needed a parent who could help her to leave her mother in a different way. She was moving into an oedipal world of competitive and adversarial triangles, princes, and wishes to have her own family. In her mind, her mother's jealousy would lead her to undermine this development or vengefully retaliate. The anxiety and emotions of this developmental phase had the potential at times to precipitate a temporary collapse. Mrs. Kaufman's presence in her dreams and fantasies enabled her to feel supported rather than attacked as she engaged oedipal yearnings.

Isabel needed a parent or analyst who could help manage her overstimulated state, filled with sexual excitement and overwhelming anxiety about bodily mutilation. Over the course of her analysis, Isabel portrayed this parental or analytic role when she re-created the character of the teacher who enacted, at different times, the needed parental functions and the ways in which Isabel felt her parents had failed her. Early on, Isabel played that she was the teacher, and Dr. Huddleston suffered as the student who was treated harshly, endured the demands of authority, and was humiliated for her ignorance. Isabel turned her passive experience into an active experience. She was no longer the vulnerable child but became the aggressive, humiliating adult. Dr. Huddleston's capacity to endure this treatment without retaliating and without crumbling or submitting was a key part of the therapeutic function of the analytic work.

This process can also be understood in terms of projective identification (Ogden, 1979). Dr. Huddleston contained the obnoxious affective experience that Isabel elicited in her, affect that Isabelle found intolerable and strove to unload. She digested it and fed it back to her patient in a way that she could tolerate, absorb, and integrate. Projective identification, like other mental processes, has its own line of development. It is a psychological phenomenon that can function in more primitive ways, serving the black-and-white mentation of dissociation or splitting, and can function in more sophisticated ways, serving the effort to contend with and communicate the intense affects of oedipal development.

The success of this engagement with the developmental object enabled Isabel to develop an object representation that was more forgiving and caring and a self-representation that was more tolerant of her confusion, her affects, and her being a little girl among adults. When she felt that her emotions were cared for, she could identify with the caring adult, which in turn enabled her to care for herself and for the other. The defense of reaction formation, taking care of your little sister rather than strangling her, is more adaptive than identification with the aggressor, but it is still a defense that represses or disavows troubling feelings. In the context of a satisfying relationship with a developmental object, this child felt less alone when dealing with the powerful feelings of hurt, fear, shame, jealousy, fury, and revenge. Dr. Huddleston was with her as they looked under the bed of her mind, and she felt less afraid. This lessened her need to inhibit herself or dominate her emotions with rigid defenses. It facilitated transformation and allowed sublimation; she could more genuinely tolerate her negative feelings and more genuinely enjoy being like the loving parent who takes pleasure in her wishes to care for others, including "Shiskapoo."

Dr. Huddleston and Isabel taught "Shiskapoo" to groom himself when faced with overpowering, messy feelings. The teacher of the chipmunks firmly set limits on the boy and girl chipmunks who went into the bathroom together. This teacher responded in a firm though caring way and took them to a place where they could talk the situation over. The analytic relationship had become one in which Isabel's sexual feelings and related anxieties could be managed and discussed. Setting limits while tolerating the child's desires, feelings, thoughts, and actions and communicating with the child in a way that she could tolerate emotionally and understand cognitively are essential parts of the task of the caring adult. No longer feeling overwhelmed by anxiety or excitement, Isabel became the child within this facilitating relationship who could talk about the birds and the bees.

INTERNAL MAPS AND STRUCTURE

Dreams of streets and maps are frequent in analysis. The analytic process can feel like a trip to unfamiliar places or finding one's way through a geographical terrain that lacks street signs, the usual way of orienting one's self. Images of streets and maps are well suited to represent internal maps or psychological structure. I discussed internal maps in chapter 5 when I considered the mental-representation model of Fonagy and colleagues (1993). I refer back, as well, to Bromberg's (1996) model of the mind, in which isolated or split-off self states become increasingly interconnected and integrated. When discussing Bromberg's model, I used the small circles within the larger circle. I compared the structure of the mind to the infrastructure that unites isolated population centers into a larger political community. These models of the mind come alive when Isabel drew maps and Ella built and played with roads. Consideration of these aspects of their play activities gives us a chance to see how children unconsciously represent psychological structure, how these structures changed over the course of Ella's and Isabel's analyses, and how the analyst and the analytic process are part of this change.

Isabel constructed a game map that helped to illustrate Harry Potter's world. Later in the analysis, she returned to this map, wanting to change it and make the paths more flexible. Later yet, when she was dealing with termination and her parents' divorce, Isabel read from the epilogue of one of the books in the collection of books titled A Series of Unfortunate Events (Handler, 1999). She again returned to the Harry Potter maps. This time she added new streets, pointing out that they were from the dark side. She and Dr. Huddleston discussed how these additions added something new and important to the history of her life. Without them, hers would have been a different life.

These maps reflected her growing capacity to consider both the good and the bad. Like Ella, Isabel reflected on the course of her analysis and the course of her life. The uncomfortable and painful events of her life were part of the landscape that could not be ignored. The changes in the maps indicated structural change, but the kind and quality of the changes were different for Isabel than Ella.

Ella at the start of her analysis had limited capacity to soothe herself or calm her anxiety and was vulnerable to fragmentation. The crumbling of her self and her psychological structure created a mental state qualitatively different from that of a child like Isabel, whose self for the most part remained cohesive. The essential therapeutic effect of the early phases of Ella's analysis was the building of psychological structure.

There were structural changes that occurred in Isabel's mind, but they were different. The internal maps and paths were not first getting laid down or totally taken apart and reconstructed. They instead became more flexible. The roads developed more branches, and buildings and landscaping became more complex and full. We often associate the capacity to tolerate ambivalence with a developmental shift from an earlier psychological structure, such as movement through the stages of separation-individuation toward object constancy or a transition from the paranoid/schizoid position to the more mature psychological structure of the depressive position. Isabel had made this transition. Yet, children like Isabel, who to a significant extent inhabit the depressive position, have not completed the task of dealing with ambivalence. We can trace a developmental line of the child's ability to manage her emotions and contend with internal conflict. This enhanced capacity to tolerate ambivalence and to integrate the good and the bad of life allowed Isabel to expand her narrative history and add depth and breadth to her internal maps. Thus, her psychological structure was both strengthened and made more flexible.

Toward the end, as they dealt with termination, Isabel drew maps for the student version of Dr. Huddleston. These internal maps, her psychological structure, could be applied in a variety of ways: She could think about her past, she could find her way in the present, she could help others and show them the way, and they provided a path to the future that facilitated her capacity to go forward.

Ella introduced roads in her play after she and Mrs. Kaufman had received a reprieve from the threat of termination. She played that Mrs. Kaufman hunted for all the food she needed and repeatedly depicted herself running away and then being found. She built a wall of blocks around her analyst so that Mrs. Kaufman could not leave. Prior to analysis, Ella was literally running away from home across a busy street. It was a dangerous situation, and her parents had to retrieve her. Later in the analysis, she turned the wall of blocks into a road over which she traveled increasingly large distances, followed by her return to her analyst.

When the separation-individuation process goes awry, when the selfobject or developmental object cannot facilitate the child's efforts to move away and return as needed, and when attachment is not sufficiently secure, the laying down of internal maps is interfered with. Investment in the awareness of her internal world is undermined. Immature, rigid, less adaptable coping mechanisms are mobilized to protect the child from catastrophe. When the relationship between the developmental object and the child is unreliable, insecure, or fraught with conflict, defensive structures are created to cope with the unstable situation. The extent to which these defensive structures are required to manage the present is inversely proportional to the capacity to lay down structures that allow greater subtlety, flexibility, and complexity and enable her to her move forward into the future. The representation of the parent or analyst is walled in or walled off, and the child must remain within the safety and restrictions of her own walls, as well. These rigid walls allow some forward developmental progress, but they make it much more difficult to build the roads that expand the infrastructure. When the relationship between child and parent or analyst seem secure, the walls can come down, internal roads can be built, infrastructure is laid down, and the child can more comfortably and confidently venture into the world and into new frontiers of development.

These girls were playing in the realm of Bollas's (1979) unconscious processing. Without realizing it, they developed metaphors that depicted the growing structure of their minds. I draw on these theorists' models of the mind in order to help us understand what has unfolded in Isabel's and Ella's

play and to help us infer meaning from the play. I also draw on the girls'
constructions and their fantasy play to infer representations of their minds in
order to see how well our models and theories fit with theirs.

Chapter Eight

Fragmentation to Cohesive Self

Edward I. Kohn

The Second Coming
W. B. Yeats

Turning and turning in the widening gyre
The falcon cannot hear the falconer;
Things fall apart; the centre cannot hold;
Mere anarchy is loosed upon the world,
The blood-dimmed tide is loosed, and everywhere
The ceremony of innocence is drowned;
The best lack all conviction, while the worst
Are full of passionate intensity.

Yeats's (1921) poem is about his view of the state of the world at the time of the First World War, when Western civilization was crumbling. I use the imagery of the first verse of this poem for my own purposes: to capture the experience of fragmentation. I don't think it is an accident that his poem about civilization can evocatively capture the experience of the individual. I have already used the expanding infrastructure of a growing political society as a model of the developing structure of the mind. Society and culture evolve in response to the needs of people. Individual minds are essential building blocks of that society, and the organization and shapes of those minds are reflected in the larger structures of society.

WHAT EXACTLY IS FRAGMENTATION?

When there is failure of the synthetic function of the ego or integration of mental processes, cohesiveness of the self, integration of the system of self states, or reliability of the representational world, the "centre cannot hold."

The gravitational force that keeps the planets of the mind in coherent orbits is not sufficient to keep them from flying off into space. As the planets lose touch with the centripetal force of their sun, they turn and turn in the "widening gyre."

When the "falcon cannot hear the falconer," the developmental object or selfobject has lost its tie to the self of the child. The parent or analyst is unable to serve the function of tethering the child's emotions within a manageable orbit, leading to the threat of fragmentation, and "things fall apart." In addition, when fragmentation occurs, meaningful communication between the falcon and the falconer is interfered with. Then, with the loss of communication, the capacity of the child to make use of the adult and the adult's capacity to engage the child is further undermined. This vicious chain reaction leads to the "widening gyre." Without a coherent center or organizational structure, unmodulated impulses are unleashed, and "mere anarchy" and the "blood-dimmed tide" are loosed. An enduring continuity of self and a sense of hope are lost: "The best lack all conviction."

In earlier chapters, I discussed the phase transition in the structure of the developing mind that leads it to function in a profoundly new way. I showed how different psychoanalytic theorists, while using different models and different languages, all come to grips with this phenomenon: cohesive self versus fragmentation (Kohut, 1968; Kohut & Wolf, 1978), paranoid/schizoid position versus depressive position (Klein, 1975), beta elements versus alpha elements (Bion, 1965/1977b; Brown, 2011), lack of versus presence of object constancy (Mahler, Pine, & Bergman, 1975), and psychic equivalence versus reflective functioning (Fonagy & Target, 1996; Target & Fonagy, 1996). In this chapter I revisit the concept of fragmentation and the point at which the cohesive structure of the mind is lost in an effort to better understand the nature of this phase transition. If we looked no further into this phenomenon, we might be apt to conclude that there is a definable moment when the tipping point has been reached and the emotional state I infer in the verse from Yeats's poem is the inevitable and paradigmatic result. We might believe that there is one identifiable essence to this psychic phenomenon or a clear point of transformation from order into disorder. Examining the concept of fragmentation with the magnifying lenses provided by these psychoanalytic thinkers, we can see that this transition point is a valuable concept, but it not so simple or straightforward.

How clear can we be about what triggers fragmentation or results from fragmentation? Can we identify the final moment that tips the individual mind into the widening gyre, or does the widening gyre throw the communication between the individual and her tethering object into an unreadable chaos? Is fragmentation the ultimate catastrophe, or is it an effort to avoid another catastrophe? Or is it both? Can we distinguish efforts to fend off fragmentation from efforts to cope with fragmentation or from efforts to reconstitute the self? When are these efforts part of the solution, and when are they part of the widening problem?

In a psychological black hole, it is difficult to distinguish cause from effect. Boulanger (2002) describes a defensive retreat into dissociation as the cause of the disruption of the core self. If this is the case, what is the defense of dissociation trying to contend with? Is this an even more catastrophically unbearable state than fragmentation? When the obliteration of connections among the different self states occurs, what happens to the individual's inner world?

Grotstein (1990a, 1990b) refers to primary meaninglessness or primary undifferentiation, a state of nonorganization. When a holding environment is available to the infant, this nonorganization retains the potential to become organized and achieve meaning. Grotstein uses the word *nothingness* to describe the empty space within the container, and nothingness retains the potential to be filled. However, if there is no viable container for experience, the potential to organize the representational world—internal and external experience—is lost. The result is catastrophic. Potential is gone. The individual is in a state of mind that Grotstein defines as "pathological secondary meaninglessness" or disorganization. Without a container, there is a vacuum of nothingness that gets filled by no-thingness, "non-substance or antimatter accumulated in the black hole as entropy" (1990a, 270). Grotstein sees Klein's (1975) paranoid/schizoid position and frank psychoses as efforts at restitution to fend off the crumbling of the container of the mind. The mother is the fabric of space and time in which the infant's mind is imbedded. If there is no space and time, there can be no objects and no events, and there can be no mind. The defensive creation of no-thingness is an effort to prevent space and time from foreclosing. Yet, this effort creates the black hole that also can foreclose space and time.

Barranger, Barranger, and Mom (1988) point out that the anxiety associated with Klein's (1975) depressive position is a more organized and modulated affect than that associated with paranoid/schizoid anxiety. They believe, however, that the paranoid/schizoid anxiety is not the bottom of the hole: "It is preferable to have a relatively localized persecutor against which the subject may take protective measures than to be at the mercy of nameless, placeless dangers whose nature remains unknown" (124). They add confusional anxiety, disintegration anxiety, and nameless anxiety to the range of affective states associated with fragmentation.

Krystal's (1978) effort to find the essence of the traumatic state includes the distinction between the adult's and child's versions of trauma. When the adult endures seemingly unbearable and never-ending affects, he fears them and dreads the return of the infantile type of trauma, but he has not reached the point of catastrophic trauma. It is when he is helpless in the face of this situation, is overwhelmed by the affective responses and surrenders, that automatic anxiety prevails, a phenomenon that is more biological than psychological. Krystal (1978) states that this is a "phylogenetically determined surrender pattern which is also a potential psychological self-destruct mechanism." This state of passive surrender, Krystal's (1978) and Stern's (1951) catatanoid reaction, is another place where it seems unclear where the initial devastating injury ends and the catastrophic inflammatory reaction begins.

Whether we talk about automatic anxiety, catatonoid state, beta elements, or black holes, at some point it appears that biological descriptions are employed in lieu of psychological descriptions. When the container of the mind crumbles, there is a body and a brain, but there is no longer a cohesive mind to experience the body.

DEGREES OF FRAGMENTATION

How relative is fragmentation? How relative is the catastrophic traumatic state? Is there a tipping point after which we would all recognize that the theater of the mind is gone? Models and metaphors get tricky here. Each takes on a life of its own and might lead us toward a different answer, depending on its structure or how we apply it. When it is sufficiently cold, we are able to agree that water has solidified to ice, and when it is sufficiently warm, we readily identify liquid water. During this phase transition of the mind, we have entered a murkier state. Throughout this book, I rely on dichotomies like cohesive versus fragmented or action versus words. The boundary lines between categories, when examined under our mental microscopes, are not thin lines. They are continua, and they are deep and wide. In chapter 11, I look carefully at the continuum from action to words and show that it is a matter of more and less rather than either and or. Actions speak, and words act. For now, I peer into the complex states of the crumbling mind.

If our metaphor of the mind is a theater that contains a stage on which the representational world is portrayed, earthquakes of differing intensities may damage the building and impact the internal world to varying degrees. Efforts to shore up the building while it trembles may be more or less successful and more or less enduring. In contrast, if fragmentation is compared to the black hole, we might conclude that there is a sudden transition or an irrevocable change, like the photon that passes the event horizon into the black hole, never to return to the outer universe. This metaphor can lead us to observe and explain the dramatic forces impinging on the photon as it approaches the event horizon, and then we can compare the breakdown of the functioning of the mind to the breakdown of the current laws of physics within the black hole. When do the laws of the mind's functioning change in a way that is qualitatively different rather than a matter of degree? What determines whether the changes in the state of mind are enduring and unrecoverable rather than temporary and recoverable? If our model is the black hole, we still need a way to conceptualize the range of organizations, like the paranoid/schizoid position and the depressive position, that represent enduring ways of functioning that maintain different distances from the black hole. The chemistry analogy, the phase transitions from ice to liquid water and water to steam, might serve us better when we think about the different ways in which the mind can be organized, but it does not provide us with a picture of the oppressive threat of fragmentation that is evoked from the looming black hole.

Krystal (1978) explains that the loss of one ego function affects all ego functions. Therefore, the threat to any ego function can trigger a feeling of psychic helplessness, a threat of the loss of all functions. This provides a model that enables us to consider degrees of trauma or fragmentation. A patient's dream of driving without brakes suggests the threat of a shift in defensive function and feeling a dangerous loss of control: She is unable to apply sufficient resistance in order to maintain a reassuring velocity of the analytic process and thereby keep it safely on the road. The structure is loosened, creating fear, but the totally uncontrolled widening of the gyre has not occurred. Images depicting the experience and fear of shifting defenses and structures in the analytic process are common. These include, among many others, dams leaking, buildings being renovated, sites being dug up, windows without shutters, confusing or changing maps, streets without street signs, and doors without locks. Other images may capture greater degrees of threat. A crumbling dam suggests a more overpowering danger than one that is merely leaking as defensive structures shift. A nuclear chain reaction and the nuclear catastrophe at Chernobyl suggest an even more devastating, out-of-control, and unstoppable psychic state, such as unmanageable rage or a loss of psychic stability, or both, that will increasingly feed on itself. When nuclear fuel releases particles of radiation, these particles strike other particles, leading to the release of more particles. Unless kept under control at some point, so many particles get released that the collisions release more and more particles that cause more and more collisions, and a geometric progression leads to the release of enormous energy—an explosion. Another image of an out-of-control and unstoppable process is a planet that drifts further and further from the gravitational pull of its sun: As the distance between the planet and the sun gets larger, the gravitational pull that sustains an orderly orbit becomes weaker and weaker, allowing the planet to drift further away.

It appears that fragmentation, or what Winnicott (1980) calls breakdown, is a term that may include more than one psychological phenomenon (Goldberg, 2016). A variety of images or narratives can capture the experience of fragmentation, and it may be that the different images reflect differences in the specifics of the loss of a cohesive psychic structure. Images of an earth-quake, a shattered mirror, or a jigsaw puzzle that has been knocked off the table or a phrase like "everything is falling apart" may reflect the experience of a psyche that is crumbling into pieces and can't come back together. Ella could not tolerate movement of the pieces in the dollhouse and later urgently needed to repair the drawing she had torn to pieces. Images of drowning, being swallowed up, or falling into quicksand might depict a self that is on the verge of feeling fused with the object. These images might alternatively suggest the experience of feeling like one is drowning in a sea of emotion. As Ella became more able to tolerate her emotions, she was able to represent the experience of being consumed by them. She told a "scary story" about sad horses that drowned. A palette of paint in which the colors have all mixed together into a muddy state might represent loss of the capacity to differen-tiate affects or losing a sense of individual identity. Depression can be a manifestation of fragmentation, a state of total depletion in which all sense of connection with a sustaining environment has been lost, and the individual has no more resources. The experience of depressive affect, when the child has progressed to Klein's (1975) depressive position, is very different from a state of total depletion or the inescapable smothering of sinking into quick-sand. Within the depressive position, the child has a self that is predominant-ly cohesive and can still feel connected in the face of negative feelings or separation. The presence of a developmental object helps the child to believe that, despite feeling at sea with her emotions, she will come back to the surface. When a child can avail herself of such an object, she can grapple more effectively with feelings of loss, guilt, and remorse. As she moves toward object constancy or a cohesive self, this function becomes part of her own mental capacities, and she can tolerate these affects more independently.

BREAKDOWN OF THOUGHT PROCESSES

Fragmentation can be a breakdown of thought processes. We might observe loose associations, tangential thinking, or flight of ideas as the patient en-dures the experience of her mind becoming unglued. Unconscious or con-scious awareness of this pending psychic catastrophe might lead to efforts to stabilize the mind, including paranoid delusions or intense symptoms of OCD. The need for stability might appear in verbal or visual images like a balloon that needs to be tethered to the ground or pieces of a structure that must be held together. This need for stability might be reflected in a child's behavior. The center could not hold for Ella when she frantically threw the toys about the room. Her efforts to tape her drawing back together, with Mrs. Kaufman's help, were manifestly intended to reconstitute her picture, but also represented the task of pulling herself back together. Preoccupation with a key might predominate when an individual is desperate to grasp what is happening, hoping for the key to the code or a key that can be turned in order to stop the chaos. Hypochondriasis can reflect a regression from the mental to the physical but also might depict, through the body, what has happened in the mind. The self is no longer an integrated structure; the different pieces are disconnected, and the different parts become dismal preoccupations.

Qualitative changes in the functioning of the psyche occur during states of fragmentation. The communicative function of the mind diminishes or might, in the extreme, disappear. In these extremes, projective identification becomes the dumping of unbearable experience, and the capacity to use it as communication or a potential therapeutic encounter shrinks to almost nothing (Brown, 2005). Unconscious communication, as well as conscious communication, gets blocked. Meaning is no longer disguised; it does not exist (Goldberg, 2016). Dreams become endless repetition rather than a manifestation of the unconscious processing of experience. Reflective function—the capacity to experience one's own behavior or the behavior of others as reflections of mental states, including beliefs, desires, and intentions—is lost. When a person functions in the mode of psychic equivalence, thought and feeling are no longer reflections of states of mind but are experienced as concrete reality. The distinction between the feeling of being a worthless human being and the reality evaporates. Ella tried to crawl between Mrs. Kaufman's legs in an effort to get literally inside her.

ELLA: FROM FRAGMENTATION TO COHESIVE STRUCTURE

Over the course of her analysis, Ella's psychic structure consolidated. We see evidence of a more cohesive self and the capacity for object constancy as the analytic work progressed. Attention to these changes provides an opportunity to examine the differences in the mind of the child before and after she has gone through this phase transition. Increasingly, the content of the material in Ella's analysis included oedipal themes, such as her distress about triangular competition. The change in content went along with an underlying change in structure. The child who inhabits the depressive position or has a more cohesive self is better able to manage the developmental challenges of the phallic and oedipal phases.

Children in all phases of development, including the oedipal phase, continue to need the support of their parents or analysts as developmental objects. Despite the consolidation of psychological structure that had occurred early in the analysis, Ella was still vulnerable to disruption. She needed Mrs. Kaufman to help her manage her affective state as well as the content of her play and conversation.

Six months into the analysis, after Mrs. Kaufman's vacation, Ella played that her mother was a queen and she was born a princess. She married the prince and was now herself the queen who sat on the throne and knew all the answers. While this vignette suggests oedipal themes, it was a fragile performance and seemed to be an effort to contend with the loss of Mrs. Kaufman during her absence. In the play, Mrs. Kaufman was to be Ella's servant and follow her orders, as if Cinderella and the wicked stepmother had changed roles. The fragility of this effort at coping was revealed when Ella "made a mistake" in her coloring. This mistake was shattering, and she tried to shore herself up by insisting, "You made an even bigger mistake. . . . I'm the queen, and queens don't make mistakes." But this effort to shore herself up was unsuccessful. With the tape she had been using to fasten her drawings, Ella flung herself at Mrs. Kaufman in an effort to tape her. Mrs. Kaufman helped Ella to understand that she was trying to keep her from leaving, and I also think this use of tape reflected a wish to keep herself together.

Reuniting after the vacation confronted Ella with the emotions of missing her analyst and longing for her. This was too much for her to bear. She tried desperately to maintain her balance and stability by insisting that she was the queen and Mrs. Kaufman was her servant. She could only sustain this if everything remained exactly in place, and when it did not, her still-fragile psychological structure tumbled. Despite this and her resort to concrete behavior, she showed evidence of a capacity to represent her emotional state. The fragmentation was not so great that the communicative functions of her mind were totally lost. Ella felt like she had been torn to pieces without sufficient emotional glue to keep her intact. She communicated this desperate need to be glued together in her concrete actions by taping Mrs. Kaufman. She used projective identification in order to imagine that the feeling of falling apart belonged to her analyst rather than to her. Under these conditions, Ella had an opportunity to repair the damage and prevent catastrophe. In the action there was meaning that could be understood.

After some discussion, Ella burst into tears and explained that, while Dr. Kaufman was away, her mother had given her extra household chores. She had to do the dishes, and when Ella broke one, her mother got angry. Her mother then broke another and made Ella clean up the mess both of them had made. This description captures something about how Ella felt when her analyst was away. Her mother was the queen who insisted she never made mistakes, and it was Ella who was blamed for the mistakes. For Ella, her mother did not ease her distress or help to repair the breach; she intensified it.

Most children feel at times like Cinderella. In their minds, they are burdened by the drudgery of what they feel are the insensitive and excessive demands made by their parents. Do the dishes; cut the grass; take out the garbage; go down to the basement and get my screwdriver. In addition, children often believe their siblings are receiving favored treatment, are spared the blame for misdeeds, and are subjected to fewer of these unreasonable demands. The wicked stepmother and stepsisters of the fairy tale Cinderella are narrative devices that readily capture the imagination of children. The split between the evil figures, such as the wicked stepmother and stepsisters, and the idealized figures, such as Prince Charming and the fairy godmother, may or may not resonate with a child's tendency to use splitting. The narrative device of portraying qualities of one person among several characters can also be a rich way to portray a range of complex and mixed feelings.

Relevant to our understanding of the selfobject or developmental object function of the analyst, Mrs. Kaufman had become the fairy godmother, whose kindness and guardian-angel qualities made possible developmental progression into the oedipal world of Prince Charming. Without Mrs. Kaufman, this Cinderella would be left in her cellar and ordered around by the wicked stepmother, whose demands and anger burdened the child further rather than sustained her growth. This is the way that Ella saw her own mother. Within the context of her relationship with Mrs. Kaufman—her selfobject, developmental object, and transformational object—she was not alone in the cellar. Within this matrix, her world was more coherent and more integrated, and things were less black and white. When they were apart, it was hard to sustain this integration and coherence.

Ella's view of her mother heightened her distress during the absence of her analyst. Not only did she have to deal with this separation, but she also described a mother who angrily turned on her. If she had felt that she and her mother were in a supportive, less conflicted relationship, she would likely have felt that her mother gave her comfort during this challenging time. It is striking that Ella's mother also was distressed by the absence of Mrs. Kaufman, which likely contributed to her less modulated responses to her daughter. Here, we see how the reality of the child's relationship with her mother, her inner world, and her analysis combine.

Early in the second year of her analysis, Ella faced the possibility that her parents would bring her work and relationship with Mrs. Kaufman to an end. Her response to this threat revealed the progress she had made since the start of the analysis as well as the vulnerability that remained. Ella's capacity to express grief was one of the developmental advances made possible by her increasing ability to rely on her analyst as a development-promoting figure. The foundation that makes grief bearable is the reassuring and comforting relationship with the parent, and without that support, the pain is disorganizing or smothering. The grief must be walled off rather than felt or expressed, and the child descends into a dark hole from which escape or even the capacity to see any light feels impossible. The parents' role in tolerating the child's affects and projective identifications provides emotional sustenance and support and facilitates movement into and maintenance of the depressive position.

When Ella's analysis was threatened with the prospect of termination, she was able to communicate her grief and despair. The importance of her tie to her analyst led Ella to talk about feeling unloved and unwanted. Despite the power of this threatened loss, Ella did not come totally undone. She communicated her state of mind in words. She also tried to be on her best behavior, which was likely related to a belief that she would be able to continue in analysis with Mrs. Kaufman if she was a good girl rather than a devil child. Despite the irrelevance of this idea to the reality of the decision, it represented a greater ability to use more adaptive defenses to cope with and try to head off great distress. Rather than crumbling into chaos or becoming destructive, Ella mobilized the resources to try and be a better, more likeable girl. Even as she absorbed the very painful news and experienced the sadness and the anger, her self remained, to a significant extent, intact. She did not cross into the black hole, where loss is no longer a meaningful event that elicits sadness but instead becomes an infinitely dense agony of depression that has no identifiable meaning. In the black hole, the agony will, as Krystal (1978) says, be never-ending. There is not even a way to peek out of the black hole to see anything different. In the mode of psychic equivalence, there is no other way it can be. Hope is more difficult to sustain. But this was not Ella's fate.

Ella brought in a book about migrants who were separated at great distance from their families, and they did not know if they would ever see each other again: "They gave up so much." The intensity of this affect, which communicated so much to the analyst and to the reader, was too much for Ella. She crumbled to the floor, saying, "This doll is falling apart. A part of it is missing. I won't leave until I find it. It will never be right." She felt like she was falling apart. Without Mrs. Kaufman, a psychological part of Ella would be missing.

This moment was similar to but also different from the very early sessions, when Ella threw things around the room or panicked about the shapes inside the house. All of these moments dealt with the experience of falling apart, of fragmentation. In the earlier sessions, however, she was less internally integrated and more chaotic, and this showed in her behavior. If Mrs. Kaufman did not keep everything exactly in place early on, Ella crumbled. Then the analyst had to weather the storm, protect them both, and allow things to come back together. Even when meaning could be inferred, it could not be processed. In the later sessions, her earlier vulnerability had not totally disappeared. She regressed and temporarily became more concrete. She really seemed concerned that the doll was missing pieces; it was not just play. Then she pushed Mrs. Kaufman to smell her feet. But this disruption was more contained than the earlier outbursts. She was less out of control, she regained her composure more easily, and meaning was evident in the action of taping Mrs. Kaufman and in her concern that her doll was falling apart. It was the doll, not Ella, that was missing pieces. Despite her distress, Ella represented the feeling of losing a part of herself through her toy. There was more opportunity to communicate and elaborate on the emotional experience.

Early in the analysis, Ella lived within a feeling of abandonment. She despaired about the tricks and lies that left her feeling that there was no one to care for her. Now, she saw the end of analysis as a broken promise, and again she faced losing a mother figure. At this point, however, something had begun to change within Ella. The fairy-godmother quality of Mrs. Kaufman had been to a significant extent internalized. Rather than assuming that she was a devil who deserved to be treated harshly, Ella believed that a promise had been made. She was someone who deserved to have kind and supportive figures in her life. When that expectation was threatened, she continued to feel justified in having that expectation. She felt betrayed and felt free to let Mrs. Kaufman know how angry she was. This kind of anger is dynamically and qualitatively different from the anger Ella expressed when her self came unglued. Her fury about the betrayal is not a moment of immediate, automatic, and total collapse. Instead, she was enduring a painful and potentially overpowering experience. Her self remained vulnerable but less fragile and less threatened by fragmentation. She was further along in the development of the capacity to have a cohesive self and object constancy, and this capacity helped to sustain her. She occupied the territory of the depressive position more consistently. She could still believe that Mrs. Kaufman was there for her, even though she felt betrayed, even though she was threatened with losing her, and even though she was furious with her. Because her self had not fully collapsed, she could modulate her emotions more effectively, and she could communicate her experience to herself and to her analyst more coherently. She could more effectively represent her experience, and her ability to elicit an empathic response from the object was enhanced. She could better tolerate a very distressing piece of data without needing to dissociate.

Chapter Nine

Therapeutic Action

Edward I. Kohn

A theory of mind, a model that illustrates the structure and functioning of the mind, informs psychoanalytic technique. The psychoanalytic situation and the analysand's responses to the analyst provide data for hypotheses about the working of the mind. Our understandings of the therapeutic action of psychoanalysis and our ideas about how the mind changes are intimately entwined with our models of the mind. In this chapter and the following two chapters, I examine the concept of therapeutic action and, in the process, elaborate a vision of the structure of the mind.

I return to my discussion of the structure of the mind in chapter 5 as I explore the ways in which our models of the mind influence our understanding of therapeutic action and the ways in which therapeutic action elucidates our models of the mind. I also refer back to chapter 7, where I discuss the developmental object, in order to examine the transformational power of the human relationship and the analytic process. In chapter 10 I examine the same principles, specifically as they emerge in child analysis, and I discuss the ways in which immersion in play and a child's imagination reveal and facilitate the transformation of a child's mind. In chapter 11, I sort through the therapeutic aspects of child analysis as we trace a continuum from action to words.

FREUD AND THEORIES OF INSIGHT

Freud's (1895/1953–1974n) first theory of abreaction assumes there are pent-up affects that need to be released. Then, with the topographic model, he concluded that insight was the curative factor. The role of insight is to make the unconscious conscious. Unacceptable thoughts, though out of awareness, continue to influence the mind, are expressed in disguised ways, and appear as symptoms. Putting words to these unconscious representations allows them to enter consciousness and frees the individual from the symptoms (Freud, 1915/1953–1974o). As Freud came to understand resistance, his understanding of the therapeutic role of insight changed. It was not sufficient to explain the wish at the root of the dream or the hidden unconscious impulses, but insight into the reluctance of the system conscious to recognize these forces had to be achieved (Freud, 1923/1953–1974d). With Freud's recognition of transference—as a resistance and as an expression of unconscious forces—insight into the analysand's perception of her relationship with the analyst took center stage.

In developing the structural model of the mind, Freud provided a new set of tools to apply to the role of insight. Insight into resistance brings unconscious aspects of the ego and superego within the ego's conscious domain and allows further understanding of the deep unconscious forces of the id. Insight facilitates the ego's capacity to use anxiety as a signal. Functioning like the reins or spurs of the rider of a horse, this allows the less powerful ego to exert control and influence over the more powerful id. He goes further, stating that the id does more than cede control to the ego; the id becomes ego: "Where id was, there shall ego be" (Freud, 1933/1953–1974k, 80).

Freud's theorizing had to contend with clinical experience in which insightful moments did not lead to change immediately or readily. He developed the concept of working through to explain the slow and gradual nature of psychological transformation (Freud, 1914/1953–1974m). Exploration of the thinking of other theorists enables us to understand more clearly how changes in the working of the mind and the structure of the mind occur in the psychoanalytic situation. The ways in which id is transformed into ego or by which ego achieves mastery over the id require further examination. The process by which affect gets modulated and the ego develops the function of signal affects is not explained simply by positing the therapeutic value of insight. How different theorists portray the mind also give us a more complex understanding of the role of insight in the transformative power of psychoanalysis. It is time to return to chapter 5 and the consideration of psychic structure.

THE MENTAL-REPRESENTATION MODEL: ANALYSIS OF TRANSFERENCE AND INSIGHT

According to the mental-representation model (Fonagy et al., 1993), procedures or patterns of action rather than individual experiences are retained from parent–child interactions. These intrinsically interlinked sequences of events, when taken together, amount to a representation of a relationship.

Mental schemata are formed in which expectations of a particular person toward the self are aggregated, and working models of representations of self and others are formed. Repeated activation strengthens the links among features such that subsequent activation of features is more likely to activate the entire representation. This process serves to integrate mental representations, while it also creates the potential to impose a representation on a variety of experiences. In the analytic situation, we see this as transference. Transference is an instantiation of the current structure of the mind, and elucidation of the transference is an essential part of the process of recognizing old, enduring connections and creating new connections, along with new structures that allow the individual to develop new and more flexible models for engaging internal and external reality.

Insight helps a patient identify the repetitive patterns created by old, enduring connections. Recognition of representations that appear dangerous brings to awareness the automatic avoidance of those representations. This process facilitates connections among isolated ideas and representations, allowing the development of new links. The availability of new links among representational structures contributes to the development of ever-larger representational units. This explains how id becomes ego and how, according to Anna Freud (1965), interpretation of transference and resistance leads to a widening of consciousness and ego dominance. Those individuals who have surpassed the stage of psychic equivalence and achieved the stage of representational thinking but are held back from further development by pathological influences from the past are especially well served by insight.

THE PROCESS OF INSIGHTFULNESS

Sugarman (2006) conceptualizes mentalization as a psychic process. He emphasizes the process of gaining insight, which he calls insightfulness, over verbal interpretations aimed at knowledge of contents of the mind. Facilitating insightfulness allows the individual to regain access to inhibited or repudiated capacities for mentalization. Love and attachment and the adult's interest in the child's representational world foster the child's interest in her own inner world. The relationship with the parent or analyst is an inseparable part of the process. For Sugarman, consideration of the process of insightfulness does away with the dichotomy of verbal insight versus relationship.

DIFFERENT VISIONS OF THE BABY

Kohut's (Kohut & Wolf, 1978) vision of the baby is different from Freud's. For Kohut, she is less an instinctual animal whose primitive drives need to be tamed or sublimated and rather an energetic and vibrant self that must be immersed in a sufficiently empathic surround so that it can grow and be actualized. Anger is not an instinct or drive but a response to frustration of the strivings of her self.

Mayes and Cohen (1993b) quote Freud's *Beyond the Pleasure Principle* (1920/1953–1974a) to demonstrate his view of the death instinct: "The inclination to aggression is an original, self-subsisting instinctual disposition in man, and I return to my view that it constitutes the greatest impediment to civilization" (122). In *Civilization and Its Discontents*, Freud (1930/1953–1974c) portrays the unending tension between the individual's drives and the society in which he lives. Mayes and Cohen state that Freud's commitment to the aggressive instinct prevented him from seeing aggression as an essential and positive influence in development. It is his contemporaries and those who followed him who worked with his theory of aggression in an effort to formulate a conception of how the drive becomes modulated or neutralized (sublimation, displacement, and restriction of aim) and thereby becomes available for the formation of psychic structures like the superego.

Mayes and Cohen (1993b, 151) state,

> Aggressivity and aggressive feelings are rooted in the earliest and most basic biologically determined patterns of behavior designed to protect the child and bring others to him in times of need. . . . The infant's cry is almost always perceived by adults as unpleasant and aversive, yet indicative of a need. . . . Early motor activity and motility are a part of the process of experiencing self as effective and autonomous. (151)

They cite other child investigators who view aggression less as a primary instinct and more as a response to frustration. Like Loewald (1960), they see the drive and the object as intricately intermingled: "How aggressivity assumes adaptive and nonadaptive forms is defined and refined in the context of the child's earliest experiences" (Mayes & Cohen, 1993, 153).

OPTIMAL FRUSTRATION AND CLASSICAL THEORY

In classical theory, optimal frustration is an essential aspect of the psychoanalytic process. Derivatives of the drives must be sufficiently frustrated—hopefully without being traumatically frustrated—in order for the patient's thoughts and affects to be accessible in the free-associative process. Structure building emerges from optimal frustration, as the mental apparatus builds structures that defend against, cope with, and redirect the frustrated impulse. The more finely tuned the system of structures, the more flexible is the apparatus. This facilitates sublimation and modulation of affects.

The ego function of signal anxiety is evidence of a more highly structured mental apparatus in which the intense flow from the id, returning to Rapaport's (1960) ideas in chapter 5, becomes manageable and usable in the system of channels and dikes of the ego. When the ego function of signal anxiety has been achieved, the individual's ability to respond to threats is enhanced. The fire alarm at school leads to an orderly and confident exit from the building rather than chaos and panic. This virtuous cycle, in which positive developments in the evolving structure of the mind facilitate subsequent positive developments, is the opposite of the widening gyre of fragmentation that I discussed in chapter 8, where the further the falcon drifts from the falconer, the less the falconer is able to contain the falcon's circular orbit.

OPTIMAL FRUSTRATION AND SELF PSYCHOLOGY

From the perspective of self psychology, empathic attunement is the foundation that facilitates the analytic process. Here, another kind of optimal frustration is essential to the curative process. Small-enough misattunements cause disruptions of the selfobject transference that are not traumatic but are bridgeable by the analysand. In the context of the selfobject transference, empathic attunement to these disruptions enables the patient to manage the disappointment, enables the analytic pair to discuss the shared experience, and facilitates the analysand's capacity to provide for herself a bit of the function that previously she had required of her analyst. New psychological structure has been laid down: This is transmuting internalization.

According to the classical model of the mind, the impulse sets the process in motion. The analyst is the object of gratification of the impulse, and the object becomes important because it is the source of gratification. Interpretations bring the impulse and the defenses into awareness, unconscious phenomena get attached to words, the complex compromise formations get reworked, and structure changes. In self psychology, the relationship is more central. The pull toward the selfobject is primary rather than secondary. Within the context of the selfobject relationship, the incomplete developmental strivings reengage, and development moves forward. Empathic failures, disruptions of the relationship, set in motion the process that can lead to transmuting internalization (Kohut, 1971, 1984; Kohut & Wolf, 1978; Tolpin, 1971).

THE ZONE OF PROXIMAL DEVELOPMENT AND OPTIMAL FRUSTRATION

Returning to chapters 5 and 7, Wilson and Weinstein (1996) build on Vygotsky's study of the process of learning and the ways in which adults facilitate language development in children. The zone of proximal development (ZPD) is a concept developed to formulate the ways in which linguistic mediation between child and adult facilitates internalization:

> Being in the ZPD "calls to life in the child, awakens and puts in motion an entire series of internal processes of development. These processes are at the time possible only in the sphere of interaction with those surrounding the child and in collaboration with companions, but in the internal course of develop-ment they eventually become the internal property of the child." (Vygotsky, 1956, 450; cited by Wertsch, 1985, 71; cited by Wilson & Weinstein, 1996, 170)

When the adult is speaking to the child within the ZPD, the child feels on solid ground, and further elaboration of meaning or comprehension is pos-sible.

Wilson and Weinstein use the ZPD to provide a subtle vision of optimal frustration. It is a perspective that allows for a moment-to-moment assess-ment of optimal frustration as the analytic process shifts over time. For Wilson and Weinstein, abstinence is not a single stance that has the same significance or meaning in a consistent way, from moment to moment, when an analytic process is set in motion. When the analyst and analysand are mutually engaged in the ZPD, abstinence serves a therapeutic purpose. Transference wishes that are associated with budding processes that are in reach of the ZPD are stimulated to grow and reorganize when contending with the frustration of abstinence. The scaffold of the internalization commu-nity is present but a bit out of reach. The breadth of the ZPD is a measure of the distance that the analysand can stretch her self in order to bridge the space between her self and the scaffold. This bridging corresponds to Ko-hut's (1971, 1984; Kohut & Wolf, 1978) and Tolpin's (1971) transmuting internalization.

When the analyst and the analysand are not mutually engaged in the ZPD, abstinence creates a fragile space that does not seem or feel bridgeable. This leads to anger, frustration, or anxiety that is difficult to tolerate. Analytic associations are less apt to reflect a creative filling in of the space and more apt to reflect responses to the distressing affects of losing connection to the scaffolding analyst. It can be compared to the mother who has ventured too far from the zone of the toddler's capacity for object constancy or to the selfobject that has failed to maintain the illusion and reality that his hand is readily in reach of the bicycle seat as the little girl tries to balance her self on her emotional two-wheeler.

When analyst and analysand are working within the ZPD, a context is provided that enables a new experience to feel hopeful rather than over-whelming. Working in this small range facilitates modulation of affect, as little bits of terror are managed in lieu of great chasms of portending catastrophe. Rather than retreat to the repetitive old solutions, a bit of progressive development can occur.

THE RELATIONSHIP

From the perspective of object relations, the human relationship between analyst and analysand is transformative. The first analysts might have seen the influence of the relationship as compromising suggestion or unanalyzed transference cure, but object-relations theorists have made this relationship the object of study. The placebo effect, the transference cure, and the power of suggestion are not just to be dismissed or merely tolerated but to be explored and their power understood.

HOLDING, CONTAINING, AND PROJECTIVE IDENTIFICATION

Ogden (1979) describes projective identification as an interactional and intra-psychic process. The patient's behavior and ways of interacting during analytic sessions unconsciously influence the analyst and elicit countertransference feelings. It is as if the analysand has placed affects or parts of herself that are intolerable within the analyst. How the analyst manages these feelings and presents them back to the patient in a digestible way greatly influences the therapeutic action of analysis. Bion (1962/1977a, 1963, 1965/1977b) refers to this as the container function of the analyst (Brown, 2011). Winnicott (1965) describes a holding environment. The patient is unable to manage or contain some of her feelings, but with the analyst's container or holding function or capacity to tolerate and think analytically about projective identifications, these feelings can be more readily expressed, recognized, reorganized, modulated, and then reinternalized. Strachey (1934) explains that the analyst is seen by the analysand as her harsh superego. The moderate and nonjudgmental stance of the analyst, as he interprets the transference, allows the development of a less harsh and more realistic superego. These authors help us to understand the modulation of affect. With the help of the analyst, the intolerable feelings can be experienced and expressed rather than suppressed, and they become more modulated.

The analyst is more than a screen on which internalized conflicts are projected and then interpreted. The relationship with the analyst is a new opportunity to contend with unmanageable feelings. This facilitates the capacity to engage experiences that have previously been unavailable. Within the context of this relationship, the opportunity to rework the influence of the past is enhanced. The analyst serves a function similar to the parent of the child.

Ella played "the people with no home" who gave away their yucky baby. She silently sobbed as she leaned against Mrs. Kaufman. Her grief was more tolerable and communicable when she could literally and metaphorically lean on her analyst. Free association, dialogue, and interpretation occur within the envelope of the relationship between the subject and her developmental object. It is within this human matrix that change occurs.

THE DEVELOPMENTAL OBJECT

I return to some of the ideas discussed in chapter 7 in order to consider further the quality of the analytic relationship and its therapeutic potential. While concepts like auxiliary ego, holding environment, or container are often associated with the earliest phases of life, especially infancy, objects continue to serve these functions throughout the life cycle. The need for holding, containing, or supporting does not disappear with the achievement of object constancy, but the quality of these needs changes, and they become more subtle and more complex. The transformational potential and development-promoting capacity of that magical experience, those moments when the child is immersed in the interest of and engagement with her parents or other significant objects, is alive throughout life, and it comes into exquisite focus in the analytic situation.

Different analysts, when discussing the analyst's involvement in the mental functioning of the analysand, describe the engagement differently. Kohut (1966, 1968, 1971; Kohut & Wolf, 1978) talks about empathy and the selfobject transference. He refers to the mirroring function of the twinkle in a mother's eye or merger with the strength of the idealized parent. Loewald (1960) explains that the patient's reciprocal involvement with the analyst's mind allows a reorganization of the patient's mind at a higher level. Despite their differences, they are both trying to come to grips with a similar phenomenon. Human beings are genetically programmed to seek relationships. Whether we understand the therapeutic encounter as a relationship with a new object, selfobject, transformational object, or developmental object or think about it as an engagement of psychic systems, we all try to understand the transformative power of this engagement.

Rather than empathy, Winnicott (1960) refers to attunement. The mother's attunement to the child enables the child to see herself. If she sees her mother instead, this becomes an impingement, and the child's self is apt to be constructed around a false representation. Fonagy and Target (1998) suggest that children develop awareness of their own psychic experience by seeing their intentions, desires, and beliefs in the minds of their parents. Sugarman (2006) and Miller (2013) agree that the adult's interest in the child's mind stimulates the child's interest and facilitates expansion of her psychic theater.

Lyons-Ruth (1999) emphasizes the parents' openness to the state of mind of the child. This allows the child's affective or emotional state to remain open and develop, while failure to be open to the mind of the child causes her mind to be overtaken and foreclosed. As a result of this failure, discontinuities in implicit, nonconscious procedures result, leading to segregated and fragmented functioning with little opportunity to update and revise these procedures.

FORWARD DEVELOPMENTAL THRUST

Embedded in many theories of the therapeutic action of psychoanalysis, including all of the theories I have discussed, is the concept of a forward developmental thrust. All people, no matter how impaired, have within themselves a movement toward health and transformation. Sigmund Freud uses the metaphor of a migrating population leaving resources behind to portray fixation of libido and ego development. For both Sigmund Freud and Anna Freud, insight has the potential to remove resistances and allow repressed ideas and wishes into awareness. This frees up libido and allows increased integration and dominance of the ego. When the people (libido) in the rear are no longer required to maintain those positions and when they are not restricted from movement, they are available to move forward, providing more resources for further (ego and libido) progression.

At the start of her analysis, following the map provided by the theory of psychosexual development, Ella had many troops in the rear, and they were a disorganized lot, prone to chaos. She inhabited a territory where oral-phase desires for caretaking and nurturance were predominant. Considering the developmental line of anxiety, she feared loss of the object and abandonment. As her analysis progressed, her play revealed that she had moved forward on this map and contended with oedipal concerns, including wishes for a boyfriend and a family of her own. Jealousy and rivalry were the dangers that predominated, and they could lead to attack or loss of love and support.

More of Isabel's troops were in the oedipal zone at the start of her analysis. Her fantasies and theories about conception and birth revealed that some troops remained in the territory she had passed through earlier in her life, and anal theories about birth and oral fantasies about conception were dominant. As the analytic work progressed, her fantasies evolved. She dreamed of a boy cracking eggs on her head, and she explained to Dr. Huddleston that baby owls come out of their mothers' vaginas.

If we accept that a drive to resume thwarted development persists, the repetition compulsion can be understood as pressure to reengage experiences in an effort to achieve mastery of trauma or resolve unresolved developmental conflicts. Object-relations schools or self psychology see within repetition and transference a drive to find the kind of relationship that can engage unmet developmental needs and facilitate forward development. Baker and Anna Ornstein suggest that resistance is the result of the patient's expectation that the traumas or failures of the past will be repeated. The individual is therefore afraid to be available to the development-promoting potential of a new object (Baker, 1993) or a selfobject (A. Ornstein, 1974) relationship. Interpretation is aimed at illuminating these fears so that the new object or selfobject transference can emerge.

It is in the context of this health-promoting relationship or transference that development of the libido, the ego, or the self can resume. For Kohut (1966, 1968, 1971; Kohut & Wolf, 1978), the thwarted developmentally appropriate yearnings of the warded-off nuclear self continue to be active. They reengage as the selfobject transference emerges. All of these ideas are based on an assumption that the seeds of growth are dormant within the mind and will resume growth under these new circumstances.

Tolpin (2002) organizes this distinction in terms of the forward and trailing edges of the transference. The task of the analyst is to recognize the crushed tendrils of the mobilizing selfobject transference (the forward edge) within the manifestly pathological presentation of the transference (the trailing edge). Focus on the pathological aspects closes off the health-promoting yearnings of the self. These healthy yearnings strive to resume growth and development by reengaging the developmentally appropriate needs that were warded off in the past and that reemerge within the selfobject transference. Recognition of these health-promoting yearnings within the transference facilitate their flowering and makes sense of the painful states when these yearnings are disappointed.

In their first session, Ella dismissed Mrs. Kaufman's overture and denied that she was afraid. She was not open to her analyst as a comforting figure and was not open to acknowledging her anxiety. By the end of the analysis, Mrs. Kaufman was a decidedly comforting figure for Ella, who was newly open to the soothing and protective functions of her analyst as a selfobject. As she assumed command of these functions, Ella developed the capacity to soothe herself.

For Bromberg (1996), the self is an illusion reliant on the integration of multiple split-off or dissociated self states. There is a tension, equilibrium, or both between stability and growth of the self. Change risks traumatic disruption of the feeling of selfhood, and reorganization risks disorganization, a loss of the integrative connections among the various self states. Fear of this traumatic disruption leads to resistance akin to Baker's (1993) and Ornstein's (1974) views that the analysand fears engagement with the new object or selfobject, anticipating repetition of the traumatic past. The manifestations of these fears are what Tolpin (2002) refers to as the trailing edge of the transference. The move toward growth and the capacity to access and process dissociated experiences, as Bromberg describes it, is the same capacity that Tolpin calls the forward edge of transference. For Bromberg, the paradox of psychoanalysis and of being human is the need to stay the same while changing.

Winnicott (1965) addresses the potential for forward movement when he says that the holding or facilitating environment provided by the analyst allows for a new beginning. Balint (1979) and Loewald (1960) state that transference interpretation provides an opportunity for new ways of relating and being.

In Fonagy and colleagues' (1993) mental-process model, their view of inhibited or underdeveloped mental processes assumes that the capacity of these inborn capabilities to resume development remains alive so that engagement with the mind of the analyst facilitates the reemergence of these processes. In their mental-representation model, insight allows connections that have been interfered with to resume.

Bollas (1979) defines *hope* as the anticipation of being transformed by an object. Each person has an existential rather than cognitive recollection of the intense affective experience of the early object that transformed the self. The drive for transformation persists, seeds future experience, and shapes the potential for new object relationships. He talks about genera, particular unconscious types of psychic organization of lived experience that result in creative new visions of life (Bollas, 1993).

THE INTERNAL NARRATIVE AND THE PSYCHOANALYTIC DIALOGUE

According to Baranger, Baranger, and Mom (1998), the repetition of traumatic experiences is in the service of an effort to heal the trauma. They see an internal, personal narrative as an essential aspect of the mind, and they state that trauma disrupts this internal dialogue. The repetition of a traumatic experience is a first attempt to historicize a mixture of real and mythic events. It fails because repetitive attraction to the traumatic event is a false historicization. The problem is not that this narration is a fantasy or unreal but that it is a closed system. Like an internally consistent paranoid delusion, the closed system allows no opportunity to expand the narrative and no opportunity to creatively integrate other possibilities.

The psychoanalytic situation leads to a change in the experience of temporality, where future, present, and the past dimensions interact dialectically. While the persistence of the past in the present is a source of distortion and repetition, the capacity of the analytic couple to sink into the states of mind where the boundaries or barriers among future, past, and present fade allows the closed system to open up and include a wider range of experience. Thus, psychoanalytic historicization has therapeutic potential. The trauma and its sequalae can be reworked and reintegrated.

Wilson and Weinstein (1996) explain that it is not possible to separate processes that promote access to the ZPD from transference repetitions. New experience emerges in the context of prior experience and existing internal structures. New linguistic capabilities emerge from the old when immersed in the internalization community, and repetition is the essential framework from which learning emerges. It is the dialogic interaction between analyst and analysand within the ZPD that facilitates growth of psychological structure in contrast to unmanageable distress or a retreat to the old, repetitive coping strategies.

For Wilson and Weinstein (1996), words and language are the fundamental units of psychological change. Through language, the mother provides a developmental zone within which the child develops new ways to apprehend the world, and expansion of the child's mind is inextricably intertwined with language. In the analytic situation, words and meanings are shared by analyst and analysand in a personal and unique way. They share a private speech community. As the analysand assumes ownership of these shared meanings in her own particular way, the previously "co-owned words are embellished intrapsychically" and "made into psychic structure" (194).

People live within a personal narrative, a system of myths or unconscious fantasies that shape and are shaped by experience. Psychoanalysis facilitates change to the extent that it frees up the myth-making capacity to be more creative. Then, myths and unconscious fantasies can be reshaped, rewritten, and transformed, and they become more flexible. When insight ties this myth-making capacity to reality, it can be elucidating, but premature introduction of such insights can interfere with the creative expression of fantasy and can be restrictive. When myth-making capacity, mentalization, insightfulness, and imagination are enhanced, they expand so that the representational world can more flexibly include fantasy and reality in its narrative. Children express this internal narrative through play.

Over and over again, Ella played that Mrs. Kaufman was the good mother who took the abandoned child into her home. Mrs. Kaufman had to say that she loved this little girl and show that she loved her unconditionally. Ella was driven to repeat this narrative in an effort to have an experience that was different from the loss of her biological mother and different from her feeling that her adoptive mother rejected her as the devil child. There was potential for this play to be endlessly repetitive, and Mrs. Kaufman deeply felt the intensity of Ella's lonely despair. Yet, Ella's desperation gradually lessened. In later play, she moved further and further from her analyst and felt in control of the return. New play themes emerged as the analysis progressed, including oedipal stories like Rapunzel.

Isabel started with a narrative about the teacher who quizzed the little boy about penises in a demeaning way. This story reflected her internal models, at the time, of child and adult relationships. Dr. Huddleston was a participant in these play-acted narratives and facilitated their transformation. Teaching and being taught were played out in many ways during the analytic work, and we can follow the changes in Isabel's model of the adult-teacher and child-student relationship. Later in the analysis, the teacher, the adult in authority, firmly though kindly engaged the sexually curious chipmunks and talked to them about these matters. At the end of the analysis, the teacher, played by Isabel, helped the girl, portrayed by Dr. Huddleston, find her way at the new school.

Mitchell (1996), from the relational perspective, describes how transference can collapse the creative myth-making potential shared by analyst and analysand. When the analysand experiences the analyst's intervention as another edition of the transference expectation, they are entangled in a knot that he refers to as bootstrapping. Pointing out an instance when a patient who is prone to criticize herself has just retreated from her "unreasonable feelings" might lead her to get more discouraged and feel criticized that she continues to respond in this "unreasonable way." Given one's necessary presence within one's own characteristic way of perceiving and experiencing, how does a person pick herself up by her own bootstraps in order to extricate herself? Together the analyst and analysand must do something new in order to free themselves from this repetition. This newness is, for Mitchell, the essence of the therapeutic action of psychoanalysis.

Bollas (1993) sees the process in which the analyst and analysand lose and then find each other as the essence of the therapeutic encounter. It is *because* we do not comprehend one another that we are *free* to reinvent one another. When we are free to misperceive, the potential to reengage in an act of creativity arises as we strive to re-find one another. Out of this gap between two human beings emerges unconscious mental life. In this space of intersubjective play, the creativity of individual psychic reality is engaged, and the two individuals are brought *closer together*. Therefore, the immersion in the moment-to-moment interpretation of one another is creative, reinventing, elucidating, and reorienting.

A moment of conflict, uncertainty, or disruption is both an opportunity for repetition and an opportunity for resolution and structural change. The analyst's response to such moments, according to Wilson and Weinstein (1996), will either allow access to a two-person internalization community or "position the analyst inside the conflict, unable to alter it" (188). When the analyst is positioned inside the conflict, the narrative has collapsed, and Mitchell's (1996) bootstrapping is in ascendance. When the analyst is in the therapeutic neighborhood (Busch, 1993) or the ZPD, Bollas's (1993) moment of losing one another has the creative potential to reinvent, elucidate, and reorient.

For Bollas (1993), most of the work of psychoanalysis occurs unconsciously, both for the analysand and the analyst. The aim of the analytic process is to facilitate this unconscious work and not to interfere with it. Bollas contrasts a "Theory of Repression" to a "Theory of Reception." Traumatic experience is repressed, and repressed contents denude the self of representational freedom, bind unwanted ideas, and feel dangerous. In the theory of repression, the analysand tries to avoid the censoring or persecutory judgment of consciousness, while the analyst tactfully aims to release such contents into a bearable consciousness.

Receptive unconscious activity, in contrast to repressive activity, aims to allow unconscious development without the intrusive effect of consciousness. The analysand withdraws ideas, feelings, or memories from narrative representation and consciousness in order to work on them from within. Premature conscious expression or premature conscious interpretation interferes with or forecloses deep unconscious work. While primary-process modes of thought can serve defense, from this perspective the ego is not functioning defensively in order to disguise. It is drawing on primary-process ways of thinking—displacement, substitution, symbolization, and condensation—in order to work on psychic experience from within as creative expressions and as part of what Bollas (1993) calls the "Jouissance of Representation" (84). The importance of unconscious processing is revisited in chapter 10, when I discuss the therapeutic significance of children's play.

Winnicott (1953) refers to the transitional object, transitional phase, and transitional space. The capacities of the child, which emerge as she begins to assume command of and manipulate the powers of the facilitating environment, allow for play, imagination, and metaphor. This capacity for illusion, for playing with reality, is an enormous accomplishment. The mother's support, of course, is still required as the child imagines her transitional object or ventures into the transitional space. By not asking if the play or the stuffed animal is real, the parent or analyst helps to sustain the illusion and allows the child to take pleasure in her new capacities. Failing to facilitate this space or prematurely confronting the child with reality leads to a collapse of this transitional space. Premature interpretation can similarly close off the unfolding analytic process.

PSYCHOANALYTIC TECHNIQUE

When Freud (1913/1953–1974l) explains the rule of free association, he uses an analogy. The analysand should look into his mind, as if he is looking out the window on a moving train, and describe as best he can what he sees.

Anton Kris (1982), in his book *Free Association*, sees attention to the stream of associations as essential to the therapeutic task of psychoanalysis. Facilitating and freeing up the capacity for associating frees up the mind. One association follows another; each association has implications for and impact on what follows. Thoughts facilitate or interfere with other thoughts.

Modern ego psychologists, modern Kleinians, and the generations of self psychologists after Kohut all listen to the stream of consciousness in order to get to know the analysand's mind, even though they may understand what they are doing in different ways. Evelyn Schwaber (1983) listens to her patients as they respond to her interpretations—not asking if she is right or wrong but listening for the patient's experience of her interpretation. This, for her, is the moment-to-moment focus of the lens of conscious insight. Betty Joseph, from a Kleinian perspective, thinks about the patient's interpretation of an interpretation in this way: "movement and change is an essential aspect of transference—so that no interpretation can be seen as a pure interpretation or explanation but must resonate in the patient in a way which is specific to him and his way of functioning; that the level at which a patient is functioning at any given moment and the nature of his anxieties can best be gauged by trying to be aware of how the transference is actively being used" (Joseph, 1985, 447). This is also where Mitchell's (1996) bootstrapping comes alive. When the analyst's interpretation of the transference is experienced as an intervention that is another instance of the transference (e.g., the patient feels criticized when the analyst notes that she felt criticized by his previous interpretation), what might feel like a quagmire can potentially be attended to in a new way.

Gray (1994) and Busch (1999) listen to the defensive shifts and to the ebb and flow of the patient's associations to the prior moments. Gray leans toward noting the shift, asking the patient to consider what anxiety had precipitated the change. Busch, like Schwaber (1983), is more apt to listen to the following associations in order help the patient understand what has been occurring in her mind. Busch pays careful attention to the patient's words and the patient's access to the meanings of her own words and thoughts, and he offers interpretations in which he explains how those thoughts and words led to his conclusion. He describes this technique as staying "in the neighborhood." Busch's neighborhood is Wilson and Weinstein's (1996) zone of proximal development.

For Wilson and Weinstein (1996), the concept of free association gives way to the concept of dialogue; "rather than one person free associating and two people examining the thematic yield, two people are speaking according to conventional pragmatic rules of discourse" (190). Within the zone of proximal development, an internalization community is established that allows a coconstructed dialogue to be shared, reworked, and reowned as new intrapsychic structure.

Our theories of psychoanalytic technique and our theories of the working of the mind inform the ways in which we attempt to enter the internal dialogue, fantasy systems, myths, narratives, and metaphors of our patients. The earlier description of free association suggests a linear sequence, the train moving past the sights on the landscape or a stream of consciousness. The narrative expressed in the play of children is more dreamlike than linear. This quality of child's play provides the analyst with remarkable ways to enter the child's inner world and brings her mind alive in the consulting room. In chapter 10, I look closely at the phenomenon of play and the play-like and dreamlike qualities of adult analysis and their roles in the therapeutic engagement.

Chapter Ten

The Play Space

Edward I. Kohn

From the earliest days of child psychoanalysis, analysts have contended with the differences between the minds of children and adults. For Melanie Klein (1975), this was an opportunity to plunge to the depths, as she believed that the earliest ways of thinking were accessible in the unconscious fantasies of children. Anna Freud (1945) and others waded in, skeptical of the deep interpretations of the Kleinians and less certain, early on, that the immature mind of the child was accessible to psychoanalysis in the way it worked with adults. Anna Freud noted that the tool of free association was not available in work with children. Play and action are their modes of operation. Play therapy was initially seen by some as a necessary though less than optimal compromise that would enable the child analyst to work therapeutically with children. This would substitute for verbal communication in the effort to understand the nature of the child's developmentally stagnating conflicts. These early analysts opened the window to the fascinating world of the child's ways of being, thinking, and communicating and the power of the therapeutic endeavor with children and adolescents.

Play can serve a protective and defensive function, as seen in Bollas's (1993) repressive model of the mind. Unconscious wishes might be expressed in displaced or symbolic form during play when they are intolerable or unacceptable to awareness. These protective and defensive stances can close off satisfaction within old pathways to objects and prevent the potential transformations that occur when pathways are open to new objects.

Play can, as well, be seen as the effort (Neubauer, 1994) to resolve normal or abnormal conflicts, restrained drive expressions, or undue environmental or superego influences. Freud (1920/1953–1974a) describes the little boy who repeatedly tossed the spool and drew it back as he contended with the absence of his mother. This activity seemed to allow him to gain mastery of feelings he passively endured.

Many writers in child psychoanalysis describe how play is much more than defense or repetition. Play potentiates transformation as it integrates past and current experience and allows the child to try out new possibilities. The play world is a serious activity (Solnit, 1998) *because* it is not real. The illusion that an activity does not have real consequences makes a child's play especially important. The gigantic realities of the world that loom over the small child can be externalized, played with, and reshaped. Myths and fairy tales of giants and stories about superheroes all reflect the universal experience of humans that as children we live in a world of giants and yearn to be powerful ourselves. Freed from the actual consequences of her activity, the child can be fully invested in the elaboration of imagination and fantasy. The child's natural immersion in play, with its closer access to primary-process thinking and lessened attunement to reality, achieves a natural suspension of disbelief that allows astounding access into unconscious fantasy but also complicates the analytic endeavor. How do you have a treatment alliance with a child? How do you, when do you, or should you bring reality to bear on these symbolic expressions?

STAYING WITHIN THE PLAY

The child plays out inner dramas, longings, attitudes, motives, and characteristics of impaired development (Cohen & Solnit, 1993). The analyst, by engaging with the child in this play, can have a development-promoting impact. Yet this may involve a minimum of conscious verbalization or interpretation (Mayes & Cohen, 1993a). Sugarman (2003b) puts it in terms of Fonagy and Target's (1998) mentalization:

> By staying within the play with our young patients, we help them to integrate the psychic equivalence and pretend modes, an integration necessary for full mentalization to occur. Our interventions allow the child to see his or her fantasies or ideas represented in our minds, to reintroject those representations, and to make them his or her own. Frightening ideas can be talked through and thought about in the play, gradually becoming recognized as inner phenomena, not real. (346)

So much more at home in the world of make-believe, the language of play and fantasy influences the child. By engaging in the play and communicating through the language of play metaphor, the analyst becomes part of the unconscious work described by Bollas (1993).

As Winnicott (1953) suggests that the parent not ask the child whether a transitional object is real, the analyst accepts the play, imagines himself into it, and need not and should not prematurely emerge from the play space and point out the reality determinants of the play. This, rather than elucidating, is likely to shut down the play space, limiting the poignant communication of the child's play-poetry and interfering with the unconscious work of transformation.

Dahl (1993, 1996) explains that play allows the child to represent thoughts, wishes, and fears in a far more complex fashion than would be possible if the child were solely to rely on her verbal ability. Imaginative play allows the child to engage with different aspects of her self and to try out varied balances among fantasies. The language of play, with its greater ability to express the complexity of the inner world, is a very important factor as we discuss the ways in which psychoanalysis facilitates structural change.

Within the analyst's creative participation in the child's play, communication with the child is no longer limited to direct interpretation. Toys, figures, or characters within play can give voice to the analyst's understanding. The analyst can make comments about the characters. Each individual character may put into words another aspect of a child's feeling state or point of view. Ambivalence, trivalence, and more can be engaged, allowing the complexity of experiences to emerge. Defensive structures and movement within the play can be subtly addressed. Degrees of distance or closeness between patient and analyst can be recognized and titrated: "When you hide under my desk, you are cozy and safe. No one could find or no one could hurt Batman in the Batcave." The analyst can address the unreality of play without fully leaving the play: "These stories are so cool. You can blow up a bomb, and no one is really hurt. If the monster were really here, it would be scary, but you can make him fight the monster in the story." The play can allow the analyst to ignore the impinging reality of the child: "Wow! Your muscle is so big. You are really strong!" in lieu of saying "You wish so much that you could be strong like your father." The analyst might play hide and seek, expressing dismay at being unable to find the child until she gleefully pops out of her hiding place.

The analyst can influence the child's object world, not only by her presence as a real object in the child's life or as an interpreter of the child's experience, but also by enacting new object relationships through the play. When the child describes the fearful bear cub that is lost in the dark woods, the analyst might introduce the park ranger who searches in the woods with her flashlight in order to help the bear cub find her way.

Despite the important recognition that play is not real and does not have real consequences, communication in the play metaphor feels compelling to the child and enables the analyst to work at a depth that would likely be defended against when addressed explicitly. If we believe that unconscious fantasy is essential in shaping an individual's experience of and relationship with reality, then the opportunity to influence a child's unconscious fantasy—even when this is never consciously addressed—can alter psychic structure and psychopathology.

Sugarman (2003b) provides an example of interpretation within the play in his work with a 3-year-old girl. He explains that staying within the metaphor of play with a young child is similar to Busch's (1993) idea about making interpretations within the neighborhood. While Busch refers to close attention to the thoughts expressed by the analysand, helping him to understand how you arrived at your interpretation, the young child's neighborhood has more to do with the structure of her mind. She comfortably lives in the realm of play.

The child analyst's comments and interpretations are manifestly about the play, but the analyst maintains in his mind the mind of the child and the analytic situation. This analytic technique is different from the traditional intervention that directly refers to the patient in that the focus is displaced to the characters and events within the play. The child is freer to explore and play with the issue at hand when she doesn't have to fully own it.

THE THEORY OF TECHNIQUE EMBEDDED WITHIN THE WORK WITHIN THE PLAY

Despite this very significant difference in technique, the child analyst carries his familiar theory of technique and theory of mind into the play space. Sugarman (2003b), for example, notes the importance of interpreting defense before impulse. This applies both to adults and to children. Analysts are generally familiar with the problems associated with efforts to bypass resistances. Under this circumstance, analysands must mobilize willpower to overcome their reluctance, while appreciation of the reasons that an impulse, a thought, or a feeling are to be avoided contributes to a sense that discussion of the warded-off content is less ominous than it had seemed. Understanding patterns of resistance and avoidance is an important part of the analytic work in and of itself, not solely to access warded-off content. Sugarman states that interpretation of defense before impulse is even more important with children than it is with adults. He explains that children are apt to hear the interpretation of impulse as permission to act (Sugarman, 2003b). Carrying out the action can be frightening to the child and distressing to the analyst. Interpretation of defense, then, is not solely designed to more easily access the impulse but to address it in a way that heightens the child's capacity for self-control.

In Sugarman's (2003b) vignette, a 3-year-old girl pretended that her pen tore up a magazine. He responded, "I told the pen (not the girl) that I thought sometimes it felt it was very bad and tried to get me to be the boss of its tearing feelings so that it did not feel so bad about itself." The young girl stopped tearing the magazine and threw a puppet into the closet, scolding it for being bad. Sugarman saw this as evidence of the validity of his interpretation. He said, "Maybe the puppet wanted us to help her to be the boss of her mean feelings so that she did not have to feel so bad about herself." The girl agreed, elaborating the need for the puppet to be the boss of its mean feelings.

Sugarman's (2003b) technique in this session was informed by his understanding of the structural theory. He pointed to a conflict with her superego when he said that the puppet struggled with feeling bad about itself. He approached the moment when the pen ripped the magazine with a "superego wish" in mind and inferred that the girl wanted help controlling her impulse. Therefore, she felt relieved to have support managing her tearing impulse, stopped the aggressive action, and scolded the misbehaving puppet.

It is also possible to infer that she responded to his interpretation as a superego prohibition and criticism. From this perspective, she stopped the bad behavior in response to the prohibition. She might have heard his interpretation as an angry rebuke and that he wanted to banish her or get rid of her angry feelings. When she threw the bad puppet into the closet, she may have been joining him in a critical and punitive attitude toward her impulse and her action. She also may have been angry with him and wanted to throw him into the closet.

Their further conversation led to her agreement that the puppet needed help in order to be the boss of her mean feelings. The data of this moment remains consistent with Sugarman's (2003b) hypothesis. Yet, the same data could be interpreted as compliance, identification with the aggressor, or a wish to please and be liked by Dr. Sugarman, the supportive restraining figure, whether she was looking for that kind of help when she initially tore the magazine or not.

In the multiply determined depths of the mind—with its reverberations of meanings expressed in the child's play, the complex and rich ambiguities of metaphor, and the symbols, displacements, and condensations of dreams or compromise formations—it is not likely that we can reduce our understanding to one meaning or the other. It is a realm of relative uncertainty and multiple possibilities. This complicates our endeavor in the displaced world of play as we struggle to understand what is happening, how we choose to intervene, and how we make sense of the consequences of our interventions. This multiplicity of meaning also has the potential to enhance our efforts, whether our understanding is precisely correct or not. The child makes her own sense of the intervention, and the play goes on. Whether we can determine which formulation was the *truth*, or whether we can assess the degree to which each dynamic contributed to the momentary equilibrium in Sugarman's (2003b) vignette, his interpretation moved the treatment process along. The little girl agreed that the puppet needed help learning to be the boss of its feelings. It appears that she was then engaged with Dr. Sugarman as a developmental object, learning to take pleasure in the mastery of her feelings and impulses.

THE RICHNESS AND COMPLEXITY OF PLAY METAPHOR

Working within the displacement of play involves thinking metaphorically. When the analyst draws a picture of a tired horse who is struggling to pull a heavy cart up a hill, she is thinking of the child who feels so burdened by the difficulties in his life. Use of play metaphor, or for that matter use of any metaphor, as a mode of communication is complicated because it is more ambiguous and more open to interpretation than secondary-process language. The analyst is likely to have a conscious idea of what he intends to communicate with the metaphor, but its ambiguity makes it more open to varied interpretations. While attending to the analytic process, when an analyst intervenes in the language of the unconscious, we must be open to what the analyst consciously intends, what he unconsciously communicates, how the analysand interprets the communication, and what the analysand's metaphors say about their communication. Bollas (1993) talks about the creative potential of the moments when analyst and analysand miss each other and the ways in which grappling with this uncertainty bring them closer together. When we move into the play of a child and live within the metaphors of her mind, we have entered the complex uncertainty of her unconscious. While this engagement is demanding of the analyst, it is the essential process of creative growth.

THE THERAPEUTIC PLAY SPACE FOR THE CHILD
AND THE ADULT

Freud (1914/1953–1974m), in the technique papers, refers to the transference as a playground, suggesting that the analytic situation allows the emergence of perceptions without the usual requirements of adherence to external reality. Free association, in the context of the nonjudgmental analytic attitude of abstinence and analysis of resistance, allows inner reality to emerge into the analytic play space without the usual attention to reality considerations. The "as if" quality of the adult analytic situation approximates the play state of the child. Approaching this childlike state of mind requires substantial work and resistance analysis on the part of the analyst and analysand. This is not a natural state of mind for the adult. Much has changed in the adult since childhood. Adults have left the imaginative play stage far behind (Dahl, 1996). The ego has become more complex; character structure maintains a firmly established relationship between id and ego; and fantasies of early childhood have been substantially layered, reworked, and reorganized by later experience.

Despite the adult's more entrenched psychic structure, as analysis frees up the creative and symbolic nature of displaced communication, associations are more revealing of the adult's inner world, as the child's play is revealing of her psychic reality. Dahl's (1996) statement about the ways in which play communicates experience with greater complexity than secondary-process verbalization also applies to the adult. The metaphor communicates richness, subtlety, depth, and complexity, in part because it is at a safer distance. The analysand can access aspects of her experience that are consciously restricted. The metaphor is also more playful, more expressive, and richer in its multiplicity of meaning, which can make secondary-process verbiage seem clunky by comparison.

Play, displacement, and transference are all ways to get what is inside to the outside. Welcoming the capacity of displacement to externalize the inner world of a child or adult enables the analysand's psychic reality to fill the room, allowing patient and analyst to be players on the stage of this inner drama. When we focus primarily or exclusively on displacement as a defense, we can be more restricted in our capacity to bring the illusion alive. Transference is, on the one hand, a displacement from awareness of internal experience and a resistance to awareness. Yet, work with transference and the access it provides to the unconscious is also the sine qua non of analytic work. Similarly, exclusive focus on the analysand's external references or a child's play as defensive movement away from the transference can be restrictive. Sometimes, rather than listen to discussion of the day-to-day world outside of the analytic hour as displacement from the transference, it is preferable to see both the transference and the other displacements as samplings of the internal world worthy of exploration in the language unconsciously communicated by the analysand.

Both free association and play are the engagement of a creative process in the transitional space—the playground of Freud's (1914/1953–1974m) transference. The analysand unconsciously fills her narrative with metaphors that communicate her internal state and the perceived relationship with the listener. The analytic situation is well served when the subject feels free to send her latent unconscious ideas and feelings to the other, and the other will reply in a like language. Bollas (1993) describes how analyst and analysand search for a common language rooted in the patient's unconscious ways of thinking in order to find narratives and metaphors that convey subjective experience. To know is not simply to understand but to play and be played by the other's idiom. Premature conversion of the subject's unconscious communication to conscious secondary-process conversation, rather than leading to evocative understanding, leads to ever more elusive displacement. In his evocative way, Bollas looks inside Tolpin's (2002) leading edge of the transference.

TRANSFERENCE

When the playground of the transference neurosis is achieved, an adult comes as close to the child's playful state of mind as possible. Neubauer (1994) notes that we can think of transference as displacement onto the analyst of patterns of early relationships, including infantile wishes, hopes, and defenses, in a way that is similar to our view that a child's play is shaped by displacement. Kern (1987) compares the transference neurosis to the dream work. A state of mind is achieved that is comparable to that of sleep and dreaming. In his paper "Transference Neurosis as a Waking Dream," he describes how the analyst or analytic situation serves as the day residue for dream formation. Primary-process mechanisms of the unconscious greatly influence construction of the dream and of the transference neurosis. Both patient and analyst are immersed in the unconscious structure of the patient. Like the play of a child, the analysand's mind fills the room, and the analytic pair lives inside this space. This is as close as we get with the adult to the state where the analyst enters the child's play world. A child's play is the stage that represents her mind, allowing us to enter this stage and her mind. When the transference neurosis is a waking dream, we are comparably immersed with the adult patient in her mind.

While transference neurosis, like play, is on the one hand a defensive displacement of internal experience, it, like play, also serves to facilitate assimilation (Solnit, 1987) of the past in an effort to find new solutions to old conflicts so that they can be integrated into the fabric of a coherent personality. As Baranger, Baranger, and Mom (1988) point out, despite the ways in which it perpetuates a closed system, repetition presents an opportunity to undo passive traumatic experience, opens the system to a new historicization, and serves transformation.

Displacement and its related capacity to think in metaphor is more than one defense or one mode of functioning among many. It represents a fundamental quality of the mind. The capacity to think symbolically is essentially human and distinguishes us from the other animals. It allows us to live beyond while we live within the concrete realities of our physical existence. It allows us to know ourselves while it makes us opaque to ourselves. It expands our experience while it makes us illogical, neurotic, or crazy.

We can broaden the view of metaphor from a particular symbolic image to a narrative and on to a complex myth. In human culture we live within a network of myths. These stories reflect our history, our present, the qualities of our minds, and our states of experience. They shape our experience. Individuals similarly live amid a network of personal myths or unconscious fantasies that are shaped by past experience and internal states, past and present. They, in turn, shape our sense of our past, our present, and our future.

These unconscious fantasy myths can range from cultural or religious myths to biographical histories to narratives (Kris, 1956a, 1956b) to vignettes or to single metaphors. These fantasy structures are lenses that engage and shape all experience. In analysis we identify, work with, and articulate these characteristic lenses and the interpretations they lend to varied experience. This repetitive feedback of experience through metaphor leads to the fractal-like layers of the phenomenon we see as transference. In analytic work we bring these myths, fantasies, and metaphors alive. Analyst and analysand become players within the expanding metaphor. Psychic change is the re-shaping of these metaphors.

Chapter Eleven

Relationship, Action, and Words

Edward I. Kohn

With so much happening between adult and child during analysis, it gets very complicated to judge precisely what we are doing, how it affects the child, and what the therapeutic implications of our interactions are. In this chapter, as I discuss the analyses of Ella and Isabel, I look closely at the ways in which the young analysands and their analysts interacted, including interventions made by the analysts, with an eye toward unpacking these interactions and examining the therapeutic and change-promoting aspects of psychoanalysis.

While the child's mind is less developed than the adult's (with her propensity to action, closeness to primary process, relative lack of observing ego, and different modes of communication), which can create confusion and uncertainty, there are ways in which the less fettered mind of the child can help us to see psychological phenomena with freshness and new clarity. While the immediacy of a child's developmental needs can knock us off balance, it also demonstrates the power and influence of the analytic relationship. This provides an opportunity to delve into the ways in which the relationship, the varieties of interplay between analyst and analysand, and the things they talk about come together and facilitate the unfolding and transformation of the child's mind.

In order to comprehend the complexity and multiplicity of the mind and the psychoanalytic process, we create categories or dichotomies: one-person versus two-person psychologies, relationship versus interpretation and insight, container versus contained, action versus language, conscious versus unconscious, self versus other, character versus symptom, or process versus content. When we look more closely at these constructs, it gets complicated, and the distinctions or lines between the dichotomies get fuzzy. It helps to consider process and content. We attend to the manifest content of a patient's associations, and we infer allusions to the analytic process. Form and content, form and function, are inextricably related. When we interpret preconscious allusions to the process, we facilitate making process into content. When we interpret the transference, we provide insight into the relationship, and we make the container of the relationship a content of our conversation and interactions. The envelope shapes the content of the letter, and the letter shapes the envelope.

Traditionally, verbal insight has been considered the change-promoting agent of psychoanalysis, in contrast to the influence of the relationship. Early in the history of psychoanalysis, the analyst's influence was considered a potential contaminant. With the shift from a one-person paradigm to a two-person paradigm, the distinction between words and the relationship can no longer be clearly made. Words are a medium of exchange between two people. Words influence the relationship and are vessels that carry aspects of the relationship. Our effort to draw a clear distinction between a one-person paradigm and a two-person paradigm is also problematic. There are two people in the room with two minds. Our understanding will be well served if we consider them as individual entities who interact, but like electrons, they also have wave functions in which we cannot clearly identify the location or behavior of either particle. A wave or field at times better explains the observable data. Despite the paradox, it is both rather than either/or.

Classically, there is a dichotomy between action and words. Transference is a resistance to the extent that it is a reliving rather than remembering. Acting out is a defense against insight. We now see that there is a continuum from action to words or symbols. Actions have meaning, and words are actions. In this chapter, I explore a continuum from actions to words to shed light on the interaction between insight and relationship. I identify positions along that continuum, recognizing that those positions are not distinct points. The distinction between action and symbolic communication is always more or less rather than either/or. Actions are embedded with meaning, and words have effects. A slam of the door might be a rage-filled act or an unanticipated burst of energy. Words at one moment might be bullets and at another moment cups of nectar. When we increase the magnification of our microscope and look deeply into any point along the continuum, we have to reassess our understanding of the more-or-less-ness of either symbols or actions.

THE CONTINUUM FROM ACTION TO SYMBOLIC THINKING AND WORDS

Gil Katz (2014) describes the ubiquity of enactment in adult psychoanalysis as the "enacted dimension of psychoanalysis." The more-dramatic action sequences that analyst and patient play out and later recognize as enactments are important to process, but they are not the only events that are enactments. All kinds of enactments go on between patient and analyst in subtler and less dramatic ways all the time. Action can be a communication or expression of meaning, and transference is a kind of enactment. Lyons-Ruth (1999) explains that implicit or procedural ways of knowing are fundamental to the minds of children and are pathways to knowing and communicating that are distinct from representational communication. The knowing is embedded in the action. By tracing the continuum from action to words, we have a compass that can help to orient ourselves when we look within the mind. Attention to the intermingling of action, enactment, fantasy, play, symbolic communication, and words helps us to understand the workings of Isabel's and Ella's minds, how their minds shaped and were shaped by the analytic process, and how their relationships with their analysts influenced their representational worlds.

Freud (1911/1953–1974e) sees thinking as experimental action. In "Formulations on the Two Principles of Mental Functioning," he describes his vision of the role of the mental apparatus in inhibiting discharge and facilitating a more complex and less immediate way of interacting with the world:

> Restraint upon motor discharge (upon action), which then became necessary, was provided by means of the process of thinking, which was developed from the presentation of ideas. Thinking was endowed with characteristics which made it possible for the mental apparatus to tolerate an increased tension of stimulus while the process of discharge was postponed. It is essentially an experimental kind of acting, accompanied by displacement of relatively small quantities of cathexis together with less expenditure (discharge) of them. For this purpose, the conversion of freely displaceable cathexes into "bound" cathexes was necessary, and this was brought about by means of raising the level of the whole cathectic process. It is probable that thinking was originally unconscious, in so far as it went beyond mere ideational presentations and was directed to the relations between impressions of objects, and that it did not acquire further qualities, perceptible to consciousness, until it became bound to verbal residues. (221)

Ekstein and Friedman's (1957) paper "The Function of Acting Out, Play Action, and Play Acting in the Psychotherapeutic Process" is an effort to trace a developmental line from action to thought. They explain that more disturbed children have difficulty engaging in play. Action often disrupts the play space:

> The preverbal period of personality development, in which motility and motor development are dominant, usually takes place in a symbiotic relationship. The mother is used as the auxiliary ego which not only gratifies and prohibits, but also thinks for the infant who, in a certain sense is capable of a kind of "thought" as expressed through impulsive action whenever need arises. As the

psychic apparatus develops, modes of problem solving grow richer, and impulsive action is supplemented by a range of modes of functioning including play action. (582)

Ekstein and Friedman chart a developmental line that proceeds along an axis of action, play action, fantasy, and play-acting (or action fantasy) on to delay and adaptive direction. They describe play action as a kind of delayed action "that combines the quasi-gratification of play with an attempt at resolution of conflict" (582). This reflects the child's early capacity to forgo immediate gratification, though it remains imbued with primary-process thinking. The authors relate play action to acting out, an unconscious attempt to resolve an unconscious conflict of the past. Play action occurs when play is interrupted and, "rather than being replaced by silence or by the change of topics, tends to erupt into acting out" (Eckstein & Friedman, 1967, 580). They use the metaphor of the stage and compare play-acting to an actor who is driven to live out his performance off the stage.

Fantasy for Ekstein and Friedman (1957) is a higher form of play, in that the need for action is given up. The capacity for fantasy allows substitution of action by thought that includes primary- and secondary-process functioning. They describe play-acting in contrast to play action as a first attempt to master the future by role taking. This involves thought, reality testing, and preconscious trial solutions.

ACTION, PLAY ACTION, PLAY-ACTING, PLAY IN THE MICROCOSM, SYMBOLS, AND WORDS

In this chapter, I draw on Ekstein and Friedman's (1957) thinking as I describe a path from action to representational thinking while also observing the intermingling of the two. My axis includes action, play action, play-acting, play in the microcosm, symbols, and words. I also discuss play interruption, a phenomenon that can occur anywhere along this continuum, whose meaning and mode of presentation varies according to the point at which the interruption occurs. Play interruptions include Ella's violence when she tried to punch and kick Mrs. Kaufman; the urgency of Isabel running to the bathroom to poop; Ella's retreat behind the couch when the biting bears growled; and more subtle shifts, like Isabel turning from one activity to the books on Dr. Huddleston's shelves.

Paying attention, as well, to action that is associated with verbal communication provides us with an elucidating perspective from which to examine the intermingling of action and symbolic thought at all points along this continuum. Action associated with verbal communication includes dancing while singing a song, shouting murderous intent while squashing a clay figure, discussing school during a game of chess, snuggling while talking, hiding in the closet while writing a secret note, and so on. This gives us another instrument to bring into focus the more-or-less-ness of action and symbolic communication at any point along the continuum.

When I refer to play in the microcosm, I am talking about play activity that is predominantly portrayed on a small stage, the sphere of toys, art supplies, and so on. Even when we enter this small stage of the play microcosm, we again look into the coexistence of symbolism, action, and words. There is still plenty of action in the microcosm, though the smallness of the stage allows attention to more subtle kinds of action and meaning. Pretend play in which the child, her playmate, or both physically enact roles on the full-sized stage is what I mean by play-acting. Play-*acting* requires the capacity for fantasy, but it occurs on a larger stage than play in the microcosm, one that is more closely tied to action. Play *action* I see as a more action-based form of play-*acting*. The game of peekaboo and the child who continually throws her spoon on the floor and waits for her mother to retrieve it are examples of play action, while a tea party is an example of play-acting. In this chapter, I discuss a vignette in which Isabel and Dr. Huddleston's interactions move from action through play action and play-acting into the realm of words.

ACTION

Action as a category is not one dimensionless point on the continuum, and it is not a monolithic phenomenon. Many different behaviors can be described as actions. The intensity of or the energy expelled in action and the degree to which an action is modulated or regulated varies. Different actions have different aims. Actions may be more or less organized, more or less goal directed, more or less adaptive, more or less enthusiastic, or more or less destructive. Different actions have different qualities. The precipitants or driving forces leading to action may be different in kind and degree. Both Ella and Isabel were action oriented. Isabel jumped on the couch, pushed for "uppies," and squished Dr. Huddleston between the doors. She took off her pants, showed her bottom, watered the flower, and told stories. Ella threw things around the room, tried to crawl between Mrs. Kaufman's legs, hid behind the couch, and read stories. In this chapter, we place ourselves in the minds of the girls as I examine their behaviors and place their actions on the continuum from action toward words. How do a specific behavior and its place on the continuum help us understand the mind of the child, and what does our understanding of her mind tell us about the behavior?

When we move into the realm of words, I discuss the meanings conveyed by words and the meanings of conveying words. Words are not only symbols, they are also actions. I go on to examine the content of verbal communications and consider the impact of verbal interpretations: interpretation of defense, attention to affect and the state of the self, and the significance of the specificity of interpretations. These discussions about the continuum from action to words provide an instrument that enables us to consider the therapeutic action of psychoanalysis and the interplay among language, action, and relationships.

ACTION ASSOCIATED WITH FRAGMENTATION

A toddler's tantrum—when she throws herself on the floor, flails her arms and legs about, and cries with rage and desperation—is a particular kind of action. It is different than the punch to a mother's thigh when she refuses to pick up her child. In both kinds of action, the child is angry. In the former, her rage is much less modulated, and her actions lack coordination. While the angry child who punches her mother in response to frustration is acting impulsively, she has more control of her body than the child immersed in a tantrum. Her aim and her intent are clearer and more purposeful. I suggest that the tantrum is a manifestation of a self that is in the neighborhood of fragmentation. The disorganization of the child's behavior reflects the disorganization of her psyche.

Ella was desperately insistent that the toys in the dollhouse remain in place. When she felt that she could not maintain this control over her world, she frantically threw the toys about. I infer that her need to keep the toys in exactly the right place reflected the fragility of the cohesion of her self. Her vulnerable psychic theater teetered on the edge of collapse. Any movement would tip it over. Functioning in psychic-equivalence mode, the movement of the toys and her inability to fully control them did exactly that. Her throwing of the toys was a manifestation of fragmentation. When she tried to crawl between Mrs. Kaufman's legs, her capacity to symbolize the wish to return to mother's inner space had substantially failed. She concretely tried to do so.

In order to think about Ella's inner world and the state of her self at that moment, I return to the understanding of fragmentation I put forth in chapters 6 and 8. When the synthetic function of the ego, cohesiveness of the self, or reliability of the representational world has failed, the "centre cannot hold" (Yeats, 1921, 184–185). The gravitational force that keeps the planets of the mind in coherent orbits is not sufficient to keep them from turning into Yeats's "ever widening gyre" (184–185), and they fly off into space. When the self falls apart, meaningful communication between the falcon and the falconer is less available, and the ability of the parent or analyst to serve the function of tethering the child's emotions within a manageable orbit is further undermined. This vicious cycle then leads to the "ever widening gyre"

(184–185). Without a coherent center or organizational structure, unmodulated impulses are unleashed. An enduring continuity of the illusion of self and a sense of hope seem unavailable.

If we adhere to a dichotomy between two states, fragmentation and cohesion of the self, we might conclude that there is a definable moment when the tipping point has been reached, and the emotional state we infer from the verse in Yeats's poem and from Ella's behavior is the inevitable and paradigmatic result. We can readily distinguish the state of mind when an analysand floods us with loose associations, lacking awareness of the discontinuities of his thought process, from one in which he is imagining our state of mind, discussing it, and commenting on the flood of memories that emerge in the process. However, there are times when this distinction is not clear. Then we have the opportunity to explore the deep and wide transition from one category to the other: in this case, the cohesive self versus the fragmented self.

"The falcon cannot hear the falconer" points us toward the complexity of this effort. How clear can we be about what triggers fragmentation or results from fragmentation? Can we identify the final moment that tips the falcon into the widening gyre, or does the widening gyre throw the message of the falconer into an unreadable chaos? Is fragmentation the ultimate catastrophe, or is it an effort to avoid another catastrophe? Or is it both? Can we distinguish efforts to fend off fragmentation from efforts to cope with fragmentation or from efforts to reconstitute the self? When are these efforts part of the solution, and when are they part of the widening problem?

In chapter 8, I described images that might represent different aspects of fragmentation, including breakdown of thought processes, crumbling to pieces, losing a sense of individual identity or a sense of continuity of self, fusing with the object, losing the capacity to differentiate affects, drowning in a sea of emotion, narcissistic rage, or depletion depression. Manifestations of fragmentation may be psychic, physical, or behavioral. I explain in chapter 6 that the individual's capacity to represent psychological phenomena is impaired when the structure of the mind is breaking down. The affective state of fragmentation can be unbearable, leading to desperate actions that serve an effort to shore up the crumbling self. A man whose grandiose self has suffered an unbearable insult might expose himself on the subway without any consideration of the risk. Until a cohesive state has been reachieved, the consequences of his actions may seem irrelevant.

When Mrs. Kaufman, in Ella's mind, failed to be the welcoming new mother as Ella dictated in her play, she was apt to lose control and would try to kick and hit. The vulnerable child needed her selfobject to sustain the activity in exactly the right way, to maintain the identity between what was in her mind and in their play. When this failed, the cohesion of her self could not be maintained. Tantrum-like behavior resulted. She lashed out in an unmodulated manner. Though this behavior was disorganized, her efforts to strike Mrs. Kaufman suggest a greater sense of direction and agency than in the first example, when she threw her toys chaotically about the room. In the session that Ella tore her drawings into pieces, I again postulate that her self was fragmenting or on the verge of doing so. However, there was more communication value in this action, and this suggests that her self was more integrated than in the other examples. This inference is supported by her capacity to readily engage when Mrs. Kaufman said that this was a job for two.

ACTION ASSOCIATED WITH OVERSTIMULATION VERSUS FRAGMENTATION

Isabel was prone to overstimulation. Earlier in her life, she endured experiences that were too powerful and anxiety-provoking to integrate: the birth of her sister in the bathroom, the attack by the dog, and her broken collarbone. She had been overwhelmed, and because of her inability to integrate those experiences, she remained vulnerable to being overwhelmed again. She could be carried away by her feelings, and this intensity drove her behavior. Like Ella, she was action-oriented, but her actions had a different driving force. While the winds of her emotions were too much for her psychic sailboat, it did not sail off the edge of the Earth.

Early in her analysis, Isabel was in constant motion. When she stood on furniture, Dr. Huddleston worried about her safety. When Isabel would clamor for "uppies," Dr. Huddleston tried to position herself in a way that limited the physical contact. She did not want to stimulate Isabel further. As a developmental object, Dr. Huddleston's task was to adjust the tiller and the sails in order to ease off the wind. Later in the analysis, a gust of wind grabbed Isabel's sails, and she showed her bottom. At another time, she sang a song, "Itsy Bitsy Teeny Weeny Yellow Polka Dot Bikini." Her sailboat went faster and faster, and it heeled dramatically, but it did not capsize. She communicated a great deal through her song while she was greatly stimulated. Ella's ship, in contrast, was prone to capsizing. The way the sailboat functions when the mast is broken, upside-down, or stuck in the mud is very different from the ship that remains intact, however out of control it may be. In this section, I compare Isabel's actions to those of Ella. Despite the manifest similarities in their behaviors, awareness of the underlying structure of their minds and the differences between them provides an understanding of the different sources for and qualities of their actions.

When Isabel squished Dr. Huddleston between the doors, her behavior was intense and potentially damaging. While this behavior was compulsively driven, it could be modulated with help from her analyst. Dr. Huddleston could manage the action, and she and Isabel could think about their play. The falcon/child, with a lot of work on the part of the falconer/analyst, could hear the falconer. When Ella would fall apart, she could not hear the falconer. Mrs. Kaufman could only try to contain the damage, wait for the affect storm to abate, and then pick up the pieces.

Isabel tried to position her analyst in such a way that the door would cut off Dr. Huddleston's abdomen and breasts. Her actions were more organized and directed than Ella's tantrum-like behavior. The meaning of Isabel's actions was more readily available than was the meaning of the less integrated behavior exhibited by Ella when she frantically threw the toys about. When Isabel threw her shoe at Dr. Huddleston's heart, there was an immediate potential threat, but we see a higher level of intention and coherent meaning in this action compared to the time that she knocked the toys off the shelf. In this example of throwing an object in a manner that could be dangerous, we see a more purposeful agent steering the action than in the examples when Ella frantically tried to hit and kick or threw the dolls. I infer different degrees of self-control and capacity to consider reality consequences if Isabel had thrown a stapler, ripped the phone out of the wall, thrown a pillow, damaged a pillow in order to get a feather to throw, or balled up a tissue and threw it at her analyst. Getting slapped in the face is different from having pieces of paper thrown at you. It made a difference to Dr. Huddleston in terms of their safety and in terms of her task of dealing with the action. Each action reveals a different degree of modulation, self-control, and consideration—consciously or unconsciously—of the consequences. Isabel's overstimulated behavior, including its out-of-control-ness, was further along the continuum from action to symbolic communication and words than Ella's frantic tantrums.

ACTION ASSOCIATED WITH COMMUNICATION

We can describe some behaviors as actions that are associated with communications. Isabel was jumping on the couch when she told the story of Purim. She ran circles around Dr. Huddleston when she asked about the Basilisk. Attention to the literal coexistence of action and language provides us with another instrument to bring to bear on the continuum from action to words. It provides us with visual images to consider the relativity of action and symbolic communication. Isabel was overstimulated when she jumped up and down on the couch. Dr. Huddleston must have wondered about Isabel's safety and the fate of her furniture. Yet, Isabel told a coherent and very meaningful story. The story of Purim provided a crucial and organizing theme that could be traced throughout Isabel's analysis. When she told this story, it was in the foreground, while her behavior of jumping up and down was in the background. Isabel's story was stimulating and filled with danger, and this moved her into rather less modulated action. The story of the Basilisk, a giant snake, was also exciting and frightening, but Isabel could talk and chew gum at the same time. Her action was the accompaniment to her conversation.

There are numerous examples in which symbolic communication occurred while, either or both, the analysand and the analyst were engaged in action. The children and their analysts made things and did activities together while they talked. Ella drew pictures and then tore them up. The two of them repaired the pictures, and Ella taped Mrs. Kaufman. Isabel watered Dr. Huddleston's plant. She asked Dr. Huddleston to help her make a Halloween costume. Ella built roads from blocks and played that the doll traveled down the road and then returned. Isabel drew maps of Harry Potter's world and discussed them with her analyst. As the analysis progressed, she and Dr. Huddleston altered the maps and considered the significance of the changes. The children and their analysts told stories to each other and read stories together. Ella leaned against Mrs. Kaufman as she told her story, and she cried.

As I further consider the continuum from action to words in this chapter, I examine the many ways in which symbolic representation and action coexist and play off one another. Both action and interpretation facilitate the change-promoting aspects of the psychoanalytic process. The relationship between these children and their analysts were often expressed in action, and their interactions led to change. It is important to understand how interactions become internalized and how the falconer's capacity to contain the action facilitates the move from action to play and to words. The next point on the continuum, play-acting, is a form of play and symbolic communication that has action at its very core.

PLAY-ACTING

Play-acting, where the child and her playmate physically play out the imagined activity, is a form of pretend that is closer to direct action than drawing or playing with toys. Play-acting has an as-if quality, but the difference between physical action and this kind of play is not distinct. It can more readily slide from fantasy to real action. It is one thing when the mother doll kisses her husband as he returns home from work. It is another thing when the little girl, playing mother, kisses the little boy, who is portrayed by the analyst. It is one thing when the child draws a picture of two dancers. It is another when the child and analyst pretend to dance or when the little girl hugs her analyst, seeking "uppies." If they touch hands, even though they are pretending that they are dancing, the touch is real. Even if the actual touch never occurs, when they turn their bodies in unison, their minds and their bodies have a more real experience than they had when the dance was displaced into the drawing.

Isabel pretended to crack eggs on Dr. Huddleston's head. While this required close physical contact, it was comfortably within the realm of fantasy play. This play was an expression of Isabel's fantasies about and infantile theory of conception. This view of conception reemerged later in the analysis in the symbolic realm, when Isabel dreamed that Daniel cracked an egg on her head. When Isabel and Dr. Huddleston pretended to cut off each other's limbs with pillows, they were again play-acting. Pillow fights are generally safe, and the softness of pillows protects the players from injury. Yet, the playmates were really swinging the pillows and really hitting each other. The whole endeavor is more real and feels more real, and the likelihood of real consequences is heightened.

In play-acting we might think of the performers inviting members of the audience onto the stage or coming down from the stage and engaging the audience directly, asking them to be part of the performance. Everyone recognizes that their activity is still a performance, but the personal engagement is heightened. A whole other range of feelings gets stirred when the observer physically becomes part of the performance. With action, in contrast to play-acting, there is no announcement or discussion. The performers descend on the audience or, as Ekstein and Friedman (1957) describe play action, they continue their role outside the theater.

In her play, Isabel pretended to stab Dr. Huddleston with a needle and plunge a knife into her back. At another time, she actually came at her with a tack. Hamlet had left the sword play on the stage, jumped down among the seats, and threatened the audience. At yet another time, Isabel abruptly slapped Dr. Huddleston in the face. Hamlet's sword had struck the person in the audience. There was little restraint and little pretend. Isabel's behavior had moved along the continuum from play-acting to action.

In the next section, I look further into the interactions between Isabel and Dr. Huddleston, when the child tried to squish her analyst between the doors, in order to see how Dr. Huddleston's analytic interventions moved them along the continuum from action to play action to play-acting and on toward words.

FROM ACTION TO PLAY ACTION TO PLAY-ACTING TO WORDS

Isabel insisted that Dr. Huddleston remain between the two doors that led to her office. She directed her to stand in a certain spot so that one of the doors would close on her breasts and abdomen. Dr. Huddleston had to contend with this action and make sure she did not get hurt. At another time or with a different child–analyst pair, it might have been necessary to interrupt this activity. During this period of analysis, Dr. Huddleston was able to contain the closing of the doors, Isabel allowed herself to be contained, and the play-like quality of the action was allowed to unfold. Their interaction, which could have stayed in the realm of Ekstein and Friedman's (1957) action, moved more into the category of play action and then toward play-acting. Dr. Huddleston's role in this engagement and her capacity to facilitate this transition illustrate her function as a developmental object. Packed into this action are a number of psychological phenomena and interactions that Miller (2013) lists in which a child analyst serves developmental functions: to be a container, to ensure safety, to provide controls and limits, to regulate affects, and to provide a narrative.

Dr. Huddleston introduced words in order to provide insight into the meanings of their interactions. She wondered aloud if Isabel didn't have some concerns about her having a woman's body and concerns about what could happen to a woman's body. Isabel did not respond directly (in words) to her analyst's interpretation/question. Instead, there was a shift in her play. Isabel directed Dr. Huddleston to take a different action: that she "Not look!" This action had fewer reality consequences than standing still as the door closed on Dr. Huddleston's body. The action was concrete in that there was a three-dimensional space between them that was to be avoided. There was also rich symbolism and meaning in the acts of looking or not looking. Seeing or not seeing the bodies of men or women and boys or girls, the primal scene, or the birth of a baby were filled with intensity and anxiety. Looking was also a stand-in for the frightening and overstimulating experience of listening to (and wishing not to hear) her mother's screams and the sirens of the ambulances when her sister was delivered in the bathroom. In response to Dr. Huddleston's interpretation, the content, the quality, and the available meaning of their shared action changed.

While Dr. Huddleston's interpretation about bodies led to a shift from more intense to less intense action, it seems that it also stirred distress. To think about, know about, not know about, or see the secrets of a woman's body was too much. It was frightening and forbidden to know and humiliating not to know. This anxiety led to a play interruption and a new play activity. Isabel mobilized defenses to contend with these emotions. In the new version of play-acting, Dr. Huddleston was the one who was forbidden to see and forbidden to know. Isabel had turned passive into active, communicating the experience of the child who does not know the secrets by inflicting it on her analyst. By playing the role of the child who was forbidden to peek, Dr. Huddleston served as a container. She tolerated the affects of the little girl who was overwhelmed by anxiety or excitement and endlessly frustrated by her lack of knowledge and understanding. Thinking of herself as the little girl who was not allowed to peek, Dr. Huddleston gave voice to her own momentary experience and to what she suspected Isabel felt. Within the context of the play-acting, Dr. Huddleston owned the feelings and said that she felt alone and confused. We see here the potential therapeutic value of projective identification. She took Isabel's affects within herself; digested them; and, like a mother bird, offered them to her nestling. She did not say that Isabel felt alone and confused. Voicing Isabel's feelings as her own enabled this understanding to be more easily digested by the child.

When Dr. Huddleston offered words to Isabel in a way that the little girl could hear, she offered insight, and she continued to be available as a developmental object. Comparing their interactions amid the forceful squishing action of the doors at the beginning of this extended play to the latter moment, when action was toned down and words were more prominent, we see a transformation. This transformation is both a product of the change-promoting aspects of their work and a facilitator of further transformation.

Action and words were aspects of both moments. Earlier, there was more action and relatively fewer words. Later, action was still on the stage, but words moved toward the foreground. When Dr. Huddleston voiced Isabel's words as her own, she continued to serve the developmental functions described on the previous page (Miller, 2013): providing controls and limits, ensuring safety, regulating affects, and serving as a container. It is a significant development that, as these functions could be taken more for granted, they became part of the reliable, less noticed structure of the theater. Then, our two protagonists could pay more attention to the performance on the stage. Dr. Huddleston's need to board up the windows in order to dampen the effects of the storm, to make sure that the props on the set did not get blown over, and to be sure that no one got hurt lessened. They could both be actors in the play performance, and they could discuss the play. When they could have these discussions, Dr. Huddleston's capacity to expand the depth and complexity of Isabel's representational world was enhanced. In Miller's (2013) words, she was able to provide the following developmental functions: "to grow capacities for self-reflection and mentalization (Fonagy and Target 1998), to give meaning to thoughts and actions, to provide language to describe states of mind, to differentiate cause and effect (A. M. Sandler, 1996), . . . to build a narrative (Knight, 2003), and to not be used as a projection (Horne, 2006)" (312–313).

This play activity went on for months. The multifaceted therapeutic process did not come to fruition in one isolated, single, "good" analytic hour (E. Kris, 1956, 446). There was an ongoing process in which the developmental relationship and the content of the analytic pair's communications helped Isabel to understand and to manage her emotions. These experiences were intense for Isabel. When it felt too intense, too stimulating, or too anxiety-provoking, she would interrupt her play. Frequently, her body responded to the stimulation, and she urgently had to rush to the bathroom in order to have a bowel movement.

There are myriad ways in which the too-much-ness of affects can be expressed and many interwoven ways in which analysts facilitate their analysands' capacities to tolerate, modulate, and articulate their internal states. Isabel's analyst helped her to constrain the intensity of her actions of squishing Dr. Huddleston between the doors. In many ways, Isabel had difficulty containing herself. Emotions drove intense activity, and she often could not contain her poop within her body. Their relationship served as a container. With Isabel's cooperation, the action became play that enabled them to interact with more complexity and subtlety. Dr. Huddleston's words furthered Isabel's capacity to enrich her representational world and move toward symbolic communication.

THE MICROCOSM

We generally distinguish the microcosm of play and the macrocosm of action, but the distinction is not pure. Such activities as doll play are more contained and at greater remove from direct action, but within the microcosm of play, there can be all kinds of action, and much goes on between the child and her analyst. While the amplitude of the action is generally greater in the macrocosm than in the microcosm, the dynamic relationship among action, symbolism, and words has a similar structure in both the macrocosm and the microcosm. This is the fractal nature of the mind. At either level of magnification, the structure is the same.

Action accompanies words, and action and symbolism play hand in hand. Isabel played with the puppets: "Troublesome Baby" crawled through the orifices of the other puppets. Dr. Huddleston looked on. Even though the play was intense and aggressive, it remained on the puppet stage. Children at play move the furniture of the dollhouse, and the dolls move and speak. Toys battle, crawl inside each other, reject another toy, fly across the room, and hide under the bed of the dollhouse or under the couch in the office.

Both girls told stories and talked about movies, books, and fairy tales. Storytelling for both of them involved an activity that was further removed from direct action, more displaced, more modulated, and more communicative than action-oriented. Yet, action occurred in a variety of ways. Isabel was jumping on the couch when she told the story of Purim. When Ella talked about the baby who was given away, she leaned against her analyst and cried. Isabel wet her pants while she played and, on multiple occasions, ran to the bathroom to poop.

Actions cannot be neatly disentangled from the fabric of symbolic meaning. Action is more noticeable on the macroscopic scale, and often we cannot avoid it, even if we wish to. It is less obvious on the microscopic scale. The common meaning of acting out, misbehaving or being disruptive, would fit this macroscopic notion of action: behavior that is hard to ignore. The kinds of enactments first described by Jacobs (1986, 2001) may be unnoticed for a time, but they loom large when they come into focus. In Katz's (2014) "enacted dimension of psychoanalysis," the action is subtler, but it is there. Transference is a kind of enactment. It is an envelope that gives shape to the message, and it brings pressure to bear on the message and its recipient. Analysis of transference increases the magnification of the moment and brings into focus increasingly subtle and minute interactions, actions, and meanings. In the microcosm of play, action persists in relatively more subtle ways than action in the macrocosm, but its presence is alive and complex. As we look into the transference and as we look into the microcosm of play, we move more deeply into the continuum of action to words and into the fractal spiral of the mind.

Play activities include interactions between the playmates, as well as interactions among the toys. Repeatedly, Ella engaged in play in which a homeless doll whose parents had died immediately after her birth came to live with a woman who lived alone. This adoptive mother was to be unambivalent in her love and desire for the little girl's company. Mrs. Kaufman felt the pressure of Ella's wish that she, Mrs. Kaufman, be that mother. She felt controlled. Anything that suggested that she was not that mother led to a breakdown in Ella's capacity to play and aggressive outbursts. Mrs. Kaufman often had to restrain Ella to keep her from hitting and kicking. Ella would dictate the scenario to be enacted, Mrs. Kaufman's role in the play, and the precise way that her character was to respond. Ella was and acted like the dictator or director of the performance, and she gave her analyst, the performer, her lines. The story was the words, and the action was in the directing. The content was the story about the girl doll, and the process was one in which Ella gave directions. Ella as the director of the performance was the envelope, and the letter was her story.

The director was most aggressive and desperate when her capacity to be the container of her own message and the structure and stage of her inner world were most vulnerable. In the early sessions, she could not tolerate any change in the position of the dolls or dollhouse furniture. Later, after Mrs. Kaufman's vacation, Ella's error in coloring was too much to bear. The envelope of her mind was less able to hold her letters. She tried to reinforce this envelope as she became the more insistent director, demanding that things remain as she needed them to be.

Unmet longings or unresolved traumatic experiences lead to repetition. Ella's feeling of abandonment drove the repetitious play of the girl who returns to a newly discovered, loving mother. Isabel persistently expressed her preoccupation with and compelling need to know about the body and sexuality. The forward edge of the transference (Tolpin, 1971), the forward developmental thrust, the search for the transformational object (Bollas,

1979) or selfobject (Kohut and Wolf, 1978), and the effort to master experience all drive this repetition. The repetitive play can, by itself, be therapeutic. It can also become a stagnant and lifeless replaying of the same old thing. This compulsive repetition can be masochistic. Because of the consequences of the object's failings and the damage to the child's self, the early developmental needs remain. The unresolved need and the yearning for a different outcome remain embedded within the repeated engagement with a hurtful (in reality and/or perception) object. Within the envelopes of the play and the analytic relationship, the therapeutic task—with all forms that this repetition may take—is to open the forward edge of the repetition and facilitate psychological development.

Ella's yearning to be loved was powerful. The pain of feeling unloved or rejected was alive in the present and stirred agonies from the past. She began the doll play about the abandoned child who found a home during the first weeks of analysis. She insisted that Mrs. Kaufman respond with exactly the right words and precisely the tone of voice that she had demonstrated. "Yes. You can come to live with me." If Ella felt that Mrs. Kaufman had failed to comply with her instructions, the doll left abruptly or ignored her new mother/analyst. During one of these sessions, Mrs. Kaufman voiced her own feelings: "This feels bad. I am getting to know what it feels like to have to do things exactly right or be left all alone." She drew upon her countertransference experience, interpreted the child's effort to turn passive into active, and identified the feeling. She contained and verbally expressed the affect associated with the projective identification and pointed out that Ella was teaching her a lesson. Mrs. Kaufman play acted the role of the lonely and shunned child. Triumphantly, Ella agreed!

PLAY INTERRUPTIONS

When play becomes too much for a child, play interruptions occur. Isabel, like many children, sought refuge in the bathroom. When Ella sadly reflected on the losses of the immigrants in her book, she dissolved into tears and fell to the floor. In the same way that an adult might begin a new line of thought in response to an uncomfortable moment, a child may simply express boredom or shift to another activity. After saying "No way" about discussing her dream, Isabel tried a different tack. She looked at the books on the shelf.

Ella played that the bad parents were to be punished for their misdeeds: "No more babies for you!" The king sent angry, biting bears instead of babies. Ella growled. She was providing a voice for the bears, but she was also growling herself. Mrs. Kaufman recognized that this was a moment when Ella was likely to leave the microcosm and shift to the macrocosm by trying to kick or bite her. Instead, Ella mobilized defenses against her biting impulses. She interrupted the play and hid behind a chair. Mrs. Kaufman offered words to capture her anxiety. "I think you are hiding because you are afraid I will send you away when you feel so yucky and bearish." After a short time, Ella returned to sit by her analyst.

Often, her unmanageable rage would have totally disrupted the play. She would have attacked or dissolved! This time, she was better able to contain her rage. The affect was more modulated, but the play still had to stop. Action again took the stage. She was not intending to play hide and seek when she moved behind the chair. It was anxiety about her rage and its consequences that drove her there. She withdrew from the scene of the play and hid from her analyst. In this action, however, her defenses were more intact, her behavior was more integrated, meaning was more evident, and her action was less disruptive. Mrs. Kaufman did not have to physically intervene. She continued to talk with the child who hid behind the chair. With some time and the interpretation, Ella could return. Enacted within this return was another version of the play in which the homeless girl finds an unambivalent, loving mother. The pattern embedded in Ella's mind of the devil child who is abandoned by her mother or flees her mother had begun its repetition. This time, however, she was able to return to the mother who could tolerate her rage, her anxiety, and her need to move away. The leading edge of the transference was open (Tolpin, 2002).

WORDS

Even when we have the luxury of verbal interchange, the impact of these verbal interventions, their meaning to the child, and their therapeutic value are not necessarily obvious. Readers may not all agree on how we decide whether an intervention is actually an interpretation or whether insight is the outcome of an interpretation. If we consider the therapeutic value of insight, we have to also consider some questions: Insight into what? Are we revealing the hidden affect or impulse, an unconscious resistance, the unnoticed shift in associations, the latent allusions to the cause of the shift, the allusions in response to the shift, or the response to the analyst's intervention? Are we explaining what has unfolded in the process? If so, are we interpreting the patient's unconscious reading of, or motivations influencing, that process? Are we offering a new way to think about such an interaction, or is our explanation in itself transformative? Are we providing insight into the dynamic unconscious and bringing a repressed thought into awareness, or are we describing an implicit procedure or nonconscious process? Are we explaining what is happening in the analysand's mind or providing a new metaphor through which she can organize her multiple and conflicting thoughts and feelings? Are we noticing an affect or a shift in state of mind or making explicit the allusions to the patient's state of mind or the state of the transference? Are we speaking directly about these things or sorting them out in the minds of the puppets, the people in the story, or the bunny rabbit in the drawing? Are we talking about the children in school, our patient, or perhaps what we know about children in general?

Our models of the mind, our theories of technique, and our own shifting internal representations of how the therapeutic encounter unfolds influence our thinking and our approaches. Mrs. Kaufman told Ella, "You don't know me yet. It could be scary to come with me to the playroom." Was she providing insight that would allow a repressed or preconscious conflict and associated anxiety into awareness by connecting them with words? Was she formulating an unformulated experience? Was she allowing dissociated parts of Ella's self to come together: the frightened little girl and the brave big girl? Was she being open to Ella's mind and therefore freeing inhibited implicit relational structures or mental processes?

Mrs. Kaufman seemed to be trying to put Ella at ease by letting her know she understood that Ella was scared, and she implicitly raised the possibility that she would not be a scary person. What do we think was in Ella's mind when she responded, "I'm not scared at all"? Was this a counterphobic stance, dictating she had to plunge forward in order to overcome her fear? Was she ashamed of being afraid, thinking that only little girls get scared, not big girls? Was she whistling in the dark, putting one foot in front of the other, hoping to get past the spooky house?

In this section I have raised a number of questions about what the analyst's words mean to the child. In the following sections, I consider these questions and examine different kinds of verbal interpretations.

INTERPRETATION OF DEFENSE

Some of the interpretations offered in our case examples fit with a one-person model of the mind. For example, when Mrs. Kaufman suggested that Ella acted bossy in order to cover up her worries or Dr. Huddleston told Isabel that her action was a way of not feeling afraid, we can readily picture Freud's (1953–1974d, 1953–1974o) topographic or structural models of the mind. Both of these interpretations can be read according to a one-person model: Her worries remain unconscious due to defenses. Children mobilize defenses against affects. It may be that the relational part of this interpretation was implicit, assumed, or taken for granted and did not require acknowledgment. Isabel responded to Dr. Huddleston's interpretation by stopping her jumping and asking why she should be afraid. Dr. Huddleston, in a close-process manner, was aware of the content during recent sessions. She pointed out that Isabel had been telling scary stories. Remaining calm, Isabel said, "Oh, yeah."

Mrs. Kaufman followed her interpretation of Ella's defensive bossiness with a statement that Ella didn't know if she, Mrs. Kaufman, could understand her feelings. We can see this as work within the transference in a one-person model of the mind, or we can see her including the two participants in a two-person model. What, when, and how does it make a difference if we talk in this way or if we don't? This kind of intervention does more directly acknowledge that the child is with you, another person. You may be a scary person, you may be unable to understand the child's distress, but maybe you will be a different kind of object who can be open to the child's mind.

What worries was Ella covering up? Is it more helpful to address the worries in general or more specific terms? When Mrs. Kaufman said, "Probably, you're not sure if you want me to know you worry about your parents," Ella opened up and complained that her mother works all the time, she has a baby brother who cries all the time, and she has to play alone. Why did this interpretation—that she worried about her parents—have a different impact than the interpretation that Ella was scared to leave her mother? I come back to this question in the next section when I discuss the specificity of interpretations.

In the previous chapter, I discussed Sugarman's (2003b) perspective on work within the displacement of play. Drawing on the work of Fonagy and Target (1996; Target & Fonagy, 1996), he explains that a young child will invest herself within the play, but she cannot recognize the relationship between her play and her own feelings or with the realities of her life. Therefore, Sugarman's technical choice is to remain within the metaphor of the play. His vignette about the little girl who pretended that the pen tore up the magazine illustrates his technique. His approach can also be understood as a way to allow the defense of displacement to modulate the child's affect without the necessity of interpreting the defense. Staying within the displacement of play allows the affective material to be tolerated. Interpretations about the characters in the play have therapeutic impact despite the fact that the child does not consciously recognize their relevance to herself.

Mrs. Kaufman provided a vignette from Ella's analysis in which she decided to make an interpretation in a way that was somewhat different from Sugarman's (2003b). While playing, Ella explained that the doll was all alone. Her parents had played a trick on her. They said they were going to work, but they went to the hospital to have a baby instead. Tears came into Ella's eyes, and she interrupted her play, stomping around the room. It was clear, in Mrs. Kaufman's mind, that Ella's play referred to her own experience. She was unsure, however, whether Ella recognized that she was talking about herself. Mrs. Kaufman had to make a technical decision as to how to address this moment. Unlike Sugarman, she did not choose to talk about how sad the doll felt. She had tried this kind of interpretation before, and it had not been effective. Neither, did she make a defense interpretation as she had in the example discussed above. She did not choose to note the interruption in the play or that Ella was stomping around the room to get away from the upsetting scene in the play. Instead, she said to Ella, "This is very sad. I see how upset you are about that baby." Mrs. Kaufman chose the phrase "that baby" in order to "bridge the possibilities." It could be understood either as a comment regarding Ella's feelings about the baby in the play or the real baby in Ella's life. Ella responded directly. "I don't know who is going to take care of me now. . . . I'm all alone."

What was it about the way Ella's mind worked, her state of mind at that moment, or Mrs. Kaufman's way of transitioning to Ella's feelings that led this little girl to seamlessly make the transition from her play to herself? Perhaps Mrs. Kaufman and Sugarman (2003b) agree that it would not have been effective, with a child Ella's age, to demonstrate the connection between her play and her reality. If our model of the mind is that a young child operates in two modes that are insufficiently integrated—psychic equivalence mode vs. pretend mode—we might think that Ella would not understand the connection or that it would have been too threatening to impose the connection on her. If we agree that making the connection between her play and reality would have been too threatening, why did she easily cross the bridge from play to reality? Perhaps Ella's propensity to function in psychic equivalence mode made her more prone to hear Mrs. Kaufman's interpretation as a direct translation of her play. Perhaps addressing the defense or staying fully within the displacement was less necessary with Ella—at least during that phase of her analysis—than it was with Isabel. Perhaps, because of the way that Ella's mind worked at that time, a defense interpretation would have been counterproductive, making her feel criticized rather than understood.

It is striking to observe, in this vignette, that Ella began to cry as she played with her dolls. She felt the sadness that her doll felt in the play. Her stomping around the room was not only an interruption of and retreat from the play. It was an expression of the emotion that both she and the doll experienced. In a significant way, Ella had already started across the bridge between the doll's sadness and her own sadness. Mrs. Kaufman stepped in and helped the little girl to get across that bridge. Ella reacted as if she didn't even notice there was a bridge to cross.

THE SPECIFICITY OF INTERPRETATIONS

In the vignette just described, the material deepens throughout the interchange between Ella and Mrs. Kaufman. They achieved more detail and specificity about Ella's experience of being the child who is left alone because of the new baby. Greater specificity is often an outcome of a deepening process, and interpretations that are more specific can facilitate a deepening of the analytic process. After crashing the baby boys into the mother's closet, Ella became panicky and reached inside the dollhouse: "It has shapes inside! I don't know where they came from." Ella was in a state of frenzy. Mrs. Kaufman addressed her affective state and noted her worry. She went on to offer herself as a developmental object when she wondered if they could figure out a way to help Ella. This didn't work, and the frenzy continued. Mrs. Kaufman kept trying and said, "I think, from what just happened in this playing, you want me to know you are confused and worried about your baby brother, where and who he came from." Ella began to calm and said all she knew was that her parents went away to have a baby. With this latter intervention, Mrs. Kaufman took her understanding of Ella's play and her history and directly addressed Ella's feelings about her brother. While both interventions included the two of them, the latter, more specific interpretation, one that addressed Ella's feelings directly, had a more facilitating impact than the less specific offer to be a new object.

A vignette from Isabel's analysis provides another example of the way in which a more specific interpretation engages the child's mind more effectively than a more general interpretation. Isabel was distressed after her father was hospitalized. When Dr. Huddleston observed how upset and angry she was, Isabel ignored her in order to follow her mother's instructions and prepare a card and gift for her father. When they discussed the fact that she didn't know how her father was, Dr. Huddleston empathized with how difficult it was when adults didn't explain what was happening. Isabel responded powerfully by peppering her analyst with questions. Isabel was worried about her father, and she felt that she was left in the dark without a way to ground her fears and fantasies. She was distressed about this particular situation, but it was also a new instance of long-standing concerns about bodily injury and secrets.

Dr. Huddleston had identified a secret, and secrets were persistent thorns in Isabel's life. Her specific concern about her father's injuries and the enduring thorny envelope of secrets engaged her. Her mind opened up, and she reported her dreams. In one dream, Daniel cracked eggs on her head. The other was about the dangerous shark and the threat of physical attack. She went on excitedly to explore the life cycle of a caterpillar. While Isabel had initially pushed past Dr. Huddleston's more general reference to her affect, the more specific interpretation—that it was difficult when adults didn't explain things fully—engaged her. The consuming secrets about conception and transformations within the life cycle emerged from her mind, as well as the intensely affect-laden threat of bodily mutilation—but she stayed in the realm of words.

In an early session, Dr. Huddleston addressed Isabel's ambivalence about discussing her dreams: "Part of you says no." Isabel's response was emphatic: "All parts say no!" When Dr. Huddleston interpreted Isabel's anger and guilt regarding her mother's intent to change her sitter and school, Isabel laughed bitterly and drew a picture of Voldemort: "I'm back!" Dr. Huddleston's interpretation was direct, and Isabel again responded emphatically. Her affect was notable, and again, the content of her response was in the metaphor. We can infer a comparison of the evil figure, Voldemort, to her mother, or to the return of her own dark and angry feelings. When Isabel's analyst followed up and interpreted that she felt callously treated and vengeful, Isabel answered by caring for "Shiskapoo." She did not respond directly in words as Ella had when she talked about her parents and her brother, nor did she stay within the verbal sphere as she had when she brought up her dreams. Instead, she moved to a different play activity. She introduced a new character and took care of him very thoughtfully. She depicted the soothing and protecting aspect of the analytic relationship, including the comforting quality of the specific verbal interpretation. Her experience of Dr. Huddleston as a helpful figure was present, and her capacity to modulate affect was growing.

The more specific interpretation closely articulated the internal metaphors that shaped Isabel's experience. It matched her experience, it opened new possibilities, and it evoked meaningful fantasy play. In the next section, I look at interventions in which the analyst instead gently points to the affective state.

ATTENTION TO THE AFFECTIVE STATE AND STATE OF THE SELF

Manifestations of a patient's affect can reveal subtly or powerfully that something important is at hand. Noticing a clouding over of the eyes or a misty look might open up meaningful content. In the previous section, I discussed vignettes in which the analysts' comments about affect did not deepen the material while specific interpretations that put the child's concerns into words did. In this section, I look at the emergence of powerful affects and the significance of the analysts' attention to the patient's emotional state and her state of mind.

Attention to affect can be done with specificity, delicacy, or both and bring into awareness feelings that are not recognized or acknowledged. As Isabel left the previously described session, where Dr. Huddleston interpreted that she felt callously treated and vengeful, she told her analyst that her friend had gotten her period. As she exited the stage, she opened the door to another powerful life event.

The next day, Dr. Huddleston commented to Isabel that "so much gets thrown at you." This was different from the interventions Dr. Huddleston had made the day before or the vignettes examined previously. Dr. Huddleston recognized that Isabel's friend's menstrual period was likely to stir a lot within her. Yet, she did not remind her of the specific event that Isabel had introduced the day before. Instead, she simply acknowledged her affective state. She addressed Isabel's propensity to feel overwhelmed. This time, Isabel did not push past the comment. She added a new aspect to her play with "Shiskapoo." Isabel provided grooming items for him. Dr. Huddleston's attention to Isabel's affect provided the child with a tool that enabled her to manage and groom her state of mind, like a mother who teaches her daughter to groom her hair or bloody genitals.

During the latter part of her analysis, Ella played that she and Mrs. Kaufman were tooth fairies, mother and daughter who looked alike. The next day she drew a picture of herself and her mother, and they looked different. Then she drew a picture in which her mother flew in and attacked Mrs. Kaufman. Ella was left injured and alone. In a fury, she destroyed the symbolic play of drawing and tore her pictures to shreds. Ella became frantic and desperately tried to piece her drawings back together. Mrs. Kaufman said that this was a job for two. Ella calmed down, and they spent the remainder of the session working together, repairing Ella's pictures.

Mrs. Kaufman's statement to Ella, that this was a job for two, was an intervention that addressed the child's emotional state and the state of her self. While Ella's state of mind, fragmentation, was not specifically put into words and Mrs. Kaufman didn't say that Ella felt like she was in pieces or overwhelmed, her state of mind was implicitly acknowledged when she said that this was a job that required both of them. This emotional state was more than Ella could manage by herself. Mrs. Kaufman put forth her willingness to help Ella with the task of repairing the drawings, she let Ella know that she was not alone with her injuries, she made herself available as a new object, and they worked together at the task of piecing together the fragments of her self.

Ella's response to the offer of help from a new object was different this time compared to the moment when Ella was in a panic about the shapes in the closet. Ella felt comforted and used Mrs. Kaufman as a developmental or selfobject who has the capacity to calm her and help her feel glued back together. The words that Mrs. Kaufman used were important, but they were the tip of a large iceberg, her actual presence as a developmental object that has the power to comfort the child.

The developmental aspect of this shared effort goes deep beneath the surface of the child's mind. Lyons-Ruth (1999) explains that, in regard to implicit relational knowing, the medium is the message. The medium was the mutual engagement in the task of putting the drawings back together, and they were putting the child's fragmenting self back together. Despite Lyons-Ruth's explanation that the impact of this interaction does not require translation into symbols or words in order to be impactful, in this instance there was also something deeply important about Mrs. Kaufman stating the seemingly simple phrase that this was a job for two. They were playing, they were repairing the drawing, and they were repairing Ella's self. Mrs. Kaufman's words were the sound of the trumpet that heralded their mutual endeavor and a communication that gave this endeavor a name.

WORDS ARE SYMBOLS AND ACTIONS

The trend outlined earlier demonstrates movement from action toward more symbolic representation and from the macrocosm to the microcosm. Direct verbal communication might follow. In the session when Isabel asked if Dr. Huddleston remembered how "Troublesome Baby" had crawled in the nose and belly of the owl, she explained that mother owls "ploop" out their eggs. She started to cry but stopped herself, saying that she was acting like a baby. Then, instead of wetting herself or going to the bathroom, she explained that bathrooms were creepy. Isabel was better able to reflect and describe her experience rather than respond somatically or shift to action.

We see over and over that verbal communication is not simply direct. Words are symbols, and condensed within them are multiple meanings. Words are also actions, and action, too, is filled with meaning. The act of communicating takes on symbolic meaning that influences process and content. We might not know to what extent the verbal communication has significance in terms of the content of the words being said, a metaphor for something latent, a reflection of an implicit and nonconscious mental process, or an action between the analyst and analysand.

When Isabel talked about how babies were "plooped" out, she was revealing her understanding of the birth process. When Ella described the violent process of birth, Mrs. Kaufman and she were engaged in an educational moment about birth, but they were also speaking to a metaphor about separation and individuation. When Ella talked about the rug in the office, she was reminiscing as part of the deep and complex process of internalizing the analytic experience.

The associative process, like play, consists of a stream of words, but it is also action that repeats internalized interactions and processes. The act of talking has meaning. An adult analysand might be angry and feel like she is biting off the head of her analyst. In contrast, her words might be an exquisitely intimate sharing. Isabel communicated a great deal when she sang "Itsy Bitsy Teeny Weeny Yellow Polka Dot Bikini," allowing us to infer an upsurge of sexual excitement. At another time, a little girl might sing "La la la la la la!" in order to drown out the words of her analyst. Falling silent can be a stubborn withholding of poop, sticking fingers in her ears, a lonely depressed isolation, an idyllic sun-filled reflection, a respite, a postcoital nap, and so on.

When Isabel, the teacher, grilled her analyst, the student, the mode of interaction spoke to us as loud as the content of the questions. Enacted between them was the experience of feeling excluded and demeaned, the child who does not know the secrets. Identifying with the aggressor and turning passive into active, Isabel strove for mastery and tried to elicit the noxious experience within her collaborator. At the end of the analysis, there was a different teaching envelope, as Isabel kindly explained the new schedule and the location of the bus to her student. Process and content, like envelope and letter, are parts of the same package. They reveal varied parts of the message, but they are intimately interrelated.

Over the course of this chapter, I have moved through the continuum from action to words. The structural dynamics among action, symbols, and words and their immersion in a two-person relationship determine the shape of the treatment and its capacity to facilitate change. Process becomes content. Content influences process. The structure of the analysand's mind shapes the treatment process, and the treatment process alters the structure of her mind. Isabel and Ella were both children, and their minds had much in common. My understanding of each of their analyses, therefore, had much in common. There were also important differences in the ways their minds were structured. Ella's psychic theater was more vulnerable to fragmentation. States of fragmentation were exhibited during her analysis, and development of psychological structure was an essential therapeutic outcome. Isabel's psychic theater, or her psychic sailboat, was less vulnerable to crumbling or capsizing. Because of the traumatic events when she was 2 years old, later events were too stormy for her to manage. Integration of those overwhelming events in a new way allowed her development to move forward.

Chapter Twelve

The Oedipal Phase and Its Earlier Determinants

Edward I. Kohn

There is oedipal material in the analyses of both girls. Isabel's world was organized primarily around oedipal-phase concerns pretty much throughout her analysis. Ella moved from a central focus on separation and abandonment to more consistent oedipal themes later in the analytic work.

SECRETS AND LIES

Both girls dealt with secrets, broken promises, and feelings of betrayal. Consideration of the meanings of these themes during the girls' analyses enables us to see the transformation of Ella's worldview as she moved forward in development, as well as the reverberations of preoedipal and separation and individuation concerns that remained embedded and added shape to her oedipal concerns. Isabel, by contrast, processed the significance of these themes in terms of intense oedipal preoccupations consistently. It was not so much the meaning of secrets, betrayals, or broken promises that changed for Isabel but the intensity of their significance. At the start, these concerns were overstimulating (she pushed Dr. Huddleston for "uppies") and terribly frightening (she threw the naked doll to the side). By the end of the analysis, with the help of her analyst (the teacher took the boy and girl chipmunks from the bathroom to talk about sexuality), Isabel could discuss these matters with considerable equanimity.

In doll play during the early phases of analysis, Ella explained that the little girl's parents played a trick on her. They said they were going to work but went to have a baby instead. She had been deceived, and she anticipated being left alone and abandoned: "I don't know who's going to take care of me now." Late in the analysis, Ella was more immersed in oedipal themes, and her oedipal narrative was revealed in her discussion of the fairy tale Rapunzel. Rapunzel, the beautiful daughter, was to marry the handsome prince. Her jealous mother, in order to prevent this marriage, tricked Rapunzel and locked her in the tower. At this point, jealousy and rivalry were on the stage, but abandonment did not totally cede the stage. When Ella felt close to her analyst, she drew a picture of her mother flying in and attacking Mrs. Kaufman. Subsequently, Ella said that she was locked out of Mrs. Kaufman's house and her own house. She was injured and alone.

This oedipal trickery of Rapunzel's jealous mother was the successor to the earlier trickery, when Ella was upset that her parents had lied about where they were going when they got the baby. At that earlier time, making babies threatened abandonment and having no one to take care of her. As Ella entered the oedipal phase, the meaning of trickery took on new significance. She wanted to go off with her own prince, but this was a threat to her mother. In her mind, her mother's distress about separation and being left behind heightened the conflict and dangers associated with Ella's oedipal interests. The oedipal girl, like the girl of separation-individuation who wants to freely move away and return, continues to rely on her mother's availability as she engages her new interests and desires. The threat that her mother will attack or withdraw her availability makes these new developments much more dangerous.

At one point, Ella coped with her anxiety about the Rapunzel story and the threats of jealousy and rivalry by moving to the story of Goldilocks. This story was safer because "there are no mothers in that story": "With a witch-like laugh, Ella said, 'I changed the story. I can trick you before you can trick me.'" In one move, Ella retreated from the danger of rivalry with her mother, got rid of her mother, and turned passive into active. She became the witch who reveled in her power to play a trick on Mrs. Kaufman.

The significance of secrets had an oedipal quality for Isabel throughout her analysis. There were mysteries to be solved, and she was upset that adults kept the answers from her. It was humiliating to be the child who did not understand sexual differences, and she subjected Dr. Huddleston to ridicule when she play-acted the role of teacher who relished demonstrating that her analyst, the student, did not know about penises. She was upset that her mother didn't let her know more about her father's injuries. She was worried about her father, as she must have worried about her mother during the delivery of her sister, and again information was withheld from her. While some things were too scary to see or know, like when she threw the naked female doll to the side, she also wanted to understand. Late in her analysis, when she was less overwhelmed by the prospect of bodily damage, Isabel turned to her mother to learn more about her own earlier injuries. While Isabel had to deal with feeling displaced by her sister, she spent much more time trying to figure out what this baby business was all about. What goes on in the Chamber of Secrets, the bedroom, or a mother's body? How are babies conceived? How do they grow inside of mother, and how do they get out?

BIRTH

Ella's fantasy of the birth process, shaped by the intensity of her separation-individuation conflicts, depicted a baby who violently tears her way out of her mother's body. Isabel, in contrast, went through a range of theories about the birth process during her analysis. Mostly, her theories were variations on anal birth. This included puppet play, where babies were pooped out; discussion of her dream, where her sister was one of the chocolate turtles; and the presence of Moaning Myrtle in the toilet.

We don't hear during this analysis of the strange sounds that come from the parental bedroom, but we do know that Isabel's mother was on the toilet when she gave birth to her baby sister. Alone in her bedroom, Isabel listened to the moans of her mother, the driven activity of her parents, and the wail of the approaching ambulance. All of this was confusing, frightening, and more than this little girl could contend with on her own. It was traumatic, at the least in that it was upsetting, it had pathological consequences, and it influenced her subsequent development (A. Freud, 1964/1967). The potty chair was central during the incident when Isabel was attacked by the family dog. It is no wonder that she became fearful when she needed to use the toilet. It is also not a surprise that Isabel's fantasies about the birth process, both their affective intensity and their content, were influenced by these events. While Ella's fantasy about birth and its associated anxiety were shaped by the conflicts of separation-individuation, Isabel was drawn to anal theories about birth and was rocked by the tsunami-like threat of violent dismemberment of one's body.

CONCEPTION

Both girls had fantasies about conception and intercourse. Ella described how the man's penis got trapped in the woman's vagina. While she recognized the roles of the penis and vagina in sexual intercourse, in contrast to Isabel's wider-ranging theories, Ella's vision was shaped by the same psychological forces that influenced her view of the birth or separation process. The man's penis, like the baby, gets trapped inside mother's body. There is something about mother or her body that tries to keep you within, not allow you to emerge, and is not receptive to your wishes to freely move in and out.

During her initial analytic sessions, Isabel's activity level was pressured, and she aggressively pretended that "Troublesome Baby" crawled into the body of the horse through his mouth, nose, and ears. This bodily penetration had multiple meanings. She went into the tummy of the horse in order to eat something. The mother's abdomen was the baby's haven and the source of nurturance. Ravenous longings to be fed like her little sister were satisfied in this play. "Troublesome Baby" crawled into the hind end of "Doggie with no Tail." Then, Isabel roughly shoved a baby bottle into the bottom of "Squirrel." The view of the primal scene as aggressive and sadistic anal penetration is another aspect of this intense play activity.

Over the course of Isabel's analysis, oral imagery transformed and became part of her oedipal vision of conception. The baby bottle, a source of milk, like a mother's breast, has a phallic shape, which makes it especially suitable as a transitional symbol representing oral and then phallic or oedipal modes of experience. At first the phallic-shaped baby bottle was the implement of anal intercourse. Later, the baby bottle gave way to a tack and a knife. When Isabel pretended and actually tried to stab Dr. Huddleston in the back, she was enacting another vision of violent and bloody penetration from behind.

Isabel's dream of eating the chocolate turtle represented, among other things, a theory of oral impregnation. The baby gets in your stomach when you eat it, and eventually it gets pooped out into the toilet. Her fantasies of impregnation included mailing away for cricket eggs and having a boy crack the eggs on your head. We can see the unfolding of this little girl's conscious and unconscious theories of the whole baby-making experience. In the latter example, she had moved away from her fantasy of anal impregnation. Making babies instead had something to do with a boy and a girl being physically intimate as they mix eggs together.

OEDIPAL TRIANGLES

Triangular relationships were portrayed in both analyses. While Ella's earlier developmental challenges influenced her oedipal experience, classical conflicts associated with the oedipal-age girl predominated in the latter part of her analysis. Consideration of triangular themes provides an opportunity to see how much Ella changed over the course of her analysis and to see the similarities in the two girls and their analyses when they were both immersed in the oedipal experience.

In Isabel's story of Esther, the king chose the beautiful young woman over his wife. In *The Wizard of Oz*, Dorothy had the support of a good witch but had to kill the evil witch. Isabel's oedipal longings were complicated by realities in her life. She had to deal with her father's physical injuries and recovery from those injuries, while Dorothy came to see that the wizard was just a man. Harry Potter dealt with good and evil witches and wizards, and oedipal rivalries became the palace intrigues of Hogwarts. In Isabel's mind, her mother's decision to seek divorce was the coup designed to settle the conflicts of the oedipal triangles in her own favor.

Ella experienced great distress over the prospect that her mother would be jealous and angry about her wish to be with her father or her growing tie to Mrs. Kaufman. She worried that Mrs. Kaufman was upset when she kissed her father in the waiting room. For Ella, triangles were complicated by the facts of her adoption. She was left to wonder about her biological mother, to try to understand why this had happened, and to deal with feeling abandoned and rejected. In addition to the pain of being the rejected one, Ella's love or loyalty to her biological mother, her adoptive mother, or Mrs. Kaufman created the potential that she would be the rejecter of the other mother. Then, she would have to deal with feelings of guilt and the potential that her feelings for one mother figure would elicit jealousy, anger, retaliation, and rejection by the other. The conflicted nature of Ella's relationship with her mother intensified the pain of both the adoptive and the oedipal triangles. The ongoing conflict with her mother and the reverberations with the adoptive triangle intensified the affects associated with her rivalry with her mother for her father. Her fantasies of marrying her own prince, having her own baby, having children who loved her and belonged to her, or having a happier family than her mother intertwined the complexities of her adoption, her separation-individuation conflicts, and her oedipal drama.

Chapter Thirteen

Termination

Edward I. Kohn

During the termination phase, the child and the analyst must adjust to a new reality. The analyst must be present for the child and attuned to the range of emotions elicited within the little girl and within herself as they prepare to part. At every developmental phase, the parent or analyst, the developmental objects, must be available to help the child deal with the losses and appreciate the gains of moving to the next phase. This is especially poignant when the task is to move on and leave the analyst behind. This availability helps the child deal with the loss, but it does more. Conflicts and developmental dilemmas worked through earlier in the analysis are apt to be repeated as analyst and child deal with the new tasks of parting and saying goodbye. This reliving and revisiting allow further reworking and resolution of internal conflict and consolidation of developmental gains.

ISABEL'S TERMINATION

Isabel exhibited distress in response to the premature termination. We learned earlier the importance of watering the flower when Isabel made tissue petals with a pencil sticking up in the middle. In response to the plan for termination, she worried that Dr. Huddleston's plants were suffering because they were not getting sufficient water. Dr. Huddleston's involvement with Isabel provided the emotional water that enabled her flower to bloom and evolve. Without her analyst, the flower was at risk. She described a movie where children were left with their inattentive grandparents. She seemed to blame her mother for much that had occurred. Her previously attentive analyst was now about to leave her behind with her inattentive mother.

In many ways she showed that she was able to deal with this pending loss. She came at her analyst with a tack but calmed down when Dr. Huddleston suggested she was angry. She showed her capacity to manage and tolerate her anger and her feelings about separation, evidence of structural change, when she made a parachute to ensure a soft landing. The parachute reflected her new capacity to modulate affect and deal with events without getting overwhelmed. She again played the role of teacher, but this teacher was supportive and helpful and showed Dr. Huddleston how to find her way in a new school. Isabel seemed genuine though impatient and a bit abrupt when she explained to Dr. Huddleston that you can't always get what you want. She seemed reasonably at ease with the need for renunciation. In her role as teacher, she could feel the pleasure of mastery of her wishes and her capacity to help the child, Dr. Huddleston, learn to find her way. Dr. Huddleston's engagement with this process helped Isabel to feel less alone with the experience of parting.

ELLA'S TERMINATION

Ella's perception of Mrs. Kaufman transformed during her analysis. In the beginning, Mrs. Kaufman was a threat who had to be controlled in order to prevent her from destabilizing the fragile structure of Ella's mind and the fragile condition of the analytic stage. As the analytic work progressed, she saw Mrs. Kaufman as a source of comfort and strength. When Ella played "the people with no home," she leaned against her analyst as she sobbed. Her dream of the friend who helped her when scared and her imagined phone call to Mrs. Kaufman during the night illustrated that she was in the process of taking into herself the essential functions provided by her analyst. In the same way that a transitional object enables a child to further the process of taking possession of mother's soothing function, Isabel's fantasy and dream were evidence that she was taking possession of her analyst's (her developmental object or selfobject) capacity ease to her anxiety and help her feel safe.

During the termination phase, Ella revisited her experiences in analysis. Facing the end of her analysis and loss of the soothing magic of Mrs. Kaufman, she was threatened with return of the discombobulation and disorganization that had been evident in the early phases of analysis. Instead of crashing cars into the closet, as she had early on, Ella played that cars were taken into a smashing machine. She explained in words that the "airplanes were scared because they did not know what would happen to them. . . . These other guys aren't scared because they are together in a team. They go into the smashing machine *together*." Ella and Mrs. Kaufman had been through a smashing machine in this analysis, and they did it together. When alone, without the support of a selfobject or developmental object or when the adult she needed was likely to turn on her, the smashing machine could not be dealt with. This machine could smash her mind to smithereens and break her into little pieces, and it had. Her own rage was also a smashing machine that threatened her object and her psychic stability. When Mrs. Kaufman could manage these feelings and help Ella with them, when it was a job for two, Ella had her team. While she insisted with bravado that she was not scared of Mrs. Kaufman in their first session, Mrs. Kaufman was now part of her team, and she genuinely felt less afraid. As a team they could deal more effectively with termination, and more importantly, Ella had developed an internal team.

With Mrs. Kaufman's help as the magical developmental object or selfobject, Ella could better mobilize her own strengths and resources, and she was able to pass through the smashing machine. Both participants emerged intact. Even more than intact, Ella was strengthened. With the support of her analyst, she had sufficient stability to engage the developmental task of building structure. The analytic situation was the stable ground for the execution of this work.

The rug in Mrs. Kaufman's office had "seen a lot." Ella was able to contemplate that rug, filled with symbolism as the foundation of their relationship and the analytic experience, and she was taking it into her own mind. It became a part of her. She was less globally reliant on her analyst to provide those functions. They belonged to her. Separation and individuation had been a smashing machine in the past, and Ella faced separation again. This time, however, termination or separation did not have to mean that she must choose between remaining trapped inside her mother or analyst or tearing apart her body in order to get free and being left to starve. Instead of facing punishment, retaliation, rejection, and abandonment that left her without any resources, instead of feeling that she had greedily and selfishly stolen from her mother and failed to pay the required allegiance, Ella could comfortably and confidently take possession of her strengthened mind. Mrs. Kaufman was now the figure who witnessed and affirmed this process as Ella took her possessions, looked them over, reflected on her memories, packed them up, and took her leave.

REMEMBERING AND REMINISCING

The processes of remembering and reminiscing were important to both girls during termination. Isabel laughed as she recalled how she had cheated Dr. Huddleston in their earlier play. She returned to previous activities, teacher and student and Harry Potter. She reviewed the old test papers, where she had judged her student/analyst harshly. She put ink into a bowl of water and watched it disappear. Was the ink there or not?

Ella played on the rug and reminisced. "It's been a house, a zoo, a world, a place to find missing things, and now a smashing machine." She and Mrs. Kaufman talked about the loss of their relationship and about being remembered. Ella was very upset when she thought about being replaced by another child and feared that her brother would take her place. She attempted to make sure that Mrs. Kaufman would think about her by hiding small items around the office, telling her that she should not look for them until after their last session. In the last hour, Ella touched various items, saying "I remember this. I remember that."

Both girls wanted to know that they would be remembered. They also wanted to remember. They were engaged in a process of establishing, in the minds of their analysts and their own minds, that their relationships were indelible. Even if you can't see the ink, it is there.

The girls and their analysts had to deal with the pain of loss. The termination phase enabled Dr. Huddleston and Mrs. Kaufman to be there with and for the girls during the grieving process. While reminiscing and remembering helped Ella and Isabel deal with the loss, we also get see how they were actively engaged in a process that facilitated internalization of their relationships with their analysts. Whether we think of the analyst as a developmental object, a selfobject, a transformational object, a new object, or a diatrophic object, each girl took possession of her experience with her analyst, and it became part of her.

Bibliography

Baker, R. (1993). The patient's discovery of the psychoanalyst as a new object. *International Journal Psycho-Analysis, 74*, 1223–1233.

Balint, M. (1979). *The basic fault*. London: Tavistock.

Baranger, M., Baranger, W., & Mom, J. M. (1988). The infantile psychic trauma from us to Freud: Pure trauma, retroactivity and reconstruction. *International Journal of Psycho-Analysis, 69*, 113–128.

Bartlett, F. C. (1932). *Remembering: A study in experimental and social psychology*. Cambridge: Cambridge University Press.

Bion, W. R. (1963). *Elements of psycho-analysis*. London: Heinemann.

Bion, W. R. (1977a). *Learning from experience*. In *Seven servants: Four works*. New York: Jason Aronson. (Original work published in 1962)

Bion, W. R. (1977b). *Transformations*. In *Seven servants: Four works*. New York: Jason Aronson. (Original work published in 1965)

Bollas, C. (1979). The transformational object. *International Journal of Psycho-Analysis, 60*, 97–107.

Bollas, C. (1993). *Being a character*. New York: Routledge.

Bonanno, G. A. (1990a). Remembering and psychotherapy. *Psychotherapy: Theory, Research and Practice, 27*, 175–186.

Bonanno, G. A. (1990b). Repression, accessibility, and the translation of private experience. *Psychoanalytic Psychology, 7*(4), 453–473.

Boulanger, G. (2002). Wounded by reality: The collapse of the self in adult onset trauma. *Contemporary Psychoanalysis, 38*, 45–76.

Brenner, C. (1982). *The mind in conflict*. New York: International Universities Press.

Bromberg, P. M. (1993). Shadow and substance: A relational perspective on clinical process. *Psychoanalytic Psychology, 10*(2), 147–168.

Bromberg, P. M. (1996). Standing in the spaces: The multiplicity of self and the psychoanalytic relationship. *Contemporary Psychoanalysis, 32*, 509–535.

Brown, L. J. (2005). The cognitive effects of trauma: Reversal of alpha function and the formation of a beta screen. *Psychoanalytic Quarterly, 74*, 397–420.

Brown, L. J. (2011). *Intersubjective processes and the unconscious: An integration of Freudian, Kleinian and Bionian perspectives*. New York: Routledge.

Burlingham, D. and Freud, A. (1943). *War and Children*. New York: Medical War Books.

Busch, F. (1993). In the neighborhood: Aspects of a good interpretation and a "developmental lag" in ego psychology. *Journal of American Psychoanalytic Association, 41*, 151–177.

Busch, F. (1999). *Rethinking clinical technique*. Northvale, NJ: Jason Aronson.

Cohen, N. J., & Squire, L. R. (1980). Preserved learning and retention of pattern analyzing skill in amnesia: Dissociation of knowing how and knowing that. *Science, 210,* 207–210.

Cohen, P. M., & Solnit, A. J. (1993). Play and therapeutic action. *Psychoanalytic Study of the Child, 48,* 49–63.

Dahl, E. K. (1993). Play and the construction of gender in the oedipal child. In A. Solnit, D. Cohen, & P. Neubauer (Eds.), *The many meanings of play* (pp. 117–134). New Haven, CT: Yale University Press.

Dahl, E. K. (1996). The concept of penis envy revisited: A child analyst listens to adult women. *Psychoanalytic Study of the Child, 51,* 303–325.

Edgcumbe, R. (1995). The history of Anna Freud's thinking on developmental disturbances. *Bulletin of the Anna Freud Centre, 18,* 21–34.

Ekstein, R., & Friedman, S. W. (1957). The function of acting out, play action, and play acting in the psychotherapeutic process. *Journal of the American Psychoanalytic Association, 5,* 581–629.

Erikson, E. H. (1968). *Identity, youth, and crisis.* New York: W. W. Norton.

Fleming, V. (Director), & LeRoy, M. (Producer). (1939). *The wizard of Oz* [Motion picture]. United States: Metro-Goldwyn-Mayer.

Fonagy, P., Moran, G. S., Edgcumbe, R., Kennedy, H., & Target, M. (1993). The roles of mental representations and mental processes in therapeutic action. *Psychoanalytic Study of the Child, 48,* 9–48.

Fonagy, P., & Target, M. (1996). Playing with reality: I. Theory of mind and the normal development of psychic reality. *International Journal of Psychoanalysis, 77,* 217.

Fonagy, P., & Target, M. (1998). Mentalization and the changing aims of child psychoanalysis. *Psychoanalytic Dialogue, 8,* 87–114.

Freud, A. (1945). Indications for child analysis. *Psychoanalytic Study of the Child, 1,* 127–149.

Freud, A. (1963). The Concept of Developmental Lines. *Psychoanalytic Study of the Child, 18,* 245–265.

Freud, A. (1965). *Normality and pathology in childhood: Assessments of development.* New York: International Universities Press.

Freud, A. (1967). Comments on psychic trauma. In *The writings of Anna Freud: Vol. 5. Research at the Hampstead Child-Therapy Clinic and other papers* (pp. 221–241). New York: International Universities Press. (Original work published 1964)

Freud, S. (1953–1974a). Beyond the pleasure principle. In *Beyond the pleasure principle, group psychology and other works. In The standard edition of the complete psychological works of Sigmund Freud, Vol. 18 (1920–1922)* (J. Strachey et al., Trans.). London: Hogarth Press. (Original work published 1920)

Freud, S. (1953–1974b). *A case of hysteria, three essays on sexuality and other works.* In *The standard edition of the complete psychological works of Sigmund Freud, Vol. 7 (1901–1905)* (J. Strachey et al., Trans.). London: Hogarth Press. (Original work published 1905)

Freud, S. (1953–1974c). Civilization and its discontents. In *The future of an illusion, civilization and its discontents, and other works* (pp. 57–146). In *The standard edition of the complete psychological works of Sigmund Freud, Vol. 21 (1927–1931)* (J. Strachey et al., Trans.). London: Hogarth Press. (Original work published 1930)

Freud, S. (1953–1974d). The ego and the id. In *The ego and the id and other works* (pp. 1–66). In *The standard edition of the complete psychological works of Sigmund Freud, Vol. 19 (1923–1925)* (J. Strachey et al., Trans.). London: Hogarth Press. (Original work published 1923)

Freud, S. (1953–1974e). Formulations on the two principles of mental functioning. In *The case history of Schreber, papers on technique and other works* (pp. 213–226). In *The standard edition of the complete psychological works of Sigmund Freud, Vol. 12 (1911–1913)* (J. Strachey et al., Trans.). London: Hogarth Press. (Original work published 1911)

Freud, S. (1953–1974f). From the history of an infantile neurosis. In *An infantile neurosis and other works* (pp. 1–124). In *The standard edition of the complete psychological works of Sigmund Freud, Vol. 17 (1917–1919)* (J. Strachey et al., Trans.). London: Hogarth Press. (Original work published 1918)

Freud, S. (1953–1974g). Inhibitions, symptoms and anxiety. In *An autobiographical study, inhibitions, symptoms and anxiety, the question of lay analysis and other works* (pp. 75–176). In *The standard edition of the complete psychological works of Sigmund Freud, Vol. 20 (1925–1926)* (J. Strachey et al., Trans.). London: Hogarth Press. (Original work published 1926)

Freud, S. (1953–1974h). Instincts and their vicissitudes. In *On the history of the psychoanalytic movement, papers on metapsychology and other works* (pp. 109–140). In *The standard edition of the complete psychological works of Sigmund Freud, Vol. 14 (1914–1916)* (J. Strachey et al., Trans.). London: Hogarth Press. (Original work published 1915a)

Freud, S. (1953–1974i). *The interpretation of dreams*. In *The standard edition of the complete psychological works of Sigmund Freud: Vols. 4 (1900) and 5 (1900–1901)* (J. Strachey et al., Trans.). London: Hogarth Press. (Original work published 1900)

Freud, S. (1953–1974j). *Introductory lectures on psycho-analysis, Parts 1 and 2* (pp. 1–240). In *The standard edition of the complete psychological works of Sigmund Freud, Vols. 15 (1916–1917) and 16 (1917)* (J. Strachey et al., Trans.). London: Hogarth Press. (Original work published 1916)

Freud, S. (1953–1974k). New introductory lectures on psycho-analysis. In *New introductory lectures and other works* (pp. 1–182). In *The standard edition of the complete psychological works of Sigmund Freud, Vol. 22 (1932–1936)* (J. Strachey et al., Trans.). London: Hogarth Press. (Original work published 1933)

Freud, S. (1953–1974l). On beginning the treatment (further recommendations on the technique of psycho-analysis I). In *The case history of Schreber, papers on technique and other works*. In *The standard edition of the complete psychological works of Sigmund Freud, Vol. 12 (1911–1913)* (J. Strachey et al., Trans.). London: Hogarth Press. (Original work published 1913)

Freud, S. (1953–1974m). Remembering, repeating and working-through (further recommendations on the technique of psycho-analysis II). In *The case history of Schreber, papers on technique and other works*. In *The standard edition of the complete psychological works of Sigmund Freud, Vol. 12 (1911–1913)* (J. Strachey et al., Trans.). London: Hogarth Press. (Original work published 1914)

Freud, S. (1953–1974n). *Studies on hysteria*. In *The standard edition of the complete psychological works of Sigmund Freud, Vol. 2 (1893–1895)* (J. Strachey et al., Trans.). London: Hogarth Press. (Original work published 1895)

Freud, S. (1953–1974o). The unconscious. In *On the history of the psycho-analytic movement, papers on metapsychology and other works* (pp. 159–215). In *The standard edition of the complete psychological works of Sigmund Freud, Vol. 14 (1914–1916)* (J. Strachey et al., Trans.). London: Hogarth Press. (Original work published 1915b)

Gitelson, M. (1962). The curative factors in psycho-analysis. *International Journal of Psycho-Analysis, 43*, 194–205.

Goldberg, P. (2016, May 4 and 5). Workshop at Cincinnati Psychoanalytic Institute.

Gray, P. (1994). *The ego and the analysis of defense*. Northvale, NJ: Jason Aronson.

Grotstein, J. S. (1990a). Nothingness, meaninglessness, chaos, and the "black hole" I: The importance of nothingness, meaninglessness, and chaos in psychoanalysis. *Contemporary Psychoanalysis, 26*, 257–290.

Grotstein, J. S. (1990b). Nothingness, meaninglessness, chaos, and the "black hole" II: The black hole. *Contemporary Psychoanalysis, 26*, 377–407.

Handler, D. (Lemony Snicket). (1999). A series of unfortunate events. New York: HarperCollins.

Hartmann, H. (1939). *Ego psychology and the problem of adaptation*. New York: International Universities Press.

Hartmann, H. (1950). Comments on the psychoanalytic theory of the ego. *Psychoanalytic Study of the Child, 5*, 74–96.

Heuves, W. (2003) Young adolescents: Development and treatment. In Green, V. (Ed.) *Emotional Development in Psychoanalysis, Attachment Theory and Neuroscience: Creating Connections* (189–208). London: Brunner-Routledge.

Horne, A. (2006) Brief communications from the edge: Psychotherapy with challenging adolescents. In Lanyado, M., Horne, A. (Eds.), *A Question of Technique: Independent Psychoanalytic Approaches with Children and Adolescents* (pp. 149–165). London: Routledge.

Hurry, A. (Ed.). (1998). *Psychoanalysis and developmental therapy.* New York: Routledge.

Jacobs, T. J. (1986). On countertransference enactments. *Journal of the American Psychoanalytic Association, 34*, 289–307.

Jacobs, T. J. (2001). On unconscious communications and covert enactments: Some reflections on their role in the analytic situation. *Psychoanalytic Inquiry, 21*(1), 4–23.

Joseph, B. (1985). Transference: The Total Situation. *International Journal of Psychoanalysis, 66*, 447–44.

Katz, G. (2014). *The play within the play: The enacted dimension of psychoanalytic process* Relational perspectives series. New York: Routledge.

Kern, J. W. (1987). Transference neurosis as a waking dream: Notes on a clinical enigma. *Journal of the American Psychoanalytic Association, 35*, 337–366.

Kernberg, O. F. (1976). *Object relations theory and clinical psychoanalysis.* New York: Jason Aronson.

Khan, M. R. (1963). The concept of cumulative trauma. *Psychoanalytic Study of the Child, 18*, 286–306.

Khan, M. R. (1964). Ego distortion, cumulative trauma, and the role of reconstruction in the analytic situation. *International Journal Psycho-Analysis, 45*, 272–279.

Klein, M. (1975). Envy and gratitude and other works 1946–1963 (M. Masud & R. Khan, Eds.). *The International Psycho-Analytical Library, 104*, 1–346. London: Hogarth Press.

Knight, R. (2003) Margo and Me II: The role of narrative building in child analytic technique. *Psychoanalytic Study of the Child 58*, 133–164.

Kohut, H. (1959). Introspection, empathy, and psychoanalysis. *Journal of the American Psychoanalytic Association, 7*, 459–483.

Kohut, H. (1966). Forms and transformations of narcissism. *Journal of the American Psychoanalytic Association, 14*, 243–272.

Kohut, H. (1968). The psychoanalytic treatment of narcissistic personality disorders: Outline of a systematic approach. *Psychoanalytic Study of the Child, 23*, 86–113.

Kohut, H. (1971). *The analysis of the self: A systematic approach to the psychoanalytic treatment of narcissistic personality disorders.* New York: International Universities Press.

Kohut, H. (1972). Thoughts on Narcissism and Narcissistic Rage. *Psychoanalytic Study of the Child, 27*, 360–400.

Kohut, H. (1977). *The restoration of the self.* New York: International Universities Press.

Kohut, H. (1984). *How does analysis cure?* (A. Goldberg, Ed.). Chicago: University of Chicago Press.

Kohut, H., & Wolf, E. S. (1978). The disorders of the self and their treatment: An outline. *International Journal of Psycho-Analysis, 59*, 413–425.

Kris, A. O. (1982). *Free association: Method and process.* New Haven, CT: Yale University Press.

Kris, E. (1956a). The personal myth: A problem in psychoanalytic technique. *Journal of the American Psychoanalytic Association, 4*, 653–681.

Kris, E. (1956b). The recovery of childhood memories in psychoanalysis. *Psychoanalytic Study of the Child, 11*, 54–88.

Kris, E. (1956c). On Some Vicissitudes of Insight in Psycho-Analysis. *International Journal of Psychoanalysis, 37*, 445–55.

Krystal, H. (1978). Trauma and affects. *Psychoanalytic Study of the Child, 33*, 81–116.

Krystal, H. (1985). Trauma and the stimulus barrier. *Psychoanalytic Inquiry, 5*, 131–161.

Krystal, H. (1997). Desomatization and the consequences of infantile psychic trauma. *Psychoanalytic Inquiry, 17*, 126–150.

Loewald, H. W. (1960). On the therapeutic action of psycho-analysis. *International Journal Psycho-Analysis, 41*, 16–33.

Loewald, H. W. (1971). On motivation and instinct theory. *Psychoanalytic Study of the Child, 26*, 91–128.

Lyons-Ruth, K. (1999). The two-person unconscious: Intersubjective dialogue, enactive relational representation, and the emergence of new forms of relational organization. *Psychoanalytic Inquiry, 19*, 576–617.

Mahler, M. S., Pine, F., & Bergman, A. (1975). *The psychological birth of the human infant: Symbiosis and individuation*. New York: Basic Books.

Mayes, L. C., & Cohen, D. J. (1992). The development of a capacity for imagination in early childhood. *Psychoanalytic Study of the Child, 47*, 23–47.

Mayes, L. C., & Cohen, D. J. (1993a). Playing and therapeutic action in child analysis. *International Journal of Psycho-Analysis, 74*, 1235–1244.

Mayes, L. C., & Cohen, D. J. (1993b). The social matrix of aggression: Enactments and representations of loving and hating in the first years of life. *Psychoanalytic Study of the Child, 48*, 145–169.

Mayes, L. C., & Cohen, D. J. (1996). Children's developing theory of mind. *Journal of the American Psychoanalytic Association, 44*, 117–142.

Miller, J. M. (2013). Developmental psychoanalysis and developmental objects. *Psychoanalytic Inquiry, 33*, 312–322.

Mitchell, S. (1993). *Hope and dread in psychoanalysis*. New York: Basic Books.

Mitchell, S. (1996). When interpretations fail: A new look at the therapeutic action of psychoanalysis. In L. E. Lifson (Ed.), *Understanding therapeutic action: Psychodynamic concepts of cure* (pp. 165–186). Hillsdale, NJ: Analytic Press.

Mitchell, S. A. (1991). Contemporary perspectives on self: Toward an integration. *Psychoanalytic Dialogue, 1*(2), 121–147.

Moore. B. E., & Fine, D. B. (1990). *Psychoanalytic terms and concepts*. New Haven, CT: Yale University Press.

Neubauer, P. B. (1994). The role of displacement in psychoanalysis. *Psychoanalytic Study of the Child, 49*, 107–119.

Ogden, T. H. (1979). On projective identification. *International Journal of Psycho-Analysis, 60*, 357–373.

Olesker, W. (1999). Treatment of a boy with atypical ego development. *Psychoanalytic Study of the Child 54*, 25–46.

Ornstein, A. (1974). The dread to repeat and the new beginning: A contribution to the psychoanalysis of the narcissistic personality disorders. *Annual of Psychoanalysis, 2*, 231–248.

Pine, F. (1994). Some impressions regarding conflict, defect, and deficit. *Psychoanalytic Study of the Child, 49*, 222–240.

Rank, O. (1929). *The trauma of birth*. New York: Harcourt, Brace.

Rapaport, D. (1960). *The structure of psychoanalytic theory: A systematizing attempt*. New York: International Universities Press.

Rowling, J. K. (1991). *Harry Potter and the chamber of secrets*. New York: Arthur A. Levine Books.

Rowling, J. K. (1998). *Harry Potter and the sorcerer's stone*. New York: Arthur A. Levine Books.

Rowling, J. K. (2004). *Harry Potter and the order of the phoenix*. New York: Arthur A. Levine Books.

Sandler, A.-M. (1996). The psychoanalytic legacy of Anna Freud. *Psychoanalytic Study of the Child 51*, 270–284.

Sandler, J. (1960). The background of safety. *International Journal of Psycho-Analysis, 41*, 352–356.

Sandler, J., & Rosenblatt, B. (1962). The concept of the representational world. *Psychoanalytic Study of the Child, 17*, 128–145.

Schwaber, E. (1983). Psychoanalytic listening and psychic reality. *International Review of Psycho-Analysis, 10*, 379–392.

Solnit, A. J. (1987). A psychoanalytic view of play. *Psychoanalytic Study of the Child, 42*, 205–219.

Solnit, A. J. (1998). Beyond play and playfulness. *Psychoanalytic Study of the Child, 53*, 102–110.

Spitz, Rene la. (1956). Countertransference: Comments on its varying role in the analytic situation. *Journal of the American Psychoanalytic Association, 4,* 256–265.

Stern, M. M. (1951). Anxiety, Trauma, and Shock *Psychoanalytic Quarterly 20,* 179–203.

Strachey, J. (1934). The nature of the therapeutic action of psycho-analysis. *International Journal of Psycho-Analysis, 15,* 127–159.

Sugarman, A. (2003a). Dimensions of the child analyst's role as a developmental object: Affect regulation and limit setting. *Psychoanalytic Study of the Child, 58,* 189–213.

Sugarman, A. (2003b). A new model for conceptualizing insightfulness in the psychoanalysis of young children. *Psychoanalytic Quarterly, 72*(2), 325–355.

Sugarman, A. (2006). Mentalization, insightfulness, and therapeutic action: The importance of mental organization. *International Journal of Psycho-Analysis, 87*(4), 965–987.

Target, M., & Fonagy, P. (1996). Playing with reality: II. The development of psychic reality from a theoretical perspective. *International Journal of Psychoanalysis, 77,* 459–479.

Tolpin, M. (1971). On the beginnings of a cohesive self: An application of the concept of transmuting internalization to the study of the transitional object and signal anxiety. *Psychoanalytic Study of the Child, 26,* 316–352.

Tolpin, M. (2002). Doing psychoanalysis of normal development: Forward edge transferences. *Progress in Self Psychology, 18,* 167–190.

Vygotsky, L. (1956). *Selected psychological investigations.* Moscow: Izdatel'stvo Akademii Pedagogicheskikh Nauk.

Vygotsky, L. (1978). *Mind in society: The development of higher psychological processes.* Cambridge, MA: Harvard University Press.

Wertsch, J. (1985). *Vygotsky and the Social Formation of Mind.* Cambridge: Harvard University Press.

Wertsch, J. (1992). *Voices of the Mind.* Cambridge: Harvard University Press.

Wilson, A., & Weinstein, L. (1996). The transference and the zone of proximal development. *Journal of the American Psychoanalytic Association, 44,* 167–200.

Winnicott, D. W. (1953). Transitional objects and transitional phenomena: A study of the first not-me possession. *International Journal of Psycho-Analysis, 34,* 89–97.

Winnicott, D. W. (1960). Ego distortion in terms of true and false self. In *The maturational processes and the facilitating environment: Studies in the theory of emotional development* (pp. 140–152). New York: International Universities Press (1965).

Winnicott, D. W. (1965). The maturational processes and the facilitating environment. *The International Psycho-Analytical Library, 64,* 1–276. London: Hogarth Press.

Winnicott, D. W. (1974). Fear of breakdown. *International Review of Psycho-Analysis, 1,* 103–107.

Yeats, W. B. (1921). "The second coming." In *The Collected Poems of W. B. Yeats.* New York: MacMillan.

Index

abandonment issues. *See* Ella
abreaction, theory of, 127–28
action: about, 157–58; communication and, 161–62; fragmentation and, 158–60; overstimulation and, 160–61. *See also* therapeutic action; words and action
adoption issues, 35–38. *See also* Ella
affect, 91–93, 174–76
aggression, 129–30
alpha and beta elements, 62, 83, 87, 88, 116
analysands. *See* Ella; Isabel
analyst-child relationship: analyst as developmental object, 97–98, 134–35; developmental functions, 108, 123–25; holding environment, 98–100; magic of analysts, 108–10; mother-child activities, 25; transformative nature of, 133. *See also* parental relationship
anxiety, 76–77. *See also* trauma
après coup, 80, 84–85
attunement, 106, 134
auxiliary ego, 99, 106
avoidance, patterns of, 146–48

Baker, R., 136, 143
Balint, Michael, 69–70, 137
Baranger, M., xiv, 117, 137–38, 150
Baranger, W., xiv, 117, 137–38, 150
Bergman, A., x, xii, 54, 73, 86–87, 90

beta and alpha elements, 62, 83, 87, 88, 116
Bion, W. R., x, xii, xiii, 73, 88, 107, 133
birth process/trauma, 54, 181. *See also* Isabel
black hole metaphor, 80–82, 93, 117, 118–19, 124
Bollas, C., xiv, 100, 109, 114, 137, 139–40, 144, 148, 149
Bonanno, G. A., 82
bootstrapping, 139, 141
Boulanger, G., xii, 82–83, 87, 117
Bromberg, P. M., xi–xii, 67–69, 73, 83, 112, 136–37
Brown, L. J., xiii, 83
Burlingham, Dorothy, 76
Busch, F., 141, 146

castration anxiety, 94
catastrophic trauma, 95, 117–18
catatonoid state, 96
chemistry analogy, 119
Cinderella story, 108–10, 122–23
classical theory and frustration, 130–31
clinical vignettes: Ella, 29–49; Isabel, 1–18
Cohen, D. J., x, xiii, 64–65, 71, 72–73, 106, 130
cohesive structure: about, 62, 88–89, 116, 121–25; opposite of. *See* fragmentation
communication: action and, 161–62; of Ella, 162; free association, 140–41;

About the Authors

Born in New York City, **Edward I. Kohn** received a B.S. in electrical engineering and computer science from the Massachusetts Institute of Technology and an M.D. from the College of Physicians and Surgeons at Columbia University. He trained in general psychiatry and child and adolescent psychiatry at the University of Cincinnati Medical Center and graduated from the Cincinnati Psychoanalytic Institute in adult psychoanalysis and from the New Orleans (now the New Orleans–Birmingham) Psychoanalytic Institute in child and adolescent psychoanalysis.

Dr. Kohn, a past director of the Cincinnati Psychoanalytic Institute (CPI), is a training and supervising analyst and a child supervising analyst at CPI. He is also a child supervising analyst at the Southeast Consortium for Child Psychoanalysis. He practices adult, adolescent, and child psychoanalysis and psychotherapy in Cincinnati, Ohio.

Christie Huddleston, MD, is a psychoanalyst in private practice in Philadelphia. In addition to her practice, Dr. Huddleston is associate clinical professor at the Hospital of the University of Pennsylvania (HUP). In this capacity she supervises HUP psychiatry residents and is co-coordinator of the applied psycho-analytic curriculum for child psychiatry fellows at Children's Hospital of Philadelphia (CHOP). As a member of the faculty of the Psychoanalytic Center of Philadelphia (PCOP), Dr. Huddleston teaches and serves as co-chair for the Gerald Pearson Lectureship in Child Psychoanalysis. She completed child analytic training with PCOP and the Southeastern Consortium. She is certified in adult psychoanalysis.

Adele Kaufman, MSW, is a psychoanalyst in private practice in Highland Park, Illinois. In addition to her practice, she is on the faculty of the Chicago

Psychoanalytic Institute, where she teaches and is a supervising and training analyst and child supervising analyst. She is the former chair of the Child and Adolescent Analysis Committee and former co-dean. She has written numerous papers on teaching, learning, and doing child analysis. She is certified in child and adult psychoanalysis and is a fellow of the American Board of Psychoanalysis.